GRAMMAR
for
GROWN-UPS

GRAMMAR

for

GROWN-UPS

Everything you
need to know but never
learnt in school

CRAIG SHRIVES

KYLE BOOKS

This edition published in Great Britain in 2012 by
Kyle Books
an imprint of Kyle Cathie Ltd
23 Howland Street
London, W1T 4AY
general.enquiries@kylebooks.com
www.kylebooks.com

First published in Great Britain in 2011 under the title *Grammar Rules*

ISBN: 978-0-85783-080-7

Text © 2011 Craig Shrives
Design © 2011 Kyle Books

Editor: Catharine Robertson
Designer: Roland Codd
Proofreader: John Westbrooke
Production: David Hearn and Nic Jones

A Cataloguing In Publication record for this title is available from the British Library.

Printed and bound in Great Britain by CPI Group (UK) Ltd, Croydon, CR0 4YY

− CONTENTS −

– FOREWORD –

While the fighting troops are bashing the enemy, the staff officers who support the fight are tucked away in the background frantically bashing out reports to help the senior decision-makers make sense of the unfolding furore. Well, that was me. I was one of the guys compiling, summarising and offering assessments for the generals on all the stuff spinning around us.

Something you notice very quickly in that job is your writing needs to be pretty credible, or else it gets ignored. As you'd expect, generals are proper grammar pedants. Worse. They're busy grammar pedants. Their diaries are "heart attack" hectic, especially when deployed on operations. To win a general's attention, your work needs to be succinct and grammatically sound. At the point in your paper when you present a grammar howler, the general's skim-reading will accelerate dramatically, or he'll push your paper to the bottom of his pile. And, it'll never resurface. On the other hand, if you offer a well-punctuated, grammatically sound paper, you might just have an impact on the war.

Over the last 25 years, I have worked on the staffs of a raft of US and UK generals (most recently General Stanley McChrystal in Kabul). I have had grammar rammed down my throat, but, as I became more senior, I slowly transformed from rammee to rammer. In this book, I have sought to categorise and answer all the grammar questions that plague not just military staff officers but managers and students in all walks of life.

It's not just the generals' whips that have instilled a "love" of grammar in me. I have studied a couple of languages while serving in the Army, and learning these has also caked me in Englishgrammarness. In my spare time (most of which should almost certainly have been spent with my wife Penny), I have been working on grammar-monster.com, which is steadily turning into one of the most popular grammar sites on the web. I expect I sound like bit of a geek, and I suppose I am. But, I'm also a through-the-ranks British officer. That means I have spent time at each soldier rank and both warrant-officer ranks before being commissioned. As a result of treading that path to officerdom, I'm probably a little rougher around the edges than your typical British Rupert and a little less geeky than most people with an interest in grammar. Mmmm? Anyway, my vision with this book was to use my experience to present a light-hearted, easily digestible grammar reference book which is well indexed and intuitive to use. We're not going to get into spelling in this book. There's no need – spellcheckers are effective. This book is about grammar – the stuff your PC doesn't help with.

It's about this sort of stuff:

> Do you put a comma before *and*? What's the difference between *if* and *whether*? How do you use semicolons? When are you actually supposed to use commas? Does *winter* have a capital W? Does *north* have a capital N? *Effecting* or *affecting*? Does my comma go inside or outside the speech marks? Double or single speech marks? What's the difference between a hyphen and a dash? When do you use square brackets? What's the difference between *into* and *in to*? *Who* or *whom*? Do people still say *whom*? Is it the same for Americans and Brits? Do you say *an RTA* or *a RTA*? Will my audience think I'm a bit thick if I get these wrong? Will they think I'm pretty sharp if I get them right?

– USING THIS BOOK –

It's a Dip-in Reference Book. This book is not designed to be read from cover to cover. You'd have to have a real hunger for grammar to do that. And, if you have, you're probably the sort of person who's looking for typos and advice you don't agree with. If that is your aim, then hopefully I've annoyed you already by starting too many sentences with conjunctions and ending too many with prepositions. (Seriously though, thanks for buying *Grammar for Grown-ups*.)

Looking up Stuff. There are two indexes:

- A basic contents at the start. Use this to look for a broad topic (e.g. "semicolons" or "prepositions").
- A detailed index at the end. This covers all the grammar points in this book. They are indexed under multiple headings to help you find them. For example, the mistake "our's" is listed under (1) absolute possessives (2) apostrophes (3) ours and (4) pronouns.

Use of Italics. All the examples in this book are written in italics. Words quoted from the examples are also in italics. I would have used speech marks, but unfortunately Americans and Brits can't agree on whether punctuation should be inside or outside speech marks. As this book seeks to cover both US and UK writing conventions, I have avoided the issue by using italics where others would probably have used speech marks. Also, to make explanations easier to read, I often use italics to group words (especially definitions). Grammar perfectionists will note I've been quite inconsistent in this practice. Each decision to use italics was based on the length and complexity of the phrase (e.g. the definition) and the structure of the sentence. Basically, if I thought it helped the explanation, I've used italics. Purists can either live with that or tut themselves to sleep each night until they get over it.

Graphics. The following tags are used throughout the book:

 GEEK SAYS To introduce grammar terminology or stuff your mates would beat you up for knowing.

 BEWARE To highlight grammar crimes that can seriously affect your credibility.

OPPORTUNITY To highlight opportunities to show off your writing skills.

 GREAT TIP To help you work around complicated grammar explanations.

 BAD TIP To highlight common misleading advice.

✔ Right (or best)
✘ Wrong (or dodgy)

Writing Voice. Unless you're writing a note to your drinking buddies, I recommend you don't copy the tone and style I use in this book in your formal documents. In an attempt to keep you engaged, I have littered the book with contractions (e.g. don't, can't), one-word "sentences" and the Anglo-Saxon version of words (e.g. *leave* not *depart*; *get* not *acquire*). Sometimes, writing in this style can be useful in formal writing but not often in my experience. You must think about the tone and style (or "writing voice") that best suit you or, more importantly, your company. This book touches upon developing your "writing voice" (see Section 52), but it's predominantly a grammar reference book.

Deliberate Repetition. To keep this book under 300 pages and to avoid too much repetition, I often send you to other sections for a more in-depth look at a subject. However, you will notice (particularly if you read this book from cover to cover) that a few topics are covered more than once. This is deliberate. My rationale is that if you want to learn about commas, you want it all in one place. If you want to learn about semicolons, you want it all in one place. So, a subject which belongs in "Commas" and "Semicolons" appears in both. Everyone who proofread this book picked me up on this point. I know proofreaders rarely do you a disservice, but – in this case – I stood my ground and kept the repetition. Within the sections, you will also notice repetition and a lack of literary variance (using two words which mean the same thing in nearby sentences to keep writing interesting). This is also deliberate. You see, repetition is the mother of learning (Russian proverb), and I wanted clarity – above all else – to determine the writing style of the explanations.

Examples and Anecdotes for Added Spice. This is a grammar book. I doubt it'll have you rolling off your chair with laughter. Worse. It's a grammar reference book. To combat that handicap, I have sought to fill it with spectacular quotes which I have been collecting for the last decade. The quotes are provided by a wide range of contributors from Homer (the Greek) to Homer (the Simpson). I've even added a few relevant anecdotes of my own to help keep your eyelids "north" of your eyes. In my explanations and recommendations, I've gone as "grammar lite" as I dare. This book is aimed at those who have reached a position that requires them to produce high-quality correspondence. I strongly suspect if you were interested in grammar, you'd know all this gumpf already. But, please plan on learning *some* grammar terminology. It's so much easier to discuss grammar when we're all using the same words.

Writing Conventions. My website, www.grammar-monster.com, has been running for around a decade. Before I wrote it, I read all the leading grammar reference books and style guides. I know that's a bit sad, but I was intrigued how much they contradicted each other. When I first launched the website, the number of people who got in touch to say the advice on my website was wrong was staggering. Their points of view were almost always backed up by only one of the reference books. However, I am very grateful to these critics, because our "arguments" have allowed me to tune this book, either by softening wording or offering alternative versions to rules. (Some of the critics, if they buy this book, will even stumble across the examples they used to make their points.) I've noticed that grammarians have different levels of leniency when it comes to grammar rulings. Until someone burns all the books and writes a grammar bible, I suspect grammarians will be at war with each other for many years to come.

If you're bit of a grammar pedant and I still haven't tuned my advice to your liking, you can write to me at file13@grammar-monster.com.

Grumpy Sod. I am aware that 25 years of being red-penned and red-penning in high-pressure environments have turned me into bit of a grumpy sod. I'm sorry if that's too evident in the book. I genuinely want to make things easier for you. It's the old chestnut: *I went through it. Therefore, you don't have to.* That's the plan. There's a plan?

PUNCTUATION

– APOSTROPHES –

1 APOSTROPHES – AN OVERVIEW

The petite apostrophe causes more errors than any other punctuation mark. It is the arch enemy of your computer's grammar checker, which will usually fail to spot its misuse.

 BEWARE Apostrophe errors will damage your credibility.

There are specific rules about when to use an apostrophe. So, if you're thinking about shoving one into a word, make sure it's for one of the following reasons:

- To show possession (e.g. *a dog's breakfast*). (See Section 3.)
- To replace a letter or letters (e.g. *can't* instead of *cannot*). (See Section 4.)
- In an expression such as *two years' misery*. (See Section 5.)
- To show the plural of an abbreviation, a letter or a number (e.g. *your 6's look like G's*). (See Section 6.)

If you use an apostrophe for anything else, it's wrong. You should expect your readers to spot your apostrophe errors. They may not say it to your face, but they'll think you're a bit of a buffoon if you let more than one slip. I'm sorry for starting this book so aggressively, but your audience will afford you no leniency when it comes to apostrophes.

2 APOSTROPHES – USED INCORRECTLY WITH PLURALS

The most common mistake with an apostrophe is to stick it before the *s* of a word that ends in *s* – usually a plural word. The plurals of words ending in vowels (e.g. *video, patio*) are extremely prone to this error. Examples:

- *Dog's look up to us, and cat's look down on us. I prefer pig's – they treat us as equal's.* ✖
  (badly transcribed version of a Sir Winston Churchill quote)
- *Anteater's prefer termite's to ant's.* ✖
- *Pearl's melt in vinegar.* ✖

- *Rent two adult video's for the price of one.* ✖
- *Once a word fly's out, you cannot catch it.* ✖
  (badly translated Russian proverb)
  (It's not just plural words that attract this error. It's all words
  ending with an *s*. This should be *flies*.)

There should be no apostrophes in any of the five examples above. Putting
a bad apostrophe before the *s* in a word is considered a grammatical howler.
Look at this example:

- *If the local tribal influences over them diminish, member's of*
  Tehrik-e Taliban Pakistan might start drifting into eastern
  Afghanistan in search of US target's. ✖
  (There should be no apostrophes in this example.)

If you riddle your work with apostrophe errors, you will damage your
credibility, and there is a danger your readers will ignore your message.

An erroneous apostrophe in a plural word is widely known as a *greengrocers'*
apostrophe, because you see it so often on their stalls (e.g. *apple's*, *banana's*,
grape's). These always remind me of a scene in Charlie and the Chocolate
Factory. Do you remember when Charlie turns to his grandpa after failing to
find a golden ticket and says: "You know, I bet those golden tickets make the
chocolate taste awful"? Well, when I see a greengrocers' apostrophe, I think:
"You know, I bet those apostrophes make the apples taste awful." And, I buy
my apples from a grocer who can resist penning an apostrophe whenever he
ends a word with an *s*. I'm not sure that's a good basis for selecting fruit. Do
you have any apostrophe-free apples?

③ APOSTROPHES – TO SHOW POSSESSION

An apostrophe and the letter *s* are often used to show possession. Examples:

- *Wagner's music is better than it sounds.* ✔ (Mark Twain)
- *A friend's eye is a good mirror.* ✔
- *A guest should be blind in another man's house.* ✔
- *A foolish woman knows a foolish man's faults.* ✔

Apostrophe before the s. In each example above, the model is:

A's B. (Wagner's music, friend's eye, man's house, man's faults.)

*When **A** is singular, the model is **A's B**. No one cares whether **B** is singular or plural.*

Notice that the apostrophe is before the *s*. It is always before the *s* when **A** is singular. (These examples are about one *Wagner*, one *friend*, one *man* and one *man*.) It doesn't matter a jot whether **B** is singular or plural. Look at the last two examples: a *man's house* (*house* is singular) and *a man's faults* (*faults* is plural). If **A** is singular, the apostrophe is before the *s*.

Of course, it is possible for the apostrophe to appear after the *s*. This happens when **A** is plural. The model becomes: **As' B**. Examples:

- *Psychiatry enables us to correct our faults by confessing our parents' shortcomings.* ✔ (Laurence J. Peter)
- *Take away the miseries and you take away some folks' reason for living.* ✔ (Toni Cade Bambara)

So, if **A** is singular, the apostrophe is before the *s*. If **A** is plural, it's after the *s*. It's still irrelevant whether **B** is singular or plural. For example:

- *Dog's breakfast* ✔ (one dog, one breakfast)
- *Dog's breakfasts* ✔ (one dog, several breakfasts)
- *Dogs' breakfast* ✔ (several dogs, one breakfast)
- *Dogs' breakfasts* ✔ (several dogs, several breakfasts)

Well, that all seems pretty straightforward. Oh, don't worry. It gets more complicated…

Exception to the Rule (Plurals Not Ending in s). Mistakes with apostrophes are very common. One reason for this is the number of exceptions to the rules above. For example, plural words which do not end in the letter *s* (e.g. *men*, *people*, *children*) have the apostrophe before the *s* when showing possession. Examples:

- *He is the people's poet.* ✔
- *Leave the childrens' presents in the hall until they have gone to bed.* ✘ (should be *children's*)
- *All television is children's television.* ✔ (Richard P. Adler)
- *Zeus does not bring all men's plans to fulfilment.* ✔ (Homer, 800–700 BC)

If **A** is a singular word ending in **s**, do whatever you like.

Another Exception to the Rule (Singular Nouns Ending s). To make things even more complicated, singular words which end in *s* (e.g. *Charles*, *Wales*, *Paris* and *Dickens*) can show possession by ending ' **or** *'s*. Examples:

- *It is Charles' birthday.* ✔ *It is Charles's birthday.* ✔ (both correct)
- *I have not seen Wales' new stadium.* ✔ *I have not seen Wales's new stadium.* ✔ (both correct)

Both *Charles' birthday* and *Charles's birthday* are grammatically correct. As a guideline, you should use the version which best matches how you would pronounce it. In other words, use *Charles's* if you pronounce it "Charlesiz," but use *Charles'* if you pronounce it "Charles." More examples:

- *Dr Evans' report* ✔
  (for those who pronounce it "Dr Evans report")
- *Dr Evans's report* ✔
  (for those who pronounce it "Dr Evansiz report")
- *Miss Williams' victory* ✔
  (for those who pronounce it "Miss Williams victory")
- *Miss Williams's victory* ✔
  (for those who pronounce it "Miss Williamsiz victory")

Another Exception to the Rule (Compound Nouns). Here is another quirk. Some compound nouns (e.g. sister-in-law) do not form their plurals by adding *s* to the end. The *s* is appended to the principal word (i.e. the plural is *sisters-in-law*). (See Section 82.) With these, the possessive form is created by adding *'s* to the end, regardless of whether it is singular or plural. For example:

- *sister-in-law's pond* ✔ *sisters-in-law's husbands* ✔
- *colonel-in-chief's arrival* ✔ *colonels-in-chief's meeting* ✔
- *maid of honour's bouquet* ✔ *maids of honour's dresses* ✔

A quirk with joint ownership

Apostrophes with Joint Ownership. One last quirk. Joint ownership is shown by making the last word in the series possessive (i.e. adding ' or *'s*). Individual ownership is shown by making both (or all) parts possessive. Examples:

- *Andrew and Jacob's factories* ✔
  (This is joint ownership – only the last part is possessive)

- *Andrew's and Jacob's factories* ✔
  (This is individual ownership – both parts are possessive)
  (Without context, it will be assumed that Andrew has one factory and Jacob has one factory. Another construction is required if this is not the case. *Andrew's factories and Jacob's factories* is one option.)
- *India and Pakistan's problems* ✔ (common to both)
- *India's and Pakistan's problems* ✔ (separate problems)

Here's something worth knowing:

> An apostrophe that shows possession never appears inside the word itself. For example:
> - *Dicken's novel* ✖ (the word is *Dickens*)
> - *The ladie's coats* ✖ (the word is *ladies*)
> - *the cat's dinner* (If the word is *cats*, then this must be wrong, because the apostrophe "never appears inside the word itself." However, for *cat* (i.e. one cat), it would be correct.)

***It's* Has Nothing to Do with Possession**. Given what you've just read, you might think it makes sense for *it's* to be the possessive form of *it*. Well, it makes sense, but it isn't. *It's* is short for *it is* or *it has*. This is a 100% rule. *It's* has nothing to do with possession. The word *its* (without an apostrophe) is used for possession. (See Section 142.)

④ APOSTROPHES – TO REPLACE LETTERS

Apostrophes can be used to replace missing letters. This is to reflect how many people speak. For example:

- *If you don't fail now and again, it's a sign you're playing it safe.* ✔ (Woody Allen)
  (In full: *do not | it is | you are*)
- *Don't look now, but there's one too many in this room, and I think it's you.* ✔ (Groucho Marx)
  (In full: *do not | there is | it is*)
- *Blood's not thicker than money.* ✔ (Groucho Marx)
  (In full: *blood is*)

Words like *don't*, *you're* and *it's* are called contractions. More often than not, writers put the apostrophes in the right places with contractions…but, not always. Here is an example of an error I found in a Christmas cracker.

The error is much funnier than the joke.

> *Q: What horse c'ant you ride?*
> *A: A clothes horse.*
> (Obviously, it should be *can't* not *c'ant*.)

Contractions in Formal Documents. It is unusual to use contractions in formal writing, but some businesses use them to portray a friendly or down-to-earth image. If you're unsure whether your boss likes them or not, avoid them in formal writing. In 25 years of military writing, I have never used a contraction in a formal document. (There is more on this at Section 52.) The most common errors associated with contractions involve *it's* and *you're*. (These are covered in Section 142 and Section 172.)

Should Of - Aaagh. The contractions *should've*, *would've* and *could've* can also cause problems. Remember, these are short for *should have, would have* and *could have*. They are not short for *should of, would of* and *could of*. You will probably get away with saying *should of* etc., but if you write it, your readers will think you're a bit dense. An example:

> *Marge: Homer, the Lord only asks for an hour a week.*
> *Homer: Well in that case he should of made the week an hour longer.*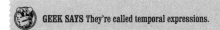
> (I should point out this is not a mistake by the writers of The Simpsons.
> I found this quote on someone's personal website.)

It's also worth noting that *can't* expands to *cannot*, which is written as one word (i.e. not *can not*). I should add there's a rule out there which states that *can not* (written as two words) is to be used for extra emphasis. Does it add extra emphasis? To me, it just looks like the writer can't spell *cannot*. Can NOT is definitely more emphatic, but I wouldn't recommend using it. Just use *cannot*, if I were you. After all, extra emphasis can come from the other words in your sentence (e.g. stick *really* before *cannot*).

5 APOSTROPHES – IN TIME EXPRESSIONS

GEEK SAYS They're called temporal expressions.

Apostrophes are used in time expressions such as *three years' insurance*. (These are also called temporal expressions.) In a temporal expression, the apostrophe is positioned before the *s* for a singular unit of time (e.g. *a minute, one day, one month*) and after the *s* for more than one (e.g. *two minutes, five days, two months*). For example:

- *I never did a day's work in my life.* ✔ (*Thomas A. Edison*)
  (one day – apostrophe before the *s*)
- *That is the equivalent of one year's pay.* ✔
  (one year – apostrophe before the *s*)
- *My car came with a years' free insurance.* ✖
  (one year – apostrophe should be before the *s*)
- *There is six months' interest-free credit on all sofas.* ✔
  (six months – apostrophe after the *s*)

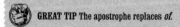

It's not always about time.

The vast majority of these expressions are time expressions, but some relate to value and distance too:

- *10 euros' worth of potatoes and 1 euro's worth of onions* ✔
  (Note the apostrophe is after the *s* for 10 but before the *s* for 1.)
- *a stone's throw away* ✔ (One stone – apostrophe before the *s*)

Beware! Do not use an apostrophe in all time expressions. The following do not have, nor should they have, any apostrophes in them:
- *The time not to become a father is eighteen years before a war.* ✔
  (E. B. White)
- *She has six months left on her loan.* ✔

This point creates great confusion for many. Here is a tip. Only use an apostrophe in an expression where the word *of* might have been used. Examples:

- *six months' insurance* ✔ (six months *of* insurance)
- *one year's pay* ✔ (a year *of* pay)
- *She has six months' left on her loan.* ✖ (She has six months *of* left on her loan. This is nonsense. It's wrong.)

GREAT TIP The apostrophe replaces *of.*

6 APOSTROPHES – THE PLURAL OF ABBREVIATIONS

It's rare, but you can use 's to show a plural.

The plurals of abbreviations, letters and numbers can be written using apostrophes. I should point out that if you ever wanted to start a fight amongst grammarians, this would be the subject to raise. There are two opposing camps: those who say apostrophes should never be used to show plurals and those who condone it if it helps the reader. I'm in the latter camp. Here are some examples of when apostrophes can help with plurals:

- *He sent three SOS's between midnight and 6 a.m.* ✔
- *There are two a's in accommodation.* ✔
- *1000's of bargains.* ✔

In these examples, the apostrophe makes the abbreviation, letter or number instantly recognisable. However, apostrophes can also be used for possession. Therefore, when an apostrophe is used to show a plural, it could lead to ambiguity. For example, look at this newspaper headline:

- *MP's plan failure* ✖ (Is this about MPs planning to fail or the failure of an MP's plan?)

Only use an apostrophe to show the plural of an abbreviation, a letter or number to assist your reader. Using *'s* to show a plural will cause your reader to pause while a mental check is performed to determine whether the apostrophe is to show a plural or possession. In the majority of cases, you should form the plural by adding just *s* (i.e. without the apostrophe).

Some more examples where the apostrophes help:

- *You use too many and's in your writing.* ✔ (The apostrophe assists the reader in this example. Of course, other versions would be possible (e.g. *"and"s, ands, ands*), but *and's* is by far the clearest.)
- *There are two consecutive i's in the words skiing and taxiing.* ✔

In most cases, the inclusion of an apostrophe doesn't make things much clearer. I think SOS's is a little clearer than SOSs, but I don't think MOT's is clearer than MOTs. Summary: Try quite hard not to use an apostrophe to show a plural, but if you're sure it helps more than it hinders, go for it. See Section 59 for guidance on when to use periods/full stops in abbreviations.

– BRACKETS –

7 BRACKETS – AN OVERVIEW

Round Brackets for Additional Information. Round brackets are used to insert additional information in text. If you were to remove the brackets and the information inside, the text would still work. For example:

- *Set in the 17th century, The Three Musketeers ("Les Trois Mousquetaires" in French) is a novel by Alexandre Dumas.* ✔
- *Although they are relatively common off Australia, California, South Africa and Mexico, great white sharks usually inhabit coastal waters where the water temperature ranges 12–24°C. They generally hunt by detecting the electrical fields (they can detect less than one billionth of a volt) emitted by the movements of their prey.* ✔

Using lots of brackets looks bad.

Using lots of brackets in your writing is usually a sign of bad sentence structure. Brackets also look a little informal in serious correspondence. Luckily, the latter issue is easily solved. You don't have to use brackets all the time. In fact, you have a choice between round brackets, commas and dashes. These are all called parentheses. The information between the parentheses is called a parenthesis. Bored? Sorry. If not, see Section 8 for more information on your options for parentheses. It's worth it. You'll become a more skilled writer.

Your additional information (i.e. your parenthesis) is often just a few words, but it can be a complete sentence or even a few sentences. (If it's any longer than that, you should probably reconsider whether it's appropriate as a parenthesis.)

If your parenthesis is a complete sentence, you should start it with a capital letter, end in a period/full stop and then close the brackets. (This sentence is an example.) However, if your parenthesis is a complete sentence that appears in the middle of another sentence, you have a choice. You can still use a capital letter and a period/full stop within the brackets if you think it makes your writing clearer, or you can use a lowercase letter and no end mark. (See the last example about great white sharks.) Using a lowercase letter and no end mark is a more common practice nowadays, because it looks less unwieldy.

Round Brackets to Denote Singular or Plural. For brevity, round brackets can be used to show that a word could be either singular or plural.

For example:
- *Please write the name(s) of your guest(s) in the section below.* ✔
- *Ensure the rod(s) is(are) aligned with the top section.* ✔

Square brackets are usually used with quotations.

Square Brackets to Make the Text Clearer. Square brackets can be used to add information that explains the text it follows. The information is usually added by someone other than the original author. Square brackets are commonly seen in quotations. For example:

- *Hedy Lamarr once said: "Most people save all their lives and leave it [their money] to somebody else."* ✔
- *"It [electricity] is really just organised lightning."* ✔

Square Brackets to Modify the Original Text. Square brackets are also used to replace text to make it clearer for the reader. The information is added by someone other than the original author. For example:

- *Hedy Lamarr once said: "Most people save all their lives and leave [their money] to somebody else."* ✔
  (The writer has replaced *it* with *[their money]*. In the similar example above, the word *it* was left in place. Both versions are okay.)

Square Brackets [sic]. The term *[sic]* is used to show that the word or words it follows featured in the original text. Often, *[sic]* is used to indicate that a grammar error in the text was committed by the original author.

 GREAT TIP *[sic]* is great for responding to snotty letters that contain grammar mistakes. Simply quote their grammar mistake verbatim in your reply and write *[sic]* afterwards. After they've looked it up, they'll be wounded. Hilarious. But, use with caution.

For example:

- *The minister believed that his statement was "appropriate and did not undermine the moral [sic] of our troops."* ✔
  (correct use of *[sic]* – should be *morale* not *moral*)
- *Your demand for a "full compliment [sic] of men" cannot be met at this time.* ✔
  (correct use of *[sic]* – should be *complement* not *compliment*)

Square Brackets [...]. Ellipsis is used to show text omitted from a quote. Ellipsis is usually written ... or [...]. It is used when an author wants to be succinct. If there are words in a sentence that don't add anything to the main point, they can be removed. It is good practice to replace the missing words with an ellipsis to show the reader that the quotation is not exactly what was said or written. For example:

- *It's no small irony that the government [...] ends up promoting precisely that which they would most like to repress.* ✔
  (The ellipsis replaces *"inevitably and invariably,"* but the author didn't feel the reader needed to know that.)
- *Andy Warhol is the only genius... with an IQ of 60.* ✔ (Gore Vidal)
  (The ellipsis replaces the words *"I've ever known."*)

8 BRACKETS – REPLACED BY COMMAS OR DASHES

 GEEK SAYS A parenthesis is separated from the rest of the sentence with parentheses.

Parenthesis? A parenthesis adds more information to a sentence. For example:

- *Mel Blanc, the voice of Bugs Bunny, was allergic to carrots.* ✔
  (The words *"the voice of Bugs Bunny"* add more information. The parenthesis is between two commas.)
- *Kent Oliver – the only professional jockey from Jersey – won his first race on Tuesday.* ✔
  (The words *"the only professional jockey from Jersey"* add more information. The parenthesis is between two dashes.)
- *Kent Oliver won his first race on Tuesday.* ✔
  (There is no parenthesis in this example.)

If you remove a parenthesis, the sentence will still work.

For Parenthesis, Use Commas, Dashes or Brackets. A parenthesis is separated from the rest of the sentence by commas, dashes or brackets (all called parentheses). When a parenthesis is completely removed, the sentence is still grammatically correct. Try reading each sentence below with its parenthesis (underlined) removed:

- *Jamie Buxton, <u>who fainted in church during his wedding</u>, apologised to his wife by booking two tickets to New York.* ✔
  (The parentheses chosen were commas. However, brackets or dashes could have been used.)
- *At midnight last night, Skip (<u>a guard dog for Bonds Ltd in Bury</u>) hospitalised two burglars before returning to eat the steaks they had thrown him.* ✔
  (The writer chose brackets, probably because there is already a comma in the sentence.)
- *Dave Jenkins' best friend, <u>Adam Wright-Smith</u>, stabbed him through the heart while testing a knife-proof jacket. Dave is expected to make a full recovery.* ✔
  (The writer chose commas, possibly because there are already two hyphens in the sentence, and dashes look similar to hyphens.)

 GREAT OPPORTUNITY Showcase your writing skills by using dashes occasionally.

However, As a Result. Inserted comments such as *however, therefore, as a result, as far as I am concerned, for all intents and purposes, subsequently,* and *so to speak*, fall into the category of parenthesis. (As a rule, brackets are not used with these.) Examples (parenthesis underlined):

- *The slow cooker I purchased at your store is, <u>for all intents and purposes</u>, utterly useless.* ✔
- *Darius, <u>on the other hand</u>, writes his own songs.* ✔
- *It rained all day, and, <u>as a result</u>, the hut collapsed.* ✔
- *On a happier note, her latest song – <u>Wind Me Up Baby</u> – is, <u>according to those in the know</u>, expected to enter the charts in the top 5.* ✔
  (*"Wind Me Up Baby"* is parenthesis and so is *"according to those in the know"*. Try reading the sentence with them removed. It still makes sense.)

Which One Should I Use? It is your choice whether to use commas, brackets or dashes for parentheses. Below are some guidelines:

Dashes. Parenthesis easily seen, but dashes look a little stark
Commas. Normal looking sentence, but commas are often confused with other commas in the sentence
Brackets. Parenthesis easily seen, but brackets make official letters look a little unorganised

– COLONS –

9 COLONS – FOR INTRODUCTIONS

A colon can be used to introduce something. The wording before the colon should introduce whatever follows. For example:

- *Visit: www.grammar-monster.com* ✔
- *The following points were noted during the fire-safety survey:*
  a. Fire exits blocked by empty boxes.
  b. Batteries dead in smoke detectors.
  c. Waste-paper bins used as ashtrays. ✔
- *Contact us by:*
  Phone: 01908 311267
  E-mail: colin@lion-tamers.co.uk ✔ (all colons correct)
- *Beer: The cause of, and solution to, all of life's problems.* ✔
  (Homer Simpson)
- *The English country gentleman galloping after a fox: the*
  unspeakable in full pursuit of the uneatable. ✔ (Oscar Wilde)

Warning – Definitely Not a Semicolon. Do not use semicolons for introductions. For example:

- *I spotted the following members of the crow family on the moors;*
  carrion crow
  magpie
  rook ✖

 BEWARE Don't use a semicolon to introduce a list.

No Hyphen. There is no need to add a hyphen to a colon. For example:

- *You will benefit from:-*
  Lower interest rates
  Free survey
  Online helpdesk ✖
  (It's a bit harsh to mark this wrong. It's just outdated. I usually think "git" whenever I see it, and it would never survive my proofreading.)

10 COLONS – TO EXTEND A SENTENCE

Extend a Sentence with a Colon. You can use a colon to expand on something previously mentioned in the sentence. For example:

- *The cat's fur was found in two rooms: the bedroom and the kitchen.* ✔
- *His success is attributed to one thing: determination.* ✔
- *It is by the fortune of God that, in this country, we have three benefits: freedom of speech, freedom of thought, and the wisdom never to use either.* ✔ (Mark Twain)
- *A single death is a tragedy: a million deaths is a statistic.* ✖ (Joseph Stalin)
  (This should be a semicolon not a colon. The words after the colon do not add more information about something previously mentioned.)

When a slight break is preferable to a new sentence, use a semicolon not a colon. Remember, a colon introduces words that explain something previously mentioned in the sentence. (This is also covered in Sections 24 and 75.) More examples:

- *I have made an important discovery: alcohol, taken in sufficient quantities, produces all the effects of intoxication.* ✔ (Oscar Wilde)
- *In this world there are only two tragedies: one is not getting what one wants, and the other is getting it.* ✔ (Oscar Wilde)
- *There are five principal actors in this conflict: the Afghan population, GIRoA, ISAF, the insurgency and the external "players." It is important to begin with an understanding of each of these actors, starting with the most important: the people.* ✔ (General McChrystal)

Treat a colon like an equals sign.

Colons Are Like Equals Signs. Think of the colon as an equals sign. In the three examples at the top of the page:

- *two rooms = bedroom and kitchen*
- *one thing = determination*
- *three benefits = freedom of speech, freedom of thought, and the wisdom never to use either*

When a colon is used in this way, the wording after the colon is an *equal phrase*. It is also known as an *appositive phrase* to something mentioned before the colon.

 GEEK SAYS They're called appositive phrases.

When Not To Use a Colon. When a slight break is preferable to new sentence, you should use a semicolon (see Section 31) and not a colon. For example:

- *John fumbled for the keyhole: the street lights had failed again.* ✖

⑪ COLONS – WITH BULLET POINTS

A colon is often used to introduce bullet points. When using bullets, be consistent throughout the document with the style (e.g. capital letters and punctuation at the start and end of each bullet). In the first example below, each bullet starts with a capital letter and ends with a period/full stop. Choose whatever format you like, but be consistent throughout your document.

- *Dr Mole won the following events:*
  Egg-and-spoon race.
  Toss the pancake.
  Apple bobbing. ✔
- *The birds listed below were spotted during the survey:*
  Dipper (two).
  bittern (one).
  Grey Wagtail (twelve). ✖
  (small *b* on *bittern* – not consistent)

Also, ensure all your bullets make sense when read with the words before the colon. Here is an example from a bottle of fluoride mouthwash:

- *OROSA Helps Fight:*
  Tooth Decay
  Plaque
  Freshens Breath ✖
  (The last bullet does not follow on from the introductory words.)

It is good practice to write your bullets in the same style. For example:

- *It is a picturesque region, but I would advise visitors to avoid:*
  Bathing in the river
  Driving in the town
  The local tapas bar ✖
  (This makes perfect sense, but it is not tidy. *Eating in the local tapas bar would* have been better.)

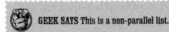

GEEK SAYS This is a non-parallel list.

When list items are written in the same style, they are said to be *parallel*. The list above is *non-parallel*. Ensuring your lists (not just bulleted lists but all lists) are parallel will test your English skills and slow you down, but they are easier to read. Creating parallel lists will portray you as a clear thinker. It's worth the investment.

12 COLONS – IN REFERENCES

Colons as Dividers. Colons are useful to divide the parts of references, titles and times. (They often make better separators than the alternative punctuation marks.) For example:

- *Learn Chapter XIV: Section 4: Paragraph 6 by tomorrow.* ✔
  (commas could be used too)
- *Have you read "Mars: The Landing"?* ✔
  (The author opted to use a colon but could have used a dash.)
- *The alarm clock is set for 07:30.* ✔
  (0730 and 07.30 are also correct)

13 COLONS – BEFORE QUOTATIONS

When introducing a quotation of more than six words, use a colon. For quotations with six or fewer words, use a comma. For example:

- *Did Albert Einstein really say: "If the facts don't fit the theory, change the facts"?* ✔
- *It was Kilgore Trout who said, "The universe is a big place, perhaps the biggest."* ✖
  (More than six words – some would prefer a colon)
- *Muhammad Ali responded: "My toughest fight? My first wife."* ✖
  (only six words – some would prefer a comma)

How much do you want your readers to pause?

This is not a rigid grammar rule. Most consider it very outdated. Nowadays, writers can choose a colon, a comma or nothing to introduce a quotation. It depends largely on the desired flow of the text (i.e. how much you want your readers to pause). This is also covered in Section 34.

– COMMAS –

14 COMMAS – AFTER "SETTING THE SCENE"

Set the 'scene,' then put a comma.

It is common to start a sentence with an introduction. An introduction can be anything from just one word to a long clause. In general, an introduction is used to state a time, a place, a condition, a frequency or a fact before the main part of the sentence. (Introductions vary hugely.) Examples (introduction underlined):

- *In the centre of London, the number of people who fell victim to pickpockets rose by 30 per cent in a month.* ✔ (sets a place)
- *As soon as the cake is golden brown, take it out of the oven.* ✔ (sets a time)
- *From the moment I picked your book up until I laid it down, I was convulsed with laughter. Some day, I intend reading it.* ✔ (Groucho Marx) (both set a time)
- *The last time I saw him, he was walking down Lover's Lane holding his own hand.* ✔ (sets a time)
- *When I was young, I used to think that money was the most important thing in life. Now that I am old, I know it is.* ✔ (Oscar Wilde) (both set a time)
- *On Tuesday 4th July a band played carols in the park for eight hours.* ✘ (*On Tuesday 4th July* sets a time. It is an introduction and should be followed by a comma. Marking this wrong is a bit harsh. See the paragraph on leniency on the next page.)
- *A band played in the park for eight hours on Tuesday 4th July.* ✔ (*On Tuesday 4th July* sets a time, but it is not an introduction – it's at the back of the sentence. No comma required.)
- *As you are aware, the latest figures do not look promising.* ✔ (states a fact)
- *After the secretary had read the minutes of the meeting, the chairman asked for the financial report.* ✔ (sets a time)
- *If you're going through hell, keep going.* ✔ (Winston Churchill) (sets a condition)
- *If I had a dollar for every time I heard "My God! He's covered in some sort of goo," I'd be a rich man.* ✔ (Homer Simpson) (sets a condition)

Only Use a Comma for an Introduction. Words that "set the scene" do not always start the sentence; they could appear at the back or in the middle. You only need a comma when these words appear at the front of the sentence.

This is very handy to know.

- *At 4 o'clock, the new manager, David Bain, will visit.* ✔
  (correct, but way too many commas)
- *The new manager, David Bain, will visit at 4 o'clock.* ✔
  (correct – much tidier)

Here is an example in the middle of a sentence:

- *I'm very proud of my gold pocket watch. My grandfather, on his deathbed, sold me this watch.* (Woody Allen)
  (Commas have been used, but they were not necessary, because the phrase that sets the scene appears in the middle not at the beginning.)

A Lot of Leniency on This Ruling. Regardless of where the scene-setting words appear (start, middle or end), there is some leniency on whether to use commas or not. The primary purpose of using a comma (or commas) to separate your scene-setting words from the rest of the sentence is to assist your readers. Especially if your introduction is short (e.g. *Yesterday*, *Today*, *Tomorrow*, *Now*, *Since then*), you can safely omit the comma. Above all else, making your text easy to read should determine whether you use a comma or not.

15 COMMAS – AFTER A TRANSITIONAL PHRASE

 GEEK SAYS "However" and "Consequently" are transitional phrases.

It is a common practice to start a sentence with an introduction that acts like a bridge from the previous sentence. The terms *However*, *As a result* and *Consequently* are examples. These are called *transitional phrases*. A *transitional phrase* is always followed by a comma. Examples:

- *Complacency towards the obesity time-bomb has been staggering. Consequently, death rates in the next 20 years will increase sharply as today's generation of fatties become middle-aged.* ✔

(*Consequently* is a transitional phrase. It acts like a bridge between the previous sentence and the new one. It is followed by a comma.)

- *Bruce Leonard spent four years in Japan studying Kung Fu and three years at the London School of Martial Arts as the senior instructor. As a result, his style is difficult to categorise.* ✔
  (*As a result* is a transitional phrase – followed by a comma.)
- *It may be hard for us to understand how overwhelming US military power appears to other countries. In summary, the world is looking for reassurance that the US is constrained by international law.* ✔
  (*In summary* – transitional phrase)
- *Of course, he never knew…* ✔
  (*Of course* – transitional phrase)
- *Therefore, the cost of each lesson…* ✔
  (*Therefore* – transitional phrase)
- *However, Bruce was unaware…* ✔
  (*However* – transitional phrase)

Semicolons Now and Again. On occasion, you may wish to use a semicolon before a transitional phrase to make the transition between sentences smoother. (See Section 32.) For example:

- *Man is always more than he can know of himself; consequently, his accomplishments, time and again, will come as a surprise to him.* ✔
  (Golo Mann)
- *It is necessary; therefore, it is possible.* ✔ (G. A. Borghese)

Never a Comma. You cannot use a comma before a transitional phrase. For example:

- *I dream, therefore I exist.* ✖ (J. A. Strindberg)
  (Yeah, very clever. The comma is dodgy though. This would have been better: *I dream. Therefore, I exist.* ✔ I can also live with: *I dream; therefore, I exist.* ✔)
- *I cannot come on Tuesday, however, Peter will be there.* ✖✖

This is a very common error – especially with *however*, which is why I've given it two crosses.

 BEWARE Don't finish a sentence, put a comma, and continue with "however."

A Comma before However. Don't get confused between transitional phrases (Section 15) and parenthesis. In the example below, the first *However* is a transitional phrase. A transitional phrase sits at the start of the sentence to act as a link to the previous sentence. You cannot precede it with a comma. The second *however* is a parenthesis and should be offset with commas.

- *I like celery soup. However, I hate celery. John, however, likes celery but hates celery soup.*

When *However* is a transitional phrase, you can replace it quite comfortably with *But*. When *however* is a parenthesis, you can't replace it with *but* comfortably (unless you're from the deepest parts of Glasgow).

16 COMMAS – AFTER AN INTERJECTION

Expressions such as *yes*, *no* and *indeed* (which often feature at the start of a sentence) are known as *interjections*. Use a comma (or commas) to separate them from the rest of the sentence. Examples:

- *Well, if I called the wrong number, why did you answer the phone?* ✔
- *Yes, she will apologise.* ✔
- *Absolutely, a fifth of all the students live in the village.* ✔

In the examples above, the interjections all appear at the start. If an interjection appears mid-sentence, offset it with commas. If it appears at the end, offset it with a comma. Examples:

- *Jesus was a Jew, yes, but only on his mother's side.* ✔
  (Stanley Ralph Ross)
- *It's cold, indeed.* ✔

An interjection can also be followed by an exclamation mark. This gives the interjection more impact. (Consider the difference between "No!" and "No,".) (This is also covered in Section 46.)

Usually Not in Business Writing. Interjections are usually used when spoken words are being quoted. You should avoid them in business writing. Most people avoid them instinctively, but I have noticed that *indeed* often creeps into formal documents. My advice? Delete it every time.

17 COMMAS – BEFORE A CONJUNCTION

 BAD TIP (1) Don't put a comma before "and." (2) Always put a comma before "and." Unfortunately, the rules are quite complicated.

Do you put a comma before *and*? Unfortunately, the rules governing this are pretty nasty, especially if you're British. It's a little easier for Americans. Here's why:

In the US. Always put a comma before *and* unless there are only two list items. For example:

- *Lisa, vampires are make-believe – just like elves, gremlins, and Eskimos.* ✔ (US) (Homer Simpson)

In this example, there are three list items (*elves, gremlins, and Eskimos*). Therefore, under US convention, the comma is required. Had Homer said *like elves and gremlins*, a comma before *and* would have been wrong.

In the UK. Don't put a comma before *and* unless it is being used to merge two sentences into one. (This is covered below.) Oh, these rules don't just apply to *and*. They apply to all conjunctions.

GEEK SAYS The word *and* is a conjunction.

Words like *and*, *or* and *but* are known as *conjunctions*. There are other conjunctions, but these three are by far the most common. (See Section 44.) As well as conjunctions being used in lists, they can be used to merge two sentences into one. This is very common. When a conjunction is used in this way, it should have a comma before it. Examples:

- *He is a great swimmer, but he prefers to play golf.* ✔
  (*He is a great swimmer. + He prefers to play golf.*)
  (This is two sentences merged into one with *but* – comma required.)
- *I may consider your plan, or I may disregard it.* ✔
  (*I may consider your plan + I may disregard it.*)
  (This is two sentences merged into one with *or* – comma required.)

- *The female applicant must be able to tell jokes and sing, and she must be able to dance.* ✔
  (*The female applicant must be able to tell jokes and sing. + She must be able to dance.*)
  (This is two sentences merged into one with *and* – comma required.)
- *The female applicant must be able to tell jokes, sing, and dance.* ✔ (Okay in US) ✖ (Wrong in UK)
  (No comma is required for Brits. Remember, US convention is to use a comma before the conjunction if the list is longer than two items. Here, it is three list items: *tell jokes, sing, and dance.*)
- *Basically, my wife was immature. I'd be at home in my bath, and she'd come in and sink my boats.* ✔ (Woody Allen)
  (The last sentence is made up of two standalone sentences – the comma before *and* is good. There is no need for the comma before the last *and*, because the list only has two things: *come in and sink my boats.*)

 GREAT TIP Use a comma before *and* if it's used to merge two sentences into one.

- *Drink is the curse of the land. It makes you fight with your neighbour. It makes you shoot at your landlord and it makes you miss him.* ✖
  (*It makes you miss him* is a sentence. The second sentence is actually two merged into one – comma required before *and*)
- *A little dog can start a hare, but it takes a big one to catch it.* ✔
  (Two sentences merged into one – the comma before *but* is good.)
- *I have nothing to offer but blood, toil, tears, and sweat.* ✖ (Winston Churchill)
  (Under UK convention, there is no need for the comma before *and*. Under US convention, the comma is fine, because there are more than two list items. In fact there are four: *blood, toil, tears, and sweat.* I'm marking this wrong, because it's a Churchill quote; i.e. it's wrong under UK convention.)
- *The play was a great success, but the audience was a disaster.* ✔ (Oscar Wilde)
  (Two sentences merged into one – the comma before *but* is good.)
- *We make a living by what we get, but we make a life by what we give.* ✔ (Winston Churchill)
  (Two sentences merged into one – the comma before *but* is good.)

Don't Worry. It Gets Worse. When sentences containing commas are merged together using a conjunction, it is possible to use a semicolon instead of a comma. (See Section 33.) However, this is quite an outdated practice in modern writing. Use it very sparingly – if at all. Example:

● *Last year, PLC provided the material; and we, L&S Ltd, built the road.* ✔ (This is two sentences merged into one with *and*. As each sentence already contains commas, the writer has decided to outrank them with a semicolon before *and*.)

Use a comma to help your readers.

Assist your Reader. On occasion, it is appropriate to put a comma before a conjunction to assist your reader. For example:

● *The emblem is an amalgamation of the Stars and Stripes, and the Hammer and Sickle.* ✔ (Under US and UK conventions, there is no need for the comma before *and* (the one after *Stripes*). However, in this case, it helps to define the two list items clearly.)

In Truth, It's Not That Well Defined. I must admit to being a little rigid in claiming these are the US and UK conventions. Generally, they are, but Americans and Brits are not consistent in sticking to them. This is covered more in Section 19. I would recommend reading Section 19 (at least the last two paragraphs).

It's old fashioned to use a semicolon before **and**.

⑱ COMMAS – TO REPLACE BRACKETS

You can use commas to separate a parenthesis from the rest of the sentence.

Parenthesis? A parenthesis is additional information in a sentence. If a parenthesis is removed, the sentence still makes sense. Examples:

● *The defendant, Mr Michael Evans, sat in silence.* ✔ (*Mr Michael Evans* is additional information. This is a parenthesis.)
● *The last owner of the Red Lion, who is my sister's friend, won over 4 million on the National Lottery.* ✔ (*who is my sister's friend* is additional information. This is a parenthesis.)

When they appear mid-sentence, comments such as *however*, *therefore*, *as a result* and *as far as I am concerned* fall into the category of parenthesis too. Examples:

- *John Winfield, on the other hand, is an experienced jockey.* ✔
- *We have really everything in common with America nowadays except, of course, language.* ✔ (Oscar Wilde)

 GREAT TIP You don't have to use commas. You can use dashes or brackets

It is also possible to use dashes or brackets, but commas look more natural. When used in this way, commas, dashes and brackets are called *parentheses*.
  Some more examples of parenthesis:

- *The second boat in the race, the six-berth Kontarka, was crewed by school children from Pembrokeshire.* ✔
- *Last year's Great Britain faggot-eating champion who works in my section came in here and ate two loaves of bread in one sitting.* ✖ (*who works in my section* is a parenthesis. It should be separated from the remainder of the sentence with commas. Oh, in the UK, faggots are a kind of meatball made from offal and vegetables. I didn't add this example for a cheap laugh from US readers. I genuinely used to work with the GB faggot-eating champion. Boy, that lad can gulp down faggots.)

Although the use of commas for parentheses makes for a normal-looking sentence, they can become confused with other commas in the sentence. Example:

- *Last night, Josie, an escaped wallaby from London Zoo, attacked two young sisters, Rebecca and Josie, which is pure coincidence, Evans, in a bid to steal their crisps.*
  (Although grammatically correct, the writer could have used a mixture of parentheses in order to make the sentence a little clearer.)
- *Last night, Josie (an escaped wallaby from London Zoo) attacked two young sisters – Rebecca and Josie (which is pure coincidence) Evans – in a bid to steal their crisps.*

Section 8 offers more on parenthesis and your options for parentheses.

19 COMMAS – IN LISTS

This subject is a nightmare. If you want the bottom line without all the brain frying, go straight to the paragraph called "The Oxford Comma" and just read the last two paragraphs in this section. Seriously, it's worth it.

Are you sure you don't want to read just the last two paragraphs? Okay then, here we go. (You might have read some of this before in Section 17.)

When there are more than two items in a list, they should be separated using commas. The last item is usually preceded with *and*, *or* or *but*. (These are called *conjunctions*.) Under UK convention, there is normally no need to put a comma before the conjunction. In the US, the convention is to use a comma before the conjunction if there are more than two lists items. Examples:

- *The old vicar, the new vicar, the pub landlord, the mayor and the chairman were at the meeting.* ✔ (UK) ✘ (US)
  (no comma before *and*)
- *I have not seen any foxes, badgers or deer in these woods this year.* ✔ (UK) ✘ (US)
  (no comma before *or*)
- *A man loves his sweetheart the most, his wife the best, but his mother the longest.* ✘ (UK) ✔ (US)
  (Under UK convention, there is no need for the comma before *but*. However, if you think its inclusion helps your reader, break the ruling and put it in.)

Use a Comma to Avoid Ambiguity or to Assist Your Reader. On occasion, it is appropriate to place a comma before the conjunction to avoid ambiguity or to assist your reader.

Examples:

- *The news will be shown after Dangermouse, and Rugrats.* ✔ (UK) ✔ (US)
  (Without the comma, readers could think that *Dangermouse and Rugrats* is one programme.)
- *The emblem is an amalgamation of the British and Irish flags, the Stars and Stripes, and the Hammer and Sickle.* ✔ (UK) ✔ (US)
  (The word *and* appears lots of times in this example. The comma before the *and* makes it easier for the reader.)
- *The parade is to recognise the achievements of DC Jones, PC Pinner, and PC Hoyles.* ✘ (UK) ✔ (US)
  (no ambiguity – comma not required under UK convention)

Using Lots of Adjectives (Enumeration of Adjectives). We need to touch upon another point. Often in creative writing, authors will use several adjectives (describing words – See Section 40). The rules about using commas in a list of adjectives are far more relaxed. For TWO adjectives:

- *vast, inhospitable moor* ✔
- *vast and inhospitable moor* ✔
- *vast, and inhospitable moor* ✖ (UK and US)
- *vast inhospitable moor* ✔

For THREE or more adjectives:
- *vast, inhospitable, windy moor* ✔
- *vast, inhospitable and windy moor* ✔
- *vast, inhospitable, and windy moor* ✖ (UK) ✔ (US)
- *vast inhospitable windy moor* ✔
- *vast inhospitable and windy moor* ✔

Okay, let's get back to the main point.

Ambiguity between List Items and Parenthesis. As covered in Section 18, commas can be used to introduce additional information (called parenthesis). For example:

- *My friend, Simon, lives near the concrete cows in Milton Keynes.* ✔
  (In this example, commas are being used to add information about *my friend*. The parenthesis is the word *Simon*.)

Beware confusion with the extra comma.

This means that when a comma is used before a conjunction in a list, it could look like parenthesis and cause confusion. For example:

- *I left the pub with my friend, Simon, and Terry.*
  (Under UK convention, it is clear that I left with pub with two people: (1) my friend called Simon (2) Terry. Under US convention, this could be three people: (1) my unnamed friend (2) Simon (3) Terry.)
- *I left the pub with my friend, Simon and Terry.*
  (In this sentence, there is no ambiguity. It's three people. However, this would be wrong under US convention.)

Both the US and UK conventions can cause ambiguity.

The last example suggests that the US convention of using a comma before a conjunction leads to ambiguity. That's not the full story. The UK convention is equally ambiguous. Here's why:

The UK Convention – Don't Use a Comma. In the UK, it is common practice not to place a comma before the conjunction in a list. For example:

- *Eggs, milk and butter* ✔ (UK) ✖ (US)
- *I left the pub with my friend, Simon and Terry.* ✔ (UK) ✖ (US)

Hooray for the UK. The word *Simon* cannot be confused as parenthesis after *my friend*.

But, check this out:

- *My uncle left me all his property, warehouses and factories.*

It's unclear whether this means:
- *all his property (i.e. warehouses and factories)*
or
- *all his (1) property (2) warehouses (3) factories.*

The US convention does not completely eliminate the ambiguity. For example:

- *My uncle left me all his property, warehouses, and factories.*

It's unclear whether this means:

- *all his property (i.e. warehouses) and factories*
or
- *all his (1) property (2) warehouses (3) factories.*

Especially given the context, the first meaning seems highly unlikely, but it is grammatically feasible.

The Oxford Comma. From what I've said so far, the second comma in the example below would be okay under US convention but dodgy under UK convention.

- *Bread, milk, and eggs.* ✖ (UK) ✔ (US)

GREAT TIP Do whatever you want – just be consistent.

In truth, the delineation between the US and UK conventions are not that clear. There are many in the UK who follow the "US" convention. In fact, the unnecessary comma (from a UK perspective) is widely known as an *Oxford Comma* – as in Oxford, England – and plenty of people use it in Great Britain. There's more confusion. US journalists tend to follow the UK convention, but the "Oxford comma" is standard in US non-journalistic writing. Basically, do what the hell you like. The English-speaking world hasn't decided one way or the other yet.

Be Consistent – The Final Advice. Follow one of the conventions, and stick to it throughout your document. If you write something ambiguous, try to reword your sentence. If that proves too cumbersome, have the confidence to switch conventions in the same document. Thereafter, be prepared to defend your comma (or otherwise).

20 **COMMAS – WITH A LONG SUBJECT**

 GEEK SAYS If your subject has more than one element, it's a compound subject.

The subject of a sentence can consist of several things. (See opposite for an explanation of *subject of a sentence*.) When a subject has more than one element, it is known as a *compound subject*.)

Sometimes, the subject is made up of so many elements that writers like to end the list with a comma to group them together. Examples:

- *A clean driving licence, the ability to operate under pressure and five years' experience in marketing, are the only criteria stipulated by the selection panel.* ✔
  (*"A clean driving licence, the ability to operate under pressure and five years' experience in marketing"* is the compound subject of this sentence.)
- *Murder is the only crime that does not increase during the full moon. Theft, disorderly conduct, larceny, armed robbery, assault and battery, and rape, all statistically increase dramatically during the full moon.* ✔

("*Theft, disorderly conduct, larceny, armed robbery, assault and battery, and rape*" is the compound subject of the second sentence.)

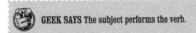

Only end a compound subject with a comma to assist your reader.

Frowned Upon. Be aware that ending a long compound subject with a comma is not popular with many grammarians. Only do it if you think it assists your reader. I can live with the commas in the examples above, but I wouldn't have used one in either example personally. I am happy with the comma in this example though:

- *Leaving a list of internet passwords, increasing your life insurance and writing a will, will give you peace of mind while you are on operations.* ✔

> **GEEK SAYS** The subject performs the verb.

What is the Subject of a Sentence? The subject of a sentence is the person or thing that is performing the verb in the sentence. (Verbs are doing words like *to dance* and *to sit*. Verbs are not all about actions though. *To think, to exist* and *to be* are also verbs. See Section 55.)

For example:

- *Balloons rose out of the stadium.*
  (The word *Balloons* is the subject of this sentence. They are performing the verb – the verb *to rise*.)
- *David Baker is a real gentleman.*
  (*David Baker* is the subject of this sentence. He is performing the verb – the verb *to be*.)
- *The man next door saw that stray dog again.*
  (*The man next door* – subject / *to see* – the verb)

21 COMMAS – WITH NUMBERS

Commas can be used to make reading numbers a little easier. They are placed every 3 decimal places for numbers comprising 4 digits or more.
For example:

- *1,234* ✔ *23,566* ✔
- *1,234,967* ✔

Do not put commas in reference numbers or years.

- *Serial number 1654880 was destroyed in 1984.* ✔

The Other Way Around in Europe. In Europe, the use of commas and periods/full stops in numbers is reversed. For example:

- *4,567.1* (British/US version)
- *4.567,1* (European version)

(This is also covered in Section 76 – Writing Numbers in Full.)

22 COMMAS – WITH SPEECH MARKS

A comma can be used before a quotation after words like *He said*, *She whispered*, *It stated*, etc. (This is also covered in Sections 13 and 34.) Examples:

- *The janitor pointed at the photograph and said, "That's me in the '60s."* ✔
- *He made a fair point when he said, "Sharks only attack wet people."* ✔
- *The sign states, "Animals drive very slowly."* ✔

Commas for Short Quotations. There are guidelines (fast becoming outdated) which state that only a quotation of six words or fewer should be introduced with a comma. Longer quotations should be introduced with a colon.
For example:

- *Lewis Grizzard once claimed: "Life is like a dogsled team. If you ain't the lead dog, the scenery never changes."* ✔

There is a lot of leniency on this. See Section 34.

23 COMMAS – WHEN ADDRESSING SOMEONE

GEEK SAYS If you address someone, their name is in the vocative case.

When addressing someone directly, separate the name being used (e.g. *John*, *Mary*, *my darling*, *you little rascal*, *my son*, *pecker head*) from the rest of the sentence using a comma or commas.

For example:

- *Alan, put your hand up if you do not understand.* ✔
  (*Alan* is being addressed directly. The word *Alan* must be separated from the rest of the sentence with a comma.)
- *Where do you think you are going, you little devil?* ✔
  (Somebody is being addressed as *you little devil*, which must be separated from the rest of the sentence with a comma.)
- *Absolutely, John, get your skates on.* ✔
  (*John* is being addressed. His name must be separated from the rest of the sentence using commas.)

Some Grammar Geekery. In the examples above, the words *Alan*, *you little devil* and *John* are all said to be in the vocative case. I reckon it was the vocative case that saved President Clinton's bacon in the Monica Lewinski scandal, but this aspect of the case is not widely reported. Intrigued? The vocative case and its possible role in the Lewinski scandal is covered more in Section 85.

– DASHES –

24 DASHES – TO EXTEND A SENTENCE

Dashes (–) look like hyphens (-), but they are a bit longer. As the dash does not feature on most keyboards, many writers use two hyphens (--) for a dash. General McChrystal is keen on this. For example:

- *We face not only a resilient and growing insurgency, there is also a crisis of confidence among Afghans -- in both their government and the international community -- that undermines our credibility and emboldens the insurgents.* (General McChrystal)

 OPPORTUNITY Show off by differentiating between dashes and hyphens.

As you hit the space bar after typing a hyphen, your PC will try to determine whether you really wanted a dash, and it may offer you one. However, PCs usually get it wrong. (One of my first jobs when I've finished writing this book is to go back and change all the hyphens that are meant to be dashes to dashes.)

Dashes are very handy.

It's worth learning about the dash, because it can be used instead of a colon, a semicolon or three dots to extend a sentence (see Section 75). Covered briefly below, the rules governing when to use a colon, a semicolon or three dots can be quite confusing, and sometimes there is a strong argument for different ones. In such cases, stop the debate, and use a dash. Job done.

Using Colons. A sentence can be extended with a colon when the writer wishes to expand on something already mentioned in the sentence. Example:

- *He blamed his divorce on one thing: beer.* ✔

Using Semicolons. A sentence can be extended with a semicolon when a slight break is preferable to a new sentence. Example:

- *No one was hurt in the accident; the only real injury was a broken finger.* ✔

Using Three Dots. If you want to create a pause for effect, use three dots. For example:

- *Bart, with $10,000, we'd be millionaires! We could buy all kinds of useful things like…love!* ✔ (Homer Simpson)

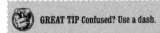 **GREAT TIP** Confused? Use a dash.

Using Dashes. Confused about colons, semicolons and three dots? Use a dash. The dash performs the functions of the colon, the semicolon and three dots. Examples:

- *He blamed his divorce on one thing – beer.* ✔
  (replaces the colon)
- *No one was hurt – the only injury was a broken finger.* ✔
  (The dash replaces the semicolon. This is a great example of a sentence that could have been extended with a semicolon or a colon. There is no need to have that debate. Use a dash.)
- *Bart, with $10,000, we'd be millionaires! We could buy all kinds of useful things like – love!* ✔
  (replaces the three dots)
- *I've been looking for a girl like you – not you, but a girl like you.* ✔
  (Groucho Marx)
  (replaces three dots)
- *I'm really a timid person – I was beaten up by Quakers.* ✔
  (Woody Allen)
  (replaces a semicolon)

25 DASHES – TO REPLACE BRACKETS

Dashes can be used to replace brackets. For example:

- *Zander (one of the fastest fish in British waters) often school together around the edges of lakes.* ✔
  (with brackets)
- *Zander – one of the fastest fish in British waters – often school together around the edges of lakes.* ✔
  (with dashes)

Commas can also be used to replace brackets. When a pair of dashes or commas is used in this way, writers often forget to end the pairing. This is as wrong as not closing a pair of brackets. For example:

- *Zander – one of the fastest fish in British waters often school together around the edges of lakes.* ✖
  (should be a dash after *waters*)
- *Zander, one of the fastest fish in British waters often school together around the edges of lakes.* ✖
  (should be a comma after *waters*)

Guidance on when to use commas, dashes and brackets is offered in Section 8.

– HYPHENS –

26 HYPHENS – IN COMPOUND ADJECTIVES

Hyphens (-) can be used to link the words in an adjective that is made up of more than one word; e.g. *ten-storey* building or *never-to-be-forgotten* experience. Let's whizz over the grammar.

Adjective? An adjective is a describing word (e.g. big, red – See Section 40).

 GEEK SAYS A compound adjective is a single adjective made up of more than one word

Compound Adjective? A single adjective made up of two or more words is called a *compound adjective*. The words in a *compound adjective* can be linked together by a hyphen (or hyphens) to show they are part of the same adjective. In the UK, this is expected. Americans are more lenient. The US ruling is: Use a hyphen if it eliminates ambiguity or helps your reader, else don't bother.

The Hyphen Might Be Essential. Sometimes a hyphen is essential to avoid ambiguity. Look at these examples:

- *a heavy-metal detector* ✔ *a heavy metal detector* ✔
  (Both are correct, but they mean different things. The first device detects heavy metals. The second detects metal, and it is heavy.)

Some more examples of compound adjectives (UK convention):

- *three-page document* ✔
  (*three-page* is a compound adjective)
- *ironing-board cover* ✔
  (*ironing-board* is a compound adjective)

The easiest compound adjectives to spot are the ones which include numbers. Examples:

- *Two-seater aircraft* ✔
- *Four-bedroom house* ✔
- *Ten stone weakling* ✖ (should be *Ten-stone*)

Not all compound adjectives include numbers. Often, a compound adjective consists of words that would not normally be joined together with a hyphen. Examples:

- *The double glazing is leaking. Can you call that double-glazing salesman?* ✔
  (*double-glazing* describes *salesman*)
- *You call this silver service? She's not a trained silver-service waitress.* ✔
  (*silver-service* describes *waitress*)
- *Carl is far too chatty. Philip is another far-too-chatty individual.* ✔
  (*far-too-chatty* describes *individual*)

More Than One Adjective or a Compound Adjective? Do not be tempted to string all adjectives together with hyphens. It is common to use more than one adjective to describe something. When you use two or more adjectives to describe one thing, it is called *enumeration of adjectives* (see Section 19). For example:

- A big maroon car ✔
  (Two adjectives: *big* and *maroon*)
- She is an intelligent-articulate lady. ✖
  (Two adjectives: *intelligent* and *articulate*. There should be no hyphen. This is also covered in Section 41.)

Don't use a hyphen with adverbs.

Adverbs with Adjectives. Adjectives are often preceded by adverbs (e.g. very, well, beautifully, extremely – see Section 42). Usually, there is no need to link an adverb to an adjective using a hyphen. Example:

- *Paula is a very talented student.* ✔ (As *very* is an adverb, it should not be linked to the adjective *talented* with a hyphen.)

Linking an adverb like *very*, *most* or *least* to an adjective with a hyphen is an uncommon error. However, when an adverb ends with the letters *ly* (and lots do), some writers feel the urge to link it to the adjective with a hyphen – there is no need.

- *It was a wonderfully-decorated tree.* ✖
  (The adverb *wonderfully* modifies the adjective *decorated*, but there is no need to join the two with a hyphen.)

However, with words like *well*, *fast* and *best* (which – rather confusingly – are both adjectives and adverbs), a hyphen can be used to avoid ambiguity. For example:

- *Alan is the best-known player on the pitch.* ✔
  (Alan is known better than any other player.)
- *Alan is the best known player on the pitch.* ✔
  (Alan could be the best player of all the known players on the pitch.)

This is covered in more detail in Section 42 – Adverbs.

Trick to Spot a Compound Adjective. Put *and* between the words. If there is a loss of meaning, you are dealing with a compound adjective. For example:

1 Here's what you're checking: *large proud rooster*
2 Put *and* in between: *large* and *proud rooster*
3 Although different in style, there is no loss of meaning. This is an example of two adjectives. No hyphen required.

Next one:
1 Here's what you're checking: *free range rooster*
2 Put *and* in between: *free* and *range rooster*
3 There is a change in meaning. The rooster is not *free* and what is a *range rooster*? This is a compound adjective and should be written as *free-range rooster*. *Free-range* is one adjective made up of two words. It's a *compound adjective*. Hyphen required.

Just hyphenate the adjective.

Just the Adjectives Get Hyphens. It is a mistake to join the adjective and whatever is being described with a hyphen. For example:

- *Biggs served only a year of his 30-year-sentence.* ✖ (should be *30-year sentence*)
- *Getting kicked out of the American Bar Association is like getting kicked out of the Book-of-the-Month-Club.* ✖
  (should be *Book-of-the-Month Club*. This could also be written without the hyphens as title case serves to group the adjective (see Section 27). In this case, the capital *C* is correct, because it forms part of the name. But, it is not part of the compound adjective, which is *Book of the Month*.)

27 HYPHENS – ALTERNATIVES IN COMPOUND ADJECTIVES

It's not all about hyphens.

You don't always have to use hyphens to link the words of a compound adjective (see the section above). You can link them using capital letters, italics or speech marks (or a mix of these). Examples:

- *Anna gave George her "don't you dare" look.* ✔ (The compound adjective could have been written *don't-you-dare*. However, for style purposes, the writer chose to group the elements of the adjective using speech marks.)
- *The actions are in accordance with Dayton Peace Accord regulations.* ✔ (When titles are used as adjectives, it is more appropriate to use title case (see Section 68) to group the adjective together. In this example, the compound adjective is *Dayton Peace Accord*.)
- It is an exclusive restaurant with an *à la carte* menu. ✔ (When foreign terms are used as an adjective, they are often grouped using italics.)
- Darren ordered a pair of *Phantom of the Opera* tickets. ✔ (combination of italics and title case)
- *Adam will be carrying a "United Colors of Benetton" bag.* ✔ (combination of quotation marks and title case)

Just Group the Adjective. It is a mistake to include the thing being described within the quotation marks, the italics or the title. For example:

- *The United Arab Emirates Spokesman stood up and left.* ✖ (There should be a small *s* on *Spokesman*.)
- It is the only *bona fide cure* on the market. ✖ (The word *cure* should not be in italics.)
- *As far as I am concerned, you can tell the House of Lords representative whatever you like.* ✔ (*House of Lords* is grouped using title case. There must be no capital *r* on *representative*.)
- You should visit the *Médecins Sans Frontières* offices in Paris and pick up an application form. ✔ (*Médecins Sans Frontières* is grouped using italics. The word *offices* must not be in italics.)

28 HYPHENS – IN COMPOUND NOUNS

A single noun that consists of two or more words is called a *compound noun* (e.g. cooking-oil, water-bottle). As with these two examples, the words in a compound noun are sometimes joined by a hyphen to eliminate ambiguity or to assist the reader by making the word stand out clearly. This is also covered in Section 48.

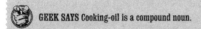

GEEK SAYS Cooking-oil is a compound noun.

There are no specific rules on forming compound nouns. For example, *ink-well* can be written *ink well* or *inkwell* – all are correct spellings. However, you should use a hyphen to eliminate ambiguity. Ambiguity is particularly prevalent when the first word of the pairing is a substance (like *water* or *ink*). Examples:

- *water-bottle* ✔ / *water bottle* ✔
  (When the first word is a substance, a hyphen is used to show that the item is not made of that substance.)
- *ice-axe* ✔ / *ice axe* ✔
  (Both are acceptable, but *ice-axe* makes it clear that the axe is not made of ice.)
- *paper-clip* ✔ / *paper clip* ✔ / *paperclip* ✔
  (All three are acceptable.)
- *Please pass me that plastic wire-fastener.* ✔
  (a fastener made of plastic not wire)

There is also some ambiguity when the first word of the pairing ends *ing*. Examples:

- *changing-room* ✔ / *changing room* ✔
  (Both are acceptable, but *changing-room* makes it clear that the room is not changing.)
- *laughing-gas* ✔ / *laughing gas* ✔
  (Both are acceptable, but *laughing-gas* makes it clear that the gas is not laughing.)

OPPORTUNITY Show your confidence by putting a hyphen in a compound noun.

Hang on a sec. An axe made of ice? A bottle made of water? Gas that is laughing? A room that is changing? Q: Isn't this all rubbish? A: Perhaps, but using the one-word or the hyphenated version means your readers do not have to perform a logic check as they're reading. I don't suspect they'll buy you a pint for being so considerate, but they might think you're pretty sharp for spotting a compound noun and being confident enough to shove a hyphen in there.

It's safe to rely on your spellchecker.

Not All Have a One-word Version. Be aware that not all compound nouns have a one-word version. Even though *inkwell* and *paperclip* are fine, *iceaxe* and *waterbottle* are spelling mistakes. There are no rules governing this – you have to know. Actually, there's good news. You don't have to know. Your spellchecker will pick this up for you. All you have to do is make the spellchecker do its job by trying the one-word version.

29 HYPHENS – IN PREFIXES

A prefix is a half-word (e.g. anti-, ex-, post-, pre-) that is placed before a word to modify its meaning.

Prefix with a Hyphen. There is often confusion about whether a hyphen should be used with a prefix. Unfortunately, there are no specific rules governing this. Examples:

- *prehistoric* ✔ | *pre-historic* ✔
  (*Prehistoric* is so widely used that many consider *pre-historic* to be wrong.)
- *ultraviolet* ✔ | *ultra-violet* ✔ (Most prefixed words exist in both forms.)
- *The attack would take place at night as the anti-government troops did not possess infrared goggles.* ✔

You can often choose when to use a hyphen in a prefixed word. In the last example, the writer did not like the look of *antigovernment* or *infra-red*. He has been inconsistent in his use of prefixes and hyphens, but that's okay.

There is a lot of leniency on this subject. For neatness, however, I would recommend consistency for similar-looking words; e.g. ultraviolent/infrared or ultra-violet/infra-red.

Other common prefixes are:

ante- (before), ex- (former), pre- (before), anti- (against), infra- (below), pro- (for), contra- (opposite to), post- (after) and ultra- (above)

Good News. For most prefixed words, both versions exist (e.g. *post-natal* and *postnatal*), but this is not true for all. For example, *pro-rata* and *pre-loved* are fine, but the non-hyphenated versions are spelling mistakes. The good news is your spellchecker will know whether the unhyphenated version exists or not. So, get it to do the work. If it doesn't like it, whack a hyphen in.

Prefixes in Titles. When names or titles (with capital letters) are prefixed, the prefix is usually written with a lowercase letter and a hyphen.

- *I am aware that ex-Bishop Zoric, who was pro-Nazi, was still teaching in the post-World War II era.* ✔

– SEMICOLONS –

30 SEMICOLONS – IN LISTS

Items in lists are usually separated with commas (as in the first and third examples below). However, if the list items themselves contain commas, then semicolons can be used as separators. For example:

- *I have been to Newcastle, Carlisle and York.* ✔
  (comma used to separate list items)
- *I went to Newcastle, Carlisle and York in week one; Bristol, Exeter and Portsmouth in week two; and Cromer, Norwich and Lincoln in week three.* ✔
  (semicolons used to separate the list items as they contain commas)
- *Bread, milk, butter, cheese, lamb, beef and onions* ✔
- *Bread, milk, butter and cheese from the corner shop; lamb and beef from the market; and onions from your uncle's stall* ✔

In complex lists like the ones below, semicolons are used to separate the list items, because commas are used within the list items. Brackets are also used to add information within the list items.

- *The guests of honour at the dinner will be Dr Alfred Peebles, the expedition leader; Mr Donald Keen, an experienced mountaineer (the latest addition to the expedition); Mrs Susan Honeywell, ornithologist from the RSPB (Mr Keen's fiancée); and Capt. John Trimble, the base-camp commander.* ✔
- *You should choose ham, chicken or char-grilled vegetable sandwiches; cups of tea, Bovril or coffee (if you don't mind them lukewarm); or red wine (one of the few options that's drinkable when lukewarm).* ✔

To make your penultimate and last list items clearly identifiable, it is normal to include the semicolon before the last list item. In the first example above, this semicolon is before *and Capt. John*. In the second, it is the one before *or red wine*.

 OPPORTUNITY Semicolons in complex lists show clarity of thought.

Using semicolons correctly in lists shows clarity of thought as well as consideration for your reader. I think semicolons in lists look impressive when they're used correctly.

31 SEMICOLONS – TO EXTEND A SENTENCE

On occasion, a writer may decide that a sentence is so closely connected to the previous one that a slight break is more appropriate than a new sentence. A semicolon can be used for this purpose. Examples:

- *Husbands never become good; they merely become proficient.* ✔
  (H. L. Mencken)
- *Like dear St Francis of Assisi I am wedded to Poverty; but in my case the marriage is not a success.* ✔ (Oscar Wilde)
- *To lose one parent, Mr Worthing, may be regarded as a misfortune; to lose both looks like carelessness.* ✔ (Oscar Wilde)
- *A pessimist sees the difficulty in every opportunity; an optimist sees the opportunity in every difficulty.* ✔ (Winston Churchill)

Semicolons Can Replace Conjunctions. Semicolons can be used to replace words like *and*, *but* and *or*. (These are called conjunctions – see Section 44.) Examples:

- *The manager did not disapprove the plan; he suggested several changes.* ✔
  (*, but* could be written in the place of the semicolon.)
- *Craig joined the Army; Darren joined the Marines.* ✔
  (semicolon replaces *, but*)

Semicolons before Transitional Phrases. Often a semicolon will sit before a short bridging phrase to the previous sentence. The terms *as a result*, *however*, *consequently* and *therefore* are common examples. This is also covered in Section 32.

Beware of Overkill. To summarise, you can merge two sentences together with a semicolon. The second sentence is usually short and always closely connected to the first. Using a semicolon in this way is very handy to control the flow of text. However, if you find yourself doing it too regularly, you should probably adjust the style of your writing. You will annoy your readers if you do it too often.

Not a Comma. You cannot use a comma to link two sentences. This is a very common mistake called a run-on error. For example:

- *Never pick a fight with an ugly person, they've got nothing to lose.* ✖
  (Robin Williams)
- *Never pick a fight with an ugly person. They've got nothing to lose.* ✔
- *Never pick a fight with an ugly person; they've got nothing to lose.* ✔

This mistake is particularly common with the word *however* (see Section 32). For example:

- *A vacation used to be a luxury, however, in today's world, it has become a necessity.* ✖
- *A vacation used to be a luxury. However, in today's world, it has become a necessity.* ✔
- *A vacation used to be a luxury; however, in today's world, it has become a necessity.* ✔

32 SEMICOLONS – BEFORE TRANSITIONAL PHRASES

This point is closely related to Sections 15, 31 and 33 (Commas after Transitional Phrases, Extending a Sentence with a Semicolon and Semicolons before Conjunctions) as it concerns merging two sentences to form one. In these examples, there is a short bridge between the first half and the second half. The bridge is known as a *transitional phrase*. There is always a comma after a transitional phrase, and – sometimes – there can be a semicolon before. The transitional phrases are underlined in the examples:

- *Everyone knows he is guilty; <u>of course,</u> it will never be proved.* ✔
  (The transitional phrase *of course* acts like a bridge between the first half and the second half.)
- *Sarah's guest was turned away by the doorman; <u>as a result,</u> she left before the presentations.* ✔
  (*as a result* – transitional phrase)
- *Business is booming; <u>for example,</u> Siemens have made 10 orders since 4 o'clock.* ✔
  (*for example* – transitional phrase)
- *I missed the early plane; <u>however,</u> I still made the meeting.* ✔
  (*however* – transitional phrase)
- *The paper is stuck; <u>consequently,</u> we cannot finish the printing.* ✔
  (*consequently* – transitional phrase)

- *She does not loathe chess, <u>on the contrary</u>, she quite likes it.* ✘
  (The term *on the contrary* is a transitional phrase. You cannot
  merge two sentences into one with a comma. You must either start
  a new sentence or use a semicolon.)
- *My security guards are not trained in fire-fighting; <u>therefore</u>, we
  paged the fire service.* ✔

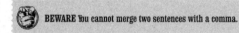

Don't go mad with semicolons.

Start a New Sentence Nine Times out of Ten. Transitional phrases are
very common. Used correctly, they demonstrate your clarity of thought by
proving you can extract the salience from your writing and develop it.
However, don't go crazy with semicolons. Transitional phrases nearly always
follow a period/full stop and start a new sentence. However, on occasion, you
can use a semicolon if you wish a smoother transition between sentences.
You should not do this too often. It is difficult to say what percentage of your
sentences should feature semicolons, but if I were to round it up to the nearest
number, it'd be 0%. What I'm saying is don't go mad with semicolons. They
look good when used correctly, but they are often misused. You could easily
get away with never using one.

> **BEWARE** You cannot merge two sentences with a comma.

Definitely Not a Comma. You cannot merge two sentences with a comma.
This is a very common mistake.

- *It is extremely foggy, <u>nevertheless</u>, the game will be played.* ✘

The Main Culprit Is However. The error described above is called a *comma
fault* or *run-on error*. This error is most commonly seen with *however*.

- *I am leaving on Tuesday, however, I will be back on Wednesday to
  collect my wages.* ✘
- *I am leaving on Tuesday; however, I will be back on Wednesday to
  collect my wages.* ✔
- *I am leaving on Tuesday. However, I will be back on Wednesday to
  collect my wages.* ✔

There is more on the *comma fault* in Sections 15 and 31.

Beware of **so**.

Comma After So. When the word *so* is used at the start of the sentence to mean *therefore*, it can be treated like a transitional phrase and is followed by a comma.

- *We are not in a position to fund the changes. So, the current system will remain until at least April when it will be reviewed again.* ✔
- *We are not in a position to fund the changes, so the current system will remain until at least April when it will be reviewed again.* ✔
  (Unlike other transitional phrases, you can precede *so* with a comma, because it is also a conjunction. See Section 44.)

When *so* means *in order that*, treat it like a conjunction. For example:

- *Go to the bridge, so you can see for yourself.* ✔
- *I have done the washing up, so you don't have to.* ✔
  (In these two examples, *so* means *in order that*. There is a lot of leniency on whether to precede it with a comma or not.)
- *I have done the washing; so, you don't have to.* ✔
  (Here, *so* means *therefore*. It has been treated like a transitional phrase.)

33 SEMICOLONS – BEFORE CONJUNCTIONS

Semicolons can be used before conjunctions (words like *and*, *but* and *or*), particularly when there are commas present.

Sometimes a conjunction (see Section 44) is used to join two sentences together to form one. For example:

- *She cannot abide tennis, but she loves watching golf.*
  (Sentence 1: *She cannot abide tennis.* Sentence 2: *She loves watching golf.*)

When a conjunction is used like this, it is usual to put a comma before. That's why there's a comma before *but* in the last example.

When the sentences being joined contain commas, it is possible to use a semicolon before the conjunction to "outrank" those commas. Examples:

- *In fact, rather surprisingly, the majestic pike is hardly used in cooking today; but, in Victorian times, pastry-topped pike was a very common dish.* ✔
  (Semicolon used before *but* to "outrank" the other commas)
- *By day, he was James Townsend Saward, esteemed barrister; but, at night, he was a master forger and frequenter of squalid taverns.* ✔
  (Semicolon used before *but* to outrank the other commas)

Old Fashioned? A comma will suffice. Many people consider it old fashioned to use a semicolon before a conjunction.

– SPEECH MARKS –

34 SPEECH MARKS – WITH COLONS OR COMMAS

Speech marks (or quotation marks) can be used to show actual words spoken or written. For example:

- *Anna looked up and said: "It's true. The dog ate the key."* ✔
  (The words within the speech marks are the exact words that Anna said.)
- *Her performance proved beyond all doubt that she was "simply the best."* ✔
  (The words *"simply the best"* are a quote from a well-known song.)
- *The sign clearly states, "Thieves will be prosecuted."* ✔
  (These are the words that are on the sign.)

Comma or Colon? When introducing a quotation with words like *He said*, *She whispered*, *It stated*, etc., you can precede the quotation with either a comma or a colon. As a guide, use commas for quotations that comprise fewer than seven words, and use colons for longer quotations. For example:

- *The prisoner uttered, "Leave me alone."* ✔
  (fewer than seven words – use a comma)
- *Granddad looked at me over the top of his glasses and said: "I've seen it all and done it all. I just don't remember any of it."* ✔
  (more than six words – use a colon)

> The choice of punctuation depends on the desired flow of text.

The majority of people do not observe these guidelines, and their inclusion in this book will doubtless annoy a few grammarians trawling through this book for stuff they don't like. (Yeah, the grammar community is a bit like that.) I think the guidelines are great, but in fairness to those who ignore them, they are outdated. Nowadays, it is very acceptable to introduce a quotation with a comma, a colon or nothing. In modern writing, the choice of punctuation depends largely on the desired flow of the text (i.e. how much you want the reader to pause). However, the guidelines are still useful as they remove the need to think about which punctuation to use. Quotation six words or shorter? Stick a comma in. Longer? Stick a colon in. Job done.

Comma after the Quotation. There is only a choice between a comma and a colon when the quotation is being introduced. Only a comma can be used after a quotation. For example:

- *Charlie looked over the hedge and shouted: "You can keep half the strawberries you pick."* ✔ (colon selected)
- *"You can keep half the strawberries you pick," shouted Charlie, looking over the hedge.* ✔ (US)
  (In this example, a colon is not an option. You will notice that the comma is inside the speech mark. This is the US convention. Under UK convention, the comma would have been to the right of the speech mark. This is covered in Section 37.)
- *"History doesn't repeat itself," says Mark Twain, "but it does rhyme."* ✔ (US)
  (When the speaker is placed mid quote, use commas throughout)

Quite often, quotations are used without introductions like *He asked*, *She yelled*, *They wrote*, etc. In these instances, no punctuation is required to introduce the quotation.

- *There really is "no place like home."* ✔
- *If this is the, "best skiing resort in France," I would hate to see the worst.* ✖
  (There should be no comma after *If this is the.*)

Not for reported speech

Be aware that speech marks are not used for reported speech. (Reported speech is usually preceded by the word *that*.) Only use them for actual quotes of speech or writing.

- *The secretary said, "The phones are dead."* ✔
  (This is an actual quote. The speech marks are correct.)
- *The secretary said that the phones were dead.* ✔
  (This is an example of reported speech.)
- *Edmund said that "he was a good boy."* ✖
  (This is reported speech. Edmund actually said, "I am a good boy." There should be no speech marks.)

 35 SPEECH MARKS – AND THREE DOTS (ELLIPSIS)

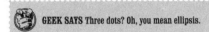 **GEEK SAYS** Three dots? Oh, you mean ellipsis.

When quoting spoken or written words, you can use three dots to show where parts of the quotation are missing. This is called ellipsis. Example:

- *Persons…with names like Sierra, Sequoia, Phoenix, and Rainbow can't sing the Blues no matter how many men they shoot in Memphis.* ✔
  (The text between *Persons* and *with* is deemed irrelevant. However, the three dots (called ellipsis) show the reader that text has been omitted.)

As covered in Section 7, you can put ellipsis in square brackets too:

- *I have no ambition to govern men; it is a […] thankless office.* ✔
  (Thomas Jefferson)

Four Dots. If an ellipsis is used to replace words that end a quoted sentence, then it is usual to use four dots: three for the ellipsis and one (a period/full stop) to end the quotation. For example:

- *"Fame is the spur…."* ✔ (John Milton)

This is quite unusual. Normally, there is no need to double up on the end punctuation. (See Section 37.)

Extend a Sentence with Three Dots. You can also extend a sentence with three dots. This is done when a pause for effect is required.

- *…and there it was…gone.* ✔
  (The first three dots are ellipsis (to show text omitted) and the second set is a pause for effect. Three dots giving a *pause for effect* is covered in Section 75.)

36 SPEECH MARKS – FOR SHIPS, PLAYS AND BOOKS

Speech marks can be used to highlight the names of books, plays, films, articles, ships, aircraft, houses and hotels. For example:

- *Jeremy stayed at "The Dorchester" for three weeks last summer.* ✔
- *"Southern Stars" was Jones's account of the trek; I have read others that contradict his version of events.* ✔
  (In this example, it is useful to group the book title with speech marks, because "Stars" is a plural word and "was" is singular.)
- *I was certain the "Spruce Goose" was too heavy to fly.* ✔

37 SPEECH MARKS – AND PUNCTUATION (INSIDE OR OUTSIDE)

Look at the first comma and the final period/full stop in the example below. Should they be inside or outside the speech marks?

- *"Bindle", to today's youth, means "a small pack of drug powder".*

To get us out of the starting blocks on this one, I'm going to say there are two conventions for determining whether punctuation should be inside or outside speech marks: the US convention and the UK convention. But, if you were to research this, you'd quickly spot that both the Brits and Americans are pretty poor at sticking to their own conventions. You'd notice instantly that many UK fiction writers and journalists follow the so-called US conventions, and you'd find plenty of US writers following the so-called UK convention. With that understood, let's move forward in ignorant bliss, calling them the US and UK conventions. (If you're in the military or in business, this categorisation works fine. If you're not, pick the convention that will annoy your readers the least and be consistent.)

See the table over the page for the rules.

What?	UK	US
. and ,	Place . and , outside (unless it appears in the original). *"Bindle", to today's youth, means "a small pack of drug powder".* ✔ *"Conquest", said Jefferson, "is not in our principles."* ✔ (Note: The . appears in the original.)	Place . and , inside. *"Bindle," to today's youth, means "a small pack of drug powder."* ✔ *"Conquest," said Jefferson, "is not in our principles."* ✔ Obviously, don't place a comma inside if it introduces the quotation (like the one after Jefferson.)
! and ?	Place ! and ? inside or outside according to logic. *Did she really say, "I love you"?* ✔ (*"I love you"* is not a question, but the whole sentence is.) *I heard him yell, "Do you love me?"* ✔ (The whole sentence is not a question, but the quotation is a question.) The second example is not a question, but it ends in a question mark. For neatness, it is acceptable to use just one end mark. Under US convention, you should only use one end mark. Under the UK convention, if you're a real logic freak, you can use two end marks (if you must). *I heard him yell, "Do you love me?".* ✔ (UK)	
: and ;	Place : and ; outside (unless it appears in the original). *On the street, there are three meanings for the word "monkey": £50, a person dependent on drugs, and a kilogram of drugs.* ✔	
?, ! and .	Don't double up with end marks. But, if you must, you can. *Did she really ask, "Do you love me?"?* (unwieldy but acceptable) ✔ (Two question marks? The sentence is a question, and the quotation is a question.) *I heard him yell, "Do you love me?".* ✔ (unwieldy but acceptable)	Don't double up with end marks. *Did she really ask, "Do you love me?"?* ✘ (too unwieldy for US tastes) *Did she really ask, "Do you love me?"* ✔
More on ?, ! and .	Don't end a quotation with . if it doesn't end the whole sentence. *"Get out!" she yelled.* ✔ *"Why me?" she asked.* ✔ *"I'll go." she said.* ✘ *"I'll go", she said.* ✔ (UK) *"I'll go," she said.* ✔ (US)	

SPEECH MARKS – DOUBLES (") OR SINGLES (')

When using speech marks, it is normal to start with doubles ("like these").
If another set of speech marks is needed within those doubles, use single
speech marks. For example:

- *Anne asked: "Are you going to see 'Phantom of the Opera'?"* ✔
- *The articles states: "A giant squid may have attacked the 'Mary
  Celeste' as the crew celebrated on the deck."* ✔
- *The Defence Secretary stood up and declared: "At 0600 hours
  tomorrow, "Ark Royal" will set sail with her full complement of
  crew."* ✖

  (*Ark Royal* should be within single speech marks. Claiming this is
  wrong is a little extreme. There is a lot of leniency on this subject.)
- *Homer Simpson said: "Maybe, just once, someone will call me 'Sir'
  without adding 'you're making a scene'."* ✔

This is not a hard and fast rule. In fact, I've seen grammar books recommend
that doubles be used within singles. In both the US and the UK, singles nested
within doubles (e.g. "shout 'bingo' clearly") is far more common than doubles
nested within singles (e.g. 'shout "bingo" clearly'). The latter is especially rare
in the US.

Example of doubles nested within singles:

- *Clapping slowly, Julian stood up and cried: 'That was even better
  than your performance of "Twelfth Night" in London last year.'* ✔

Also of note, many writers prefer to use single quotation marks in the first
instance because they look less unwieldy.

- *The 'a' has fallen off the sign.* ✔
  (This looks a little tidier than the version below.)
- *The "a" has fallen off the sign.* ✔

 GREAT TIP Use doubles within singles (or vice versa) – just be consistent.

The bottom line is this:
> You can use doubles or singles in the first instance. But, whichever style
> you choose, its use should be consistent throughout the document.

To make the point, I deem the example below to be wrong:

- *My dog may not be able to add up, spell my name or say "sausages" like the ones you see on 'That's Life,' but he can hold his own in a fight with a badger.* ✖
  (The words *sausages* and *That's Life* are at the same level in this sentence; i.e. one is not nested within the other. Therefore, they should both be written using double speech marks or singles. There should not be a mix of doubles and singles.)

39 SPEECH MARKS – ALLEGED OR SO-CALLED

Speech marks can be used to indicate *supposed*, *alleged* or *so-called*. For example:

- *Peter's "mates" left him on the path to die.* ✔
  (so-called mates)
- *Using his father's equipment, Alexander found over 50,000 bacteria on a "clean" chopping board.* ✔
  (so-called clean)
- *My sheep were noticeably stressed. It must've been a big "cat."* ✔
  (In this example, the speech marks play two roles. They show a quotation of somebody who claimed the culprit was a cat and also allude to the idea of it not being a cat.)

 GEEK SAYS An unnecessary repetition of words or ideas, whether intentional or unintentional, is called a tautology.

Just Say It Once. We know speech marks indicate *supposed*, *alleged* or *so-called*. So, there is no need to use these actual words with speech marks used for this purpose. For example:

- *Peter's so-called "mates" left him on the path to die.* ✖
  (In this example, *so-called* and the speech marks are doing the same job. This is a tautology. I don't think it's a hideous grammar error, but I reckon it warrants some red ink during proofreading.)
- *Peter's so-called mates left him on the path to freeze.* ✔
- *Peter's "mates" left him on the path to freeze.* ✔
- *I booted out the bunch of supposed "professionals" and finished the job myself.* ✖

You can commit a tautology without using speech marks. For example, *single bachelor* is tautological. (Bachelors are always single.) There's a little more on tautology at the end of this section.

Not for emphasis

Don't use speech marks for emphasis. Your readers may confuse it with *so-called*.

- *We stock a large selection of "fresh" fish.* ✖

You can also use speech marks to show that a word is not being used in its accepted sense. For example:

- *These waves "know" when you've dropped your paddle.* ✔

Tautology eats up your word count and adds no value.

Some More on Tautology. It's worth saying a little more about tautology. Often in business writing, the aim is to keep your text as short as possible. Tautological phrases eat up your word count without adding meaning. Worse, they portray you as a writer who is unable to think clearly. Here are some examples:

- *No one can earn $1,000,000 dollars honestly.* ✖
  (*$* and *dollars*)
- *In my opinion, I think invention arises directly from idleness.* ✖
  (*In my opinion* and *I think*)
- *You will receive a free gift.* ✖
  (*gifts* are always *free*)
- *Enter your PIN number in the ATM machine.* ✖
  (The *N* stands for *Number* and the *M* stands for *machine*.)
- *Eat a live toad at 7 a.m. in the morning, and nothing worse will happen to you for the rest of the day.* ✖
  (*a.m.* means *in the morning*)

It's not always clear whether something is a tautology:

- *I will offer a short summary of the article.* ✖
  (You don't need *short*. *Summary* already conveys the idea of *short*. Does it? What if it's a 20-page summary?)

The bottom line: Be wary of unintentionally saying stuff twice.

PARTS OF SPEECH

– ADJECTIVES –

40   ADJECTIVES – WHAT ARE ADJECTIVES?

You will remember from school that adjectives are describing words. *Large*, *grey* and *friendly* are all adjectives. In the example below, these adjectives are used to describe an elephant. Examples:

- *Large elephant – grey elephant – friendly elephant*

When you use more than one adjective to describe something, it is called *enumeration of adjectives*. Example:

- *Large, grey and friendly elephant*

With enumeration of adjectives, the big question is when to use commas and *and*. Luckily, the rules are very lenient. This is covered in Section 19.

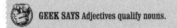

GEEK SAYS Adjectives qualify nouns.

Adjectives Qualify Nouns. The word *elephant* is a noun (see Section 47). Adjectives are added to nouns to state what kind, what colour, which one or how many. Adjectives are said to qualify nouns and are necessary to make the meanings of sentences clearer or more exact. Examples:

- *Drawing on my fine command of the English language, I said nothing.* (Robert Benchley)
  (adjective *fine* qualifies the noun *command*)
- *If you want results, press the red button. The rest are useless.*
  (adjective *red* qualifies the noun *button*)

Adjectives Qualify Pronouns. Although less common, adjectives can also qualify pronouns (see Section 53). Examples:

- *Press the red one.*
  (adjective *red* qualifies the pronoun *one*)
- *Only a brave few have received a recommendation.*
  (adjective *brave* qualifies the pronoun *few*)

The Different Types of Adjective. We've just read that adjectives are describing words. That's true, but lots of words classified as adjectives do not fall easily under that description. For example:

Personal Titles. Personal titles such *Mr*, *Mrs*, *Auntie*, *Uncle*, *Dr* and *Lord* are classified as adjectives when they are attached to a name.

- *The day after tomorrow, you can visit Auntie Pauline and Uncle Joe.*
- *The lecture will be presented by Dr Ingols and Prof. Munro.*

The question with personal titles is whether to put a period/full stop at the end of the abbreviated version. For example, is Dr. or Dr correct? There's a great rule for this – see Section 56.

A personal title is written with a capital letter when it is attached to someone's name (e.g. Auntie Dawn, Prof. Jones). This is the basis of a joke in the Mike Myers' film "The Love Guru":

- *"Would you help your Uncle Jack off the donkey?"*

A personal title with a name is classified as a proper noun (see Section 62).

Possessive Adjectives. Possessive adjectives are used to show possession. They are *my*, *your*, *his*, *her*, *its*, *our* and *their*. These don't really cause problems for native English speakers. However, some people confuse *its*, *their* and *your* with *it's*, *they're/there* and *you're*. (These are grammatical howlers – see Sections 142, 164 and 172.)

The Articles. The words *a*, *an* and *the* are known as *articles*. They are classified as adjectives too. *A* and *an* are called the *indefinite articles*, as they do not indicate a specific noun; whereas, *the* is called the *definite article*, because it does point to a specific noun. Examples:

- *A cup* (i.e. any cup)
- *The cup* (i.e. a specific cup)
- *I'm not a boxer. I'm the boxer.*

Sometimes writers are unsure whether to use *an* or *a*, especially with abbreviations. This is covered in Section 61.

Demonstrative Adjectives. Demonstrative adjectives are used to demonstrate or indicate specific things. *This*, *that*, *these* and *those* are all demonstrative adjectives.

Examples:
- *I told the doctor I broke my leg in two places. He told me to quit going to those places.* (Henny Youngman)
  (*Those* is a demonstrative adjective. It refers to specific *places*.)
- *If I were two-faced, would I be wearing this one?* (Abraham Lincoln.)
  (*This* is a demonstrative adjective. It refers to a specific face.)

Associated Howler:
- *I like these kind of birds.* ✖ (*These* and *those* can only sit before plural things. It should be: *I like these kinds of birds.*)

 BEWARE These and those must be used with plural words.

Indefinite Adjectives. Unlike demonstrative adjectives, which indicate specific items, indefinite adjectives do not point out specific things. They are formed from indefinite pronouns (see Section 54). The most common indefinite adjectives are *no*, *any*, *many*, *few* and *several*. Examples:

- *Everyone is born with genius, but most people only keep it a few minutes.* (Edgard Varese)
  (The indefinite adjective *most* qualifies the noun *people*. The indefinite adjective *few* qualifies the noun *minutes*.)
- *According to a council spokesman, there are no wallabies left in Derbyshire. However, over the past few months, many walkers have reported seeing several adults with young.*
  (The indefinite adjectives in this example are *no*, *few*, *many* and *several*. Okay, I've got to tell you this. I was camping with a mate on the Derbyshire Dales in the 90s when something smashed into our tent in the early hours of the morning. Wondering what on Earth it could be, I put my head out the tent and then got back into my sleeping bag. "Well?" my mate asked. "It's a kangaroo," I said nonchalantly. With a disbelieving tut, he looked outside the tent and then got back into his sleeping bag. "Well?" I asked. "There's no kangaroo," he reassured me. "There is!" I insisted. "Okay, keep your hair on. Maybe it was behind the wallaby," he outnonchalanted. (That's not a real word by the way.) Oh, *no* as in *no kangaroo* is an indefinite adjective. Story justified.

Numbers. Numbers are classified as adjectives too.

- *I just drank 18 whiskies. That must be a record.* (Dylan Thomas)
  (adjective *18* qualifies the noun *whiskies*)
- *All we could muster was nine cans of beans.*
  (adjective *nine* qualifies the noun *cans*)
- *When you're in love it's the most glorious two and a half days of
  your life.* ✖ (Richard Lewis)
  (In this example *two and a half* is one adjective. It should be
  joined together with hyphens to make that clear. It should be *most
  glorious two-and-a-half days of your life.* This is called a compound
  adjective. It's covered in Section 41. I should say that marking this
  wrong is a little harsh.)

41 ADJECTIVES – WHAT ARE COMPOUND ADJECTIVES?

> **GEEK SAYS** A compound adjective is an adjective that is made up of more than one word.

A compound adjective is an adjective made up of more than one word. In the
UK, it is normal to link the words of a compound adjective to show it is one
adjective. This is usually done with hyphens (also covered in Section 26).
Americans are a little more lenient on the use of hyphens. The US ruling is:
Use a hyphen in a compound adjective if it helps your reader. Examples of
compound adjectives with hyphens:

- *Please request a four-foot table.*
  (*Four-foot* is an adjective describing *table*. A hyphen is used to link
  four and *foot* to show that it is one adjective.)
- *It is a six-page document.*
- *Claire worked as a part-time keeper at the safari park.*
- *That is an all-too-common mistake.*

It's Not All about Hyphens. All the compound adjectives above are grouped
together using a hyphen or hyphens. However, compound adjectives can be
grouped in other ways too. Below are some examples. (This is also covered
in Section 27.)

Compound Adjectives with Capital Letters. Often adjectives are formed from proper nouns (i.e. the names of things), which should be written using capital letters (or least title case – see Section 68). In these circumstances, there is no need to group the words together using hyphens. Examples:

- *Did you manage to get the Billy Elliot tickets?*
  (The words *Billy Elliot* are one adjective describing the tickets. As the capital letters group the words, there is no need to use a hyphen.)

Compound Adjectives with Speech Marks and Italics. Although a less common practice, it is also possible to group the words in a compound adjective using speech marks, italics or a combination of the two. (Italics tend to be used for foreign words.) Examples:

- It is an *ab initio* course (i.e. for beginners).
  (italics used to group the adjective)
- Amber looked at the stick in the water, looked me in the eye and then turned away, having given me a "get it yourself" look.
  (speech marks used to group the adjective)
- For over ten years, Jack claimed to be part of the "*Mary Celeste*" crew before admitting to his cousin at a party that he was not.
  (capital letters, italics and speech marks used to group the adjective)

Don't join an adverb to an adjective with a hyphen.

Adverbs and Compound Adjectives. An adjective is often preceded by a word like *very, well, beautifully* or *extremely*. (These are adverbs – see Section 42.) Usually, there is no need to link an adverb to an adjective using a hyphen. Examples:

- *Electricity is actually made up of extremely tiny particles called electrons. You cannot see them with the naked eye unless you have been drinking.* ✔
  (The adverb *extremely* modifies the adjective *tiny* but is not part of it. There is no need to group *extremely* and *tiny* together with a hyphen.)
- *It was a beautifully painted portrait in a skilfully carved frame.* ✔
  (The adverb *beautifully* adds to the adjective *painted* but is not part of it. Likewise, *skilfully* adds to *carved* but is not part of it. There is no need for hyphens.)

Beware ambiguity

Ambiguous Adverbs. However, with words like *well* and *fast* (which are both adjectives and adverbs), a hyphen can be used to avoid ambiguity. Example:

- *Jacob took the well-fatted calf to the riverside.* ✔
  (*well-fatted calf* as in a very plump calf)
- *Jacob took the well fatted calf to the riverside.* ✖ (ambiguous)
  (*well fatted calf* could be construed as a *well* (i.e. healthy) and *fatted* calf. In the first example, the *well-fatted calf* could be ill.)

– ADVERBS –

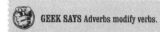 42 ADVERBS – WHAT ARE ADVERBS?

> **GEEK SAYS** Adverbs modify verbs.

Adverbs are nasty things to explain, because they are so diverse. The classic explanation is an adverb is a word that modifies a verb (see Section 55 – Verbs). Usually, an adverb tells you *when*, *where*, *how*, *in what manner* or *to what extent* an action is performed. Very many adverbs end in the letters *ly* – particularly those that are used to express *how* an action is performed. Although many adverbs end *ly*, lots do not; e.g. *fast*, *never*, *well*, *very*, *most*, *least*, *more*, *less*, *now*, *far* and *there*. Examples:

- *Tara walks gracefully.*
  (*gracefully* – adverb. It modifies the verb *to walk*.)
- *He runs fast.*
  (*fast* – adverb. It modifies the verb *to run*.)
- *I have learned a great deal from listening carefully. Most people never listen.* (Ernest Hemingway)
  (*carefully* – adverb. It shows how he listened.)
- *You can set your watch by him. He always leaves at 5 o'clock.*
  (*always* – adverb. It modifies the verb *to leave*.)
- *I am the only person in the world I should like to know thoroughly.*
  (Oscar Wilde)
  (*thoroughly* – adverb; modifies *to know*)

Types of Adverbs. Although there are thousands of adverbs, each adverb can usually be categorised in one of the following groupings:

Adverbs of Time
- *Press the button now.*
  (*now* – adverb of time)
- *Never explain. Your friends do not need it, and your enemies will not believe you anyway.*
  (*never* – adverb of time)

Adverbs of Place

- *I take my children everywhere, but they find their way back home.*
  (Robert Orben)
  (*everywhere* – adverb of place)
- *I did not put it there.*
  (*there* – adverb of place)

Adverbs of Manner

- *He passed the exam easily.*
  (*easily* – adverb of manner)
- *Learn to bear bravely changes of fortune.* (Cleobulus)
  (*bravely* – adverb of manner)

Adverbs of Degree

- *That is the farthest I have ever jumped.*
  (*farthest* – adverb of degree)
- *He boxed more cleverly.*
  (*more cleverly* – adverb of degree and manner)
  (This is covered more in Sections 69 and 70.)

 GREAT TIP Put a comma at the end a long adverb if it starts your sentence.

When you use an adverb to set the scene at the start a sentence, it is common to separate it from the rest of the sentence with a comma. Example:

- *Sometimes, I think we're alone. Sometimes, I think we're not. In either case, the thought is staggering.* (R. Buckmaster Fuller)

When your adverb is just one word (as it is here with *sometimes*), it is less common to use a comma. But, look at this:

- *In either case, the thought is staggering.*
- *Whenever the moon is full, the dog barks.*

An adverb that sets the scene is usually made up of several words, and it is usual to use a comma after it. These adverbs are called adverbial phrases or clauses. This is covered in Sections 14 and 43.

Adverbs Can Modify Adjectives and Other Adverbs. Although the term *adverb* implies that they are only used with verbs, adverbs can also modify adjectives and other adverbs. Examples:

- *The heavenly blue light shone on the water.*
  (adverb *heavenly* modifies the adjective *blue*)
- *Peter had an extremely ashen face.*
  (adverb *extremely* modifies the adjective *ashen*)
- *Peter Jackson finished his assignment remarkably quickly.*
  (The adverb *quickly* modifies the verb *to finish*. The adverb *remarkably* modifies the adverb *quickly*.)

When adverbs modify adjectives, there is no need to join the two with a hyphen. Example:

- *She wore a beautifully-designed dress.* ✖

However, with words like *well* and *fast* (which are both adjectives and adverbs), a hyphen can be used to avoid ambiguity.

- *She wore a well-designed dress.* ✔

This is also covered in Sections 26 and 41.

43 ADVERBS – WHAT ARE ADVERBIAL CLAUSES AND PHRASES?

Quite often, an adverb in a sentence consists of several words. These types of adverbs are called *adverbial phrases* or *adverbial clauses*. Adverbial phrases and clauses (underlined in the examples below) can usually be categorised as one of the following:

Adverbs of Time
- *A crow attacked your cat <u>while I was waiting for the bus</u>.*
- *<u>When I told the people of Northern Ireland that I was an atheist</u>, a woman in the audience stood up and said: "Yes, but is it the God of the Catholics or the God of the Protestants in whom you don't believe?"* (Quentin Crisp)
  (Note the comma after *atheist*. This is explained on the next page.)

Adverbs of Place
- *It is colder and wetter <u>in the north of Germany</u>.*

- *In a world where there is so much to be done, I felt strongly impressed that there must be something for me to do.* (Dorothea Dix)

Adverbs of Manner
- *That dog is walking around like he owns the place.*
- *We act as though comfort and luxury were the chief requirements of life.* (Charles Kingsley)

Adverbs of Degree
- *Your attempts to hide your flaws don't work as well as you think they do.* (Julie Morgenstern)
- *He is as modest as is he is brilliant.*

Adverbs of Condition
- *If you shoot at mimes, you should use a silencer.* (Steven Wright)
- *If you want to know what God thinks of money, just look at the people he gave it to.* (Dorothy Parker)

Adverbs of Concession
- *Although only four years old, Oliver can do long multiplication.*
- *Aristotle maintained that women have fewer teeth than men. Although he was twice married, it never occurred to him to verify this statement by examining his wives' mouths.* (Bertrand Russell)

Adverbs of Reason
- *We were forced to abandon the match because the skies opened up.*
- *I failed to make the chess team because of my height.* (Woody Allen)

Use a Comma When It's at the Front. There are very few problems associated with adverbial clauses and phrases. The main grammar point is whether to use a comma or not. When an adverbial clause or phrase is at the front of a sentence, it is usual to use a comma to assist your reader. (This is also covered in Sections 14 and 42.)

- *A crow attacked your cat while I was waiting for the bus.* ✔
  (no comma required – adverbial clause at the end of the sentence)
- *While I was waiting for the bus, a crow attacked your cat.* ✔
  (comma required – adverbial clause at the start)
- *It is colder and wetter in the north of Germany.* ✔
  (no comma required – adverbial clause at the end of the sentence)
- *In the north of Germany, it is colder and wetter.* ✔
  (comma required – adverbial clause at the start)

– CONJUNCTIONS –

44 CONJUNCTIONS – WHAT ARE CONJUNCTIONS?

Conjunctions are used to join words or groups of words together. The most common ones are *and*, *or* and *but*. Often, a conjunction sits before the last item in a list. Examples:

- *Lisa, vampires are make-believe, just like elves, gremlins and Eskimos.* (Homer Simpson)
  (conjunction *and* groups *elves, gremlins* + *Eskimos*)
- *It is a small but practical kitchen.*
  (conjunction *but* groups *small* + *practical*)
- *A little sincerity is a dangerous thing, and a great deal of it is absolutely fatal.* (Oscar Wilde)
  (conjunction *and* joins both halves of this sentence)
- *We are all in the gutter, but some of us are looking at the stars.*
  (Oscar Wilde)
  (conjunction *but* joins both halves of this sentence)
- *History will be kind to me, for I intend to write it.*
  (Winston Churchill)
  (conjunction *for* joins both halves of this sentence)
- *A dog owns nothing yet is seldom dissatisfied.*
  (conjunction *yet* joins both parts of this sentence)

Pitfalls with Conjunctions. Conjunctions do not normally cause serious errors, but writers are sometimes confused about when to place a comma before a conjunction. Unfortunately, there is no simple rule, such as: Never put a comma before *and*. (This is also covered in Sections 17 and 19.)

> **OPPORTUNITY** Show your confidence by starting a sentence with And or But. Don't do it too often though. It gets a bit annoying.

Starting a Sentence with a Conjunction. In the past, schools were rigid in their ruling that sentences could not start with conjunctions, such as *and* or *but*. But, nowadays, you can. For example:

- *I've had a perfectly wonderful evening. But, this wasn't it.* ✔
  (Groucho Marx)

The two most common conjunctions used in this way are *and* (meaning *in addition*) and *but* (meaning *however*). It is usual to follow each with a comma.

Although it is acceptable to use *and* or *but* to start a sentence, this practice should be limited and only used for impact. If you find yourself using them regularly at the start of sentences, you should consider changing the style of your writing. Your audience will accept, and even approve of, the occasional sentence starting with a conjunction, but it is still considered a little risqué. If you do it too often, you'll just annoy people.

 GEEK SAYS There are three kinds of conjunction.

More on Conjunctions. Okay, here's some grammar geekery (just for the record). Conjunctions can be categorised into one of three groupings:

> **Correlative Conjunctions.** Correlative conjunctions appear in pairs. For example, *either...or, neither...nor, whether...or* and *not only... but also.*
>
> ● *Either this man is dead or my watch has stopped.* (Groucho Marx)
>
> **Coordinating Conjunctions.** Coordinating conjunctions include *and, but, or, nor, for, so* and *yet.* They are used to join individual words, phrases and clauses.
>
> ● *[Drink] makes you shoot at your landlord, and it makes you miss him.*
>
> **Subordinating Conjunctions.** Subordinating conjunctions include *after, although, as, because, before, if, once, since, than, that, though, till, until, when, where, whether* and *while.* They are used to show the relationship between the independent clause (i.e. one that's a standalone sentence – underlined in the example below) and the dependent clause (one that isn't a standalone sentence).
>
> ● <u>*Keep your hand on the wound*</u> *until the nurse asks you to take it off.*

– INTERJECTIONS –

45 INTERJECTIONS – WHAT ARE INTERJECTIONS?

Interjections are words used to express strong feeling or sudden emotion.
They are included in a sentence – usually at the start – to express a sentiment
such as surprise, disgust, joy, excitement or enthusiasm. Examples:

- *Hey! Get off that floor!*
- *Oh, that is a surprise.*
- *Good! Now we can move on.*
- *Jeepers, that was close.*

Yes and No. Introductory expressions such as *yes*, *no*, *indeed* and *well* are also
classed as interjections. Examples:

- *Indeed, this is not the first time the stand has collapsed.*
- *Yes, I do intend to cover the bet.*
- *I'm sure I don't know half the people who come to my house.
  Indeed, from all I hear, I shouldn't like to.* (Oscar Wilde)
- *Well, it's 1a.m. Better go home and spend some quality time with
  the kids.* (Homer Simpson)

Phew! Some interjections are sounds. Examples:

- *Phew! I am not trying that again.*
- *Humph! I knew that last week.*
- *Mmmm, my compliments to the chef.*
- *Ah! Don't say you agree with me. When people agree with me, I
  always feel that I must be wrong.* (Oscar Wilde)

46 INTERJECTIONS – WITH COMMAS AND EXCLAMATION MARKS

Use a comma or an exclamation mark with an interjection.

Punctuation with Interjections. An interjection can be followed by either a comma or an exclamation mark. A comma is used for a mild interjection. An exclamation mark is used for a more abrupt display of surprise, emotion or deep feeling. It's not a crime to follow an interjection with a full stop/period. In fact, it's becoming quite fashionable. If a full stop/period gives you the desired flow of text, go for it.

- *Hurry! The bus is about to leave!* ✔
- *Jeepers! That is the largest beetle I have ever seen.* ✔
- *No, I'm not going tomorrow night.* ✔
- *Well, the lava moves more quickly than you would expect.* ✔
- *Absolutely, a fifth of them do not count.* ✔

Very often (as in the first example), an interjection with an exclamation mark is followed by a sentence with an exclamation mark.

Don't use more than one exclamation mark.

More Than One Exclamation Mark. It's worth quickly covering the use of exclamation marks. I'm pretty sure I've never used an exclamation mark in a formal document. They are considered a bit crass. Exclamation marks only belong in emails and hand-written notes as far as I'm concerned. They're pretty powerful things though. Imagine receiving this from someone who doesn't generally use exclamation marks:

- *Achieving the deadline is imperative!*

That's pretty clear, isn't it? Used sparingly, exclamation marks can be pretty effective. Don't use more than one.

- *Achieving the deadline is imperative!!!!*

Is that clearer? I don't think so. It's certainly ruder. Just use one exclamation mark.

– NOUNS –

47 NOUNS – WHAT ARE NOUNS?

Nouns are naming words. Everything we see or are able to talk about is represented by a word which names it – that word is called a *noun*. There are names for people, animals, places, objects, substances, qualities, actions and measures. Examples:

- *soldier - Alan - cousin - Frenchman*
  (names for people)
- *rat - zebra - lion - aardvark*
  (names for animals)
- *house - London - factory – shelter*
  (names for places)
- *table - frame - printer - chisel*
  (names for objects)
- *lead - nitrogen - water - ice*
  (names for substances)
- *kindness - beauty - bravery - wealth - faith*
  (names for qualities)
- *rowing - cooking - barking - reading - listening*
  (names for actions)
- *month - inch - day - pound - ounce*
  (names for measures)

The noun family is quite large, and there are different types of nouns. These are covered in the next section.

48 NOUNS – DIFFERENT TYPES

There are several different kinds of nouns.

Common Nouns. A common noun is the word used for a class of person, place or thing. Examples:

- *car*
- *man*
- *bridge*

- *town*
- *water*
- *metal*

 BEWARE Don't give a common noun a capital letter.

Unless it starts a sentence, a common noun is not normally written with a capital letter. There are some quirks with this though – words like Director and Manager tend to attract capital letters, and only a very strict grammarian would contest this practice (see Section 62).

Proper Nouns. A proper noun is the name of a person, place or thing (i.e. its own name). Proper nouns are written with capital letters (see Section 62). Examples:

- *Michael*
- *Africa*
- *Bejing*
- *Dayton Peace Accord*
- *United Nations*
- *The Tower of London*
- *Uncle George*
    (Note: *Uncle* is written with a capital letter because it is part of his name. Look at this example: *My favourite auntie is Auntie Sally*. Here, the first *auntie* is a common noun. The second *Auntie* is part of a proper noun. This is also covered in Section 40.)

Collective Nouns. A collective noun is the word used for a group of people or things. Examples:

- *choir*
- *team*
- *jury*
- *shoal*
- *cabinet (of ministers)*
- *regiment*

The big question with collective nouns is whether to treat them as singular or plural. In other words, do you say *the choir is* or the *choir are*? Well, you can do either – see Section 83.

Pronouns. A pronoun is a word used to replace a noun.

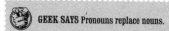

- *James is the first choice for the post. He has applied for it twice already.*
  (*He* is a pronoun. In this example, it replaces the proper noun
  James. *It* is also a pronoun. It replaces the common noun *post*.)

The term *pronoun* covers lots of words. *Some*, *who* and *this* are all pronouns.
(Sections 53 and 54 are dedicated to pronouns.)

Verbal Nouns. Verbal nouns are formed from verbs. They are a type of
common noun. Examples:

- *Walking is man's best medicine.* (Hippocates, 460–377 BC)
  (*Walking* is verbal noun. It's the name of an activity. It is formed
  from the verb *to walk*.)
- *Lateral thinking is required to solve this problem.*
  (*Thinking* is a verbal noun. It's the name of an activity. It is formed
  from the verb *to think*.)

Compound Nouns. A compound noun is the name given to a noun that is
made up of two or more words. Examples:

- Mother-in-law
- Board of members
- Court-martial
- Forget-me-not
- Manservant
- Paper-clip

To form the plural of a compound noun, pluralise the principal word in the
compound. When there is no obvious principal word, add *s* (or *es*) to the end
of the compound. Example:

- *Two mothers-in-law*

In this example, *mother* is the principal word in the compound. Forming the
plurals of compound nouns is covered in Section 82. Also, some compound
nouns are hyphenated and some aren't (see Section 28).

– PREPOSITIONS –

49 PREPOSITIONS – WHAT ARE PREPOSITIONS?

The following are all prepositions:

- *above, about, across, against, along, among, around, at, before, behind, below, beneath, beside, between, beyond, by, down, during, except, for, from, in, inside, into, like, near, of, off, on, since, to, toward, through, under, until, up, upon, with and within.*

Preposition *means* positioned before.

Preposition just means *positioned before*. A preposition sits *before* a noun to show the noun's relationship to another word in the sentence. (See Section 47 – Nouns.) Examples:

- *It is a container for butter.*
  (The preposition *for* shows the relationship between *butter* and *container*.)
- *The eagle soared above the clouds.*
  (The preposition *above* shows the relationship between *clouds* and *soared*.)

A preposition can also sit before a pronoun, which is a type of noun. (See Section 53 – Pronouns.)

- *A present for her* (Preposition *for* before pronoun *her*)
- *Give it to whom?* (Preposition *to* before pronoun *whom*)

Pitfalls with Prepositions. To understand the major pitfalls with prepositions, we will cover:

- Can you end a sentence in a preposition? (See Section 50.)
- What follows a preposition? (See Section 51.)
- Is the preposition absolutely necessary? (See Section 52.)
- Confusion over:
  Accept and *except* (See Section 86.)
  Into, *onto* and *up to* (See Section 141.)
  Past and *passed* (See Section 150.)

50 PREPOSITIONS – AT THE END OF A SENTENCE

> **GREAT TIP** Avoid ending a sentence in a preposition.

Ending a Sentence with a Preposition. Avoid ending a sentence with a preposition. This is sound guidance, but it is becoming outdated. Still, I guarantee a fair proportion of your readers won't like it if you end a sentence with a preposition. So, don't. As we've just covered in the last section, *preposition* means *positioned before*. Prepositions are supposed to sit before nouns. This is why grammar pedants don't like putting them at the end of sentences – prepositions are supposed to be before stuff not after stuff. To be honest, I'm not keen on ending a sentence with a preposition. It's a bit sloppy in formal writing. Examples:

- *That is a situation I have not thought of.* ✖
  (The word *of* is a preposition. Marking this wrong is a bit harsh. If I had a graphic for "naughty" instead of just ✖, I'd have used that.)
- *She is a person I cannot cope with.* ✖
  (The word *with* is a preposition.)
- *It is behaviour I will not put up with.* ✖
  (This example ends in two prepositions: *up* and *with*.)

If you can, reword your sentence.

Not a Serious Error. I recommend you don't end a sentence in a preposition. However, you will notice that after shuffling your words so the preposition is not at the end, your re-structured sentence often sounds contrived and unnatural. Examples:

- *That is a situation of which I have not thought.*
  (This version is grammatically more pure than the one above.)
- *She is a person with whom I cannot cope.*

This old joke captures some of the sentiment surrounding this subject:

> *"Do you know where I can catch the bus at?"*
> *"You know, here in Cambridge, we don't end our sentences in prepositions."*
> *"Do you know where I can catch the bus at, you posh git?"*

Reword to Avoid. Often, the best solution is to reword the sentence. Examples:

- *That is a situation I have not considered.* ✔ (There are no prepositions in this sentence, and it has the same meaning as the one on the previous page.)
- *It is behaviour I will not tolerate.* ✔

Leave the Preposition at the End. If the sentence sounds too contrived after it has been reworded, another option is to leave the preposition at the end of the sentence.

- *There is only one thing in the world worse than being talked about, and that is not being talked about.* ✔ (Oscar Wilde) (This is an example of a sentence that should be left with the preposition at the end.)

Your Choice. In summary, if you cannot find an alternative without a preposition, you have a choice whether to leave the preposition at the end or to re-structure your sentence. Some readers will frown at the first example below, because it ends in a preposition. But the second example sounds, for many people, way too contrived.

- *She is a person I cannot cope with.*
- *She is a person with whom I cannot cope.*

Pick the one that suits your audience.

Finally, you can't cover this subject without mentioning this famous quote about this very subject:

- *This is the type of arrant pedantry up with which I will not put.*

(This is often attributed to Winston Churchill, who may well have said it, but there is evidence it pre-dates him. It's a complaint about the ruling that adheres to it.)

51 PREPOSITIONS – AND WHAT FOLLOWS

The words after a preposition are said to be the *object of the preposition*.
For example:

- *The cat ran under the car.* ✔
  (The words *the car* are the object of the preposition *under*.)
- *Whose cruel idea was it for "lisp" to have an s in it?* ✔
  (The word *lisp* is the object of the preposition *for*. The word *it* at
  the end is the object of the preposition *in*.)

As covered in the last section, a preposition usually sits before a noun (i.e.
a word like *dog, man, house, Alan* – see Section 47). However, a preposition
can also sit before a pronoun (i.e. a word like *him, her, which, it, them* – see
Section 53). This is important because the object of a preposition is always in
the *objective case*, and some pronouns change in this case. (In general, native
English speakers have little trouble forming the objective case.) Examples:

- *Can you give the parcel to him?* ✔
  (*He* changes to *him* in the objective case.)
- *I went to the cinema with them.* ✔
  (*They* changes to *them* in the objective case.)

Who and Whom. The word *whom* is the objective case of *who*, and this
pairing causes some confusion. (See Section 170.) Examples:

- *Andy saw the scouts, at least one of whom was armed, through the
  mist.* ✔
  (*whom* – objective case after the preposition *of*)
- *Against whom did you protest if there was nobody present?* ✔
  (*whom* – objective case after the preposition *against*)

 GEEK SAYS About whom? Whom is the object of the preposition about.

Whether after a Preposition. Some writers are unsure when to use *whether*
and when to use *if*. After a preposition, only *whether* can be used:

- *A decision about whether the elections were legal is pending.* ✔
  (*about* is the preposition)

- *Will you raise the question of whether we are investing in the system or withdrawing?* ✔
  (*of* is the preposition)

There is more about *whether* and *if* in Section 134.

You and I / My Wife and I. Many people use *I* in expressions like *you and I* and *my wife and I* when, in some instances, they should be using *me*. This mistake is particularly painful to witness, because there's usually an air of "look at me being grammatically correct" when they use *I* incorrectly. (To prevent their embarrassment and utter contempt for me, I have trained myself to stop correcting them.)

 BAD TIP You should say "between you and I."

- *It is a present from my wife and I.* ✖
  (Nah, wrong. The preposition *from* governs the objective case. The objective case of *I* is *me*. It should be: *my wife and me* or *me and my wife*.)
- *Keep this between you and I.* ✖
  (Wrong again. You can't use *I* after *between*. This is as wrong as saying *between I and the post*.)

Remember, prepositions govern the objective case. Therefore, the word *I* must change to *me* when it is the object of a preposition. (It is irrelevant that it is preceded by *you and* or *my wife and*.)

You should only use *I* in an expression like *"you and I"* when it is the subject of the verb (see Section 55). For example:

- *You and I argue on this subject on a daily basis.* ✔
  (*You and I* – subject of the verb *to argue*)
- *My wife and I were happy for 20 years. Then we met.* ✔
  (Rodney Dangerfield)
  (*My wife and I* – subject of the verb *to be, i.e. were*)
- *My husband and I are either going to buy a dog or have a child. We can't decide whether to ruin our carpet or ruin our lives.* ✔
  (Rita Rudner)
  (*My husband and I* – subject of the verb *to be, i.e. are*)

Just try it with I.

If you are not confident of remembering the terms *objective case* and *subject of a verb*, don't worry. There is a neat trick to determine whether to use the *you and I* form or the *you and me* form. Simply remove everything apart from the *I* and try your sentence again. You will naturally use the correct version. For example:

- *It was proposed by my husband and I/me.*
  Question: *I or me?*
  Step 1: Remove *"my husband and"*
  Step 2: Try the sentence again with both versions
  Step 2a: It was proposed by *"I"* ✘
  Step 2b: It was proposed by *"me"* ✔

Therefore:
- *It was proposed by my husband and me.* ✔
- *It was proposed by my husband and I.* ✘

52 PREPOSITIONS – AND VERBS (SUCCINCT WRITING)

Some verbs, like *to face up to*, have unnecessary prepositions (underlined in the examples below). For more succinct sentences, omit the redundant prepositions. Redundant prepositions are usually not wrong. They're just… redundant.

- *I cannot face up to this problem.* ✘ / *I cannot face this problem.* ✔
  (Both are grammatically correct, but the second version is more succinct. The prepositions *up to* do not add anything.)
- *Try this new garlic dip out.* ✘ / *Try this new garlic dip.* ✔
- *Heat the soup up.* ✘ / *Heat the soup.* ✔
- *Give up the chase.* ✔ / *Give the chase.* ✔
  (Often, the preposition is required. These two versions have different meanings.)
- *She will not stand for shoddy work.* ✘ / *She will not stand shoddy work.* ✔
- *Where are you going to?* ✘ / *Where are you going?* ✔

Choose a Better Verb in Formal Writing. Verbs with more than one word (e.g. *to get away*, *to look after*, *to put off*) are known as *phrasal verbs*. Why do you care? Well, these are usually used in informal circumstances, such as speaking or writing notes and emails. The single-word versions (usually deriving from Latin) are often more appropriate in formal writing. Examples:

- *We will get together at 6.*
- *We will congregate at 1800 hrs.*
  (*to congregate*: Latinate version of *to get together*)

- *We've put the meeting off until Tue.*
- *We have postponed the meeting until Tuesday.*
  (*to postpone*: Latinate version of *to put off*)

The Latinate versions of verbs can sometimes sound a bit pompous. If you're super confident in your writing, stick to the non-Latinate versions (i.e. the phrasal verb, which is often the Anglo-Saxon version). The three main elements to your writing are: (1) your document structure (2) your grammar (3) your choice of words. Your audience will prefer the Anglo-Saxon words to Latinate ones. This is because the Anglo-Saxon ones are more natural sounding – they're less stuffy. However, you can only get away with these if your structure and grammar are sound. If they're poor, you'll be crucified for using Anglo-Saxon words. The bottom line: You have to leave your reader with the impression you chose the Anglo-Saxon words over the Latinate ones.

Latinate words can be a bit pompous.

The Words *Get* and *Don't*. Over the years, my bosses have always changed the word *get* to something else, and now I am one of those bosses, I do the same. But, *get* is hugely versatile. You can get up, get lost, get a bus, get a bonus, get lunch, get stuffed, get results, etc. It's a great word. It's just too informal for many, who assert that *get* shows a lack of vocabulary. Well, that view is becoming outdated.

Teachers of business writing encourage their students to write how they speak. The most talented business writers use *get* and contractions (e.g. *don't* and *isn't*) all the time.

 GREAT TIP There's an old adage: If your writing reads like writing, then re-write it.

I would offer a huge word of warning here. I never use *get* or contractions in formal writing, because I'm not confident my audience knows I'm doing it for their sake. I think there are three standards of writing.

Level 1 (the worst writers) – People who use *get* and *don't*
Level 2 – People who use *acquire* and *refrain*
Level 3 (the best writers) – People who use *get* and *don't*

If you think you're at Level 3 and you know your audience knows you are, then crack on *getting*, *gotting*, *don'ting* and *won'ting*. But, if you're unsure, play safe and write at Level 2. And, that's where I am when it comes to formal writing. I'm not confident my audience would recognise the difference between Level 1 and Level 3. I'm not sure Level 3 even exists in some fields. I don't think a brochure about *over-the-horizon radar* ought to be written in a speaking style. Many topics deserve a level of seriousness and respect that *gets* and *don'ts* would undermine.

This is not grammar, but I had to cover this topic, because so many books on executive writing skills will tell you to write how you speak. Yeah, that's great if you're selling surfboards to the local cider guzzlers. Harsh. But, you see my point. My advice: Don't use *get* and don't use contractions unless you're in a business that allows it, or you're pursuing a specific Richard Branson-style image. Look at your company's mission statement and use the "writing voice" that best represents its values.

 BAD TIP Use your thesaurus to find impressive words.

Impressive Words. Oh, and while we're on this subject, don't use obscure or long words to impress. This practice always has the opposite effect. I still remember some clown writing "sub-optimal paradigm" in a document I was reading. As it happens, I was reading it by torchlight in the back of a Land Rover in the middle of Basra in 50 degrees heat. I was far from impressed. Frustrated and flustered, I asked the crew, "What's a sub-optimal paradigm?" The only answer I got was "I bet Jenks wrote that – he's such a pretentious sod!" When I saw "axiomatic" in the same paragraph, I had to agree.

– PRONOUNS –

53 PRONOUNS – WHAT ARE PRONOUNS?

Pronouns replace nouns (see Section 47 – Nouns). Pronouns are usually short words. Examples:

- *I took a speed-reading course and read 'War and Peace' in 20 minutes. It involves Russia.* (Woody Allen)
  (*It* is a pronoun. It replaces *War and Peace.*)
- *Clutching the coin, Maria ran to the shops. She went straight to the counter and bought the sweets.*
  (*She* is a pronoun. In this example, it replaces the noun *Maria.* Pronouns are used for brevity. Imagine how wearisome a long prose would be if the writer used the full noun (in this case *Maria*) every time.)
- *One of the best things about this pen is you can write almost anything with it.*
  (*It* is a pronoun. In this example, it replaces *pen.*)

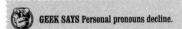

GEEK SAYS Personal pronouns decline.

Personal Pronouns. *I, you, he, she, it, we, they* and *who* are all pronouns. As these pronouns often replace nouns representing people, they are called the *personal pronouns.* Personal pronouns change (or *decline* as it's called) depending on what role they play in your sentence. Don't worry, that sounded way worse than it is. I'm just talking about stuff like *he* becoming *him*, and *she* becoming *her.* The two biggest issues relating to personal pronouns are:

Who and whom – See Section 170
Expressions like "my wife and I" – See Section 51

Unfortunately, not all pronouns are as easy to spot as personal pronouns, and there are several different types of pronouns. These are covered in the next section.

54 PRONOUNS – DIFFERENT TYPES

The term *pronoun* covers many words, some of which do not fall easily under the description given in the last section. There are many different kinds of pronouns. In general, these do not cause difficulties for native English speakers. The list below is mainly for reference purposes. I've also chucked in a few associated grammatical howlers to keep you awake.

Demonstrative Pronouns. Demonstrative pronouns are used to point out specific things. *This, that, these* and *those* are all demonstrative pronouns. (Imagine a game-show assistant demonstrating something; e.g. <u>*This is the prize you could win.*</u>) Examples:

- *This is the one I left in the car.*
  (*This* = specific item)
- *Shall I take those?*
  (*Those* = specific items)
- *What if this weren't a hypothetical question?*
  (*This* = specific question)

Indefinite Pronouns. Unlike demonstrative pronouns, which point out specific items, indefinite pronouns are used for non-specific things. This is the largest group of pronouns. *All, some, any, several, anyone, nobody, each, both, few, either, none, one* and *no one* are the most common. Examples with an associated point:

- *We are all in the gutter, but <u>some</u> of us are looking at the stars.*
  (Oscar Wilde)
- *I have <u>nothing</u> to declare except my genius.* (Oscar Wilde)

Associated Point:
- *None of the factors are relevant.* ✖
  (Many of your readers will expect you to treat *none* as singular. See Section 84 for more on this. They would have preferred: *None of the factors* is *relevant.* ✔)

 OPPORTUNITY Be confident. Treat none as singular. E.g. None of them is here.

Interrogative Pronouns. These pronouns are used in questions. Although they are classified as pronouns, it is not easy to see how they replace nouns. *Who, which, what, where* and *how* are all interrogative pronouns. Example:

- *You can't have everything. Where would you put it?* (Steven Wright)
- *If there is no God, who pops up the next Kleenex?* (Art Hoppe)

Possessive Pronouns. Possessive pronouns are used to substitute nouns and show possession. The possessive pronouns are *mine, yours, his, hers, its, ours, theirs* and *whose*. Unlike possessive adjectives (see below), which are adjectives to nouns, possessive pronouns sit by themselves. For this reason, they are sometimes called absolute possessive pronouns. Examples:

- *We cherish our friends not for their ability to amuse us, but for ours to amuse them.* (Evelyn Waugh)
- *Humans are the only animals that have children on purpose with the exception of guppies, who like to eat theirs.* (P. J. O'Rourke)

Associated Howler:
- *Try shooting their's instead of our's.* ✖
  (There are no apostrophes in any absolute possessive pronouns.
  It should be: *Try shooting theirs instead of ours.* ✔)

Even though they don't really replace nouns, possessive adjectives (see Section 40) are also classified by some as possessive pronouns. The possessive adjectives are *my, your, his, her, its, our, their* and *whose*. Examples:

- *She got her looks from her father. He's a plastic surgeon.*
  (Groucho Marx)
- *Brass bands are all very well in their place – outdoors and several miles away.* (Sir Thomas Beecham)
- *A country can be judged by the quality of its proverbs.*
  (German Proverb)

Associated Howler:
- *I could see it's eyes glistening.* ✖
  (There's no apostrophe in the possessive pronoun *its*. See Section
  142 for more on this error.
  It should be: *I could see its eyes glistening.* ✔)

Relative Pronouns. Relative pronouns are used to add more information to a sentence. *Which*, *that*, *who* (including *whom* and *whose*), *when* and *where* are all relative pronouns. Examples:

- *The man who first saw the comet reported it as a UFO.*
  (The relative pronoun *who* introduces the clause *who first saw the comet* and refers back to *the man*.)
- *How can you govern a country which has 246 varieties of cheese?*
  (Charles de Gaulle)
  (The relative pronoun *which* introduces the clause *which has 246 varieties of cheese* and refers back to *country*.)
- *A bore is a man who, when you ask how he is, tells you.*
  (Bert Leston Taylor)
  (The relative pronoun *who* introduces the clause *who, when you ask how he is, tells you* and refers back to *man*.)

Associated Howler:
- *She loves eggs. Which is why I'm buying a chicken.* ✖
  (You can't start a sentence with a relative pronoun. The more lenient grammarians will tell you it's okay these days. I can't agree. Your readers won't like it. It should be: *She loves eggs, which is why I'm buying a chicken.* ✔)

Reciprocal Pronouns. Reciprocal pronouns are used for actions or feelings that are reciprocated. The two most common reciprocal pronouns are *each other* and *one another*. Examples:

- *We are, each of us, angels with only one wing; and we can only fly by embracing one another.* (Luciano de Crescenzo)
- *They talk to each other like they're babies.*

Reflexive Pronouns. A reflexive pronoun ends with *self* or *selves* and refers to another noun or pronoun in the sentence. The reflexive pronouns are: *myself, yourself, herself, himself, itself, ourselves, yourselves* and *themselves*. Example:

- *A kleptomaniac is a person who helps himself because he can't help himself.* (Henry Morgan)
  (In this example, the first reflexive pronoun (*himself*) refers back to the noun *person*. The second (*himself* again) refers back to the pronoun *he*.)

– VERBS –

55 VERBS – WHAT ARE VERBS?

Verbs are doing words. A verb usually expresses an action (e.g. *to run*, *to jump*, *to bake*, *to play*). Verbs are not all about actions though. *To think*, *to calculate*, *to exist* and *to be* are also verbs. *To be* is the most common verb. (That's the one that goes: *I am*, *you are*, *he is*, etc. In the past tense, it goes: *I was*, *you were*, etc. In the future tense, it goes: *I will be*, *you will be*, etc.) You knew all that. Here are some examples:

- *The doctor wrote the prescription.*
  (*Wrote* is a verb. It expresses the action *to write*.)
- *A man paints with his brains and not with his hands.*
  (Michelangelo Buonarroti)
  (*paints* – verb.)
- *In politics, your enemies can't hurt you, but your friends will kill you.* (Ann Richards)
  (*hurt*, *will kill* – both verbs)

Verbs Express Mental Actions Too. Verbs do not necessarily express physical actions. They can express mental actions too. Example:

- *Peter guessed the right number.*
  (*guessed* – verb from *to guess*)
- *I like the dreams of the future better than the history of the past.*
  (Thomas Jefferson)
  (*like* – verb)

Verbs Express a State of Being. A small but extremely important group of verbs do not express any action at all. The most important verb in this group is the verb *to be*. Examples:

- *The report of my death was an exaggeration.* (Mark Twain)
  (*was* – the verb *to be*)
- *Things are only impossible until they are not.* (Jean-Luc Picard)
  (*are*, *are* – the verb *to be*)
- *Duct tape is like the force. It has a light side, a dark side, and it holds the universe together.* (Carl Zwanzig)
  (*is* – the verb *to be*. The words *has* and *holds* are also verbs.)

Often, verbs are not so easy to spot:

* *Blame the guy who can't speak English if something goes wrong at the plant.*
  (The words *blame* and *speak* are obviously verbs, but so is *goes*. In this example, I think *goes* should be classified somewhere between verbs that express a state of being and verbs that express an action.)

Verb Terminology. There is a lot of grammatical terminology associated with verbs. Next, we'll look at the most common verb-associated terms and cover some associated errors as we go through them.

Infinitive Form. When a verb is preceded by the word *to*, it is said to be in its infinitive form (i.e. most basic form).

* *I have to smoke that!*
  (*to smoke* – infinitive form of the verb)

Beware Split Infinitives. Placing another word between *to* and its verb is called a *split infinitive*. A split infinitive is considered by some to be a mistake. For example:

* *You have to really try.*
  (The infinitive verb *to try* is split by the word *really*.)
* *...to boldly go where no man has gone before.*
  (The infinitive verb *to go* is split by the word *boldly*.)

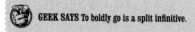 **GEEK SAYS** To boldly go is a split infinitive.

This is also covered in Section 166.

Past Tense. Verbs which express actions in the past are in the *past tense*.

* *He talked with more claret than clarity.* (Susan Ertz)

Present Tense. Verbs which express present actions are in the *present tense*.

* *He is the kind of a guy who lights up a room just by flicking a switch.*

Future Tense. Verbs which express actions in the future are in the *future tense*. These are usually formed by preceding the verb with *will*.

- *Give me where to stand, and I will move the earth.* (Archimedes, 287–212 BC)

Subject of a Verb. The person or thing performing the action of the verb is said to be the *subject of the verb*.

- *Tony stole the boat.*
  (Tony – subject of the verb *to steal*)
- *Tony is guilty.*
  (Tony – subject of the verb *to be* (i.e. *is*))
- *Who was that?*
  (*Who* – subject of the verb *to be* (i.e. *was*))
  (*Who* is always the subject of a verb. *Whom* is never the subject of a verb. That's the difference between the two. See Section 170.)

Direct Object of a Verb. Many verbs perform an action on something. This is called the *direct object* of the verb.

- *Terry kissed her hand.*
  (*her hand* – direct object of the verb *to kiss*)
- *Beverly will eat a whole chicken.*
  (*a whole chicken* – direct object of the verb *to eat*)

You can often spot a direct object by finding the verb and asking *what*.

- *Kissed* what? (*her hand*)
- *Will eat* what? (*a whole chicken*)

Intransitive Verbs. Some verbs cannot have a direct object. These verbs are called *intransitive verbs*.

- *As his new girlfriend looked over, Jack sneezed on his pizza.*
  (*Jack sneezed*, but he did not perform an action on anything. In this example, the verb *to sneeze* is an intransitive verb.)

- *Nancy Reagan fell and broke her hair.* (Johnny Carson)
  (She *fell* but did not perform an action on anything. Here, the verb *to fall* is an intransitive verb. Note: The verb *broke* did something to *her hair*. *Broke* is a transitive verb. More on that in a second.)

When you ask *what* with an intransitive verb, there is no answer.

- *Jack sneezed* what? (Err, nothing. He just sneezed.)
- *Nancy Reagan fell* what? (Nothing. She just fell.)

Verbs that can have a direct object (most of them) are called *transitive verbs*.

- *Barney copied the answer.*
  (*the answer* – direct object of the transitive verb *to copy*)
- *I hate women because they always know where things are.* (James
  Thurber)
  (*women* – direct object of the transitive verb *to hate; where things
  are* – direct object of the transitive verb *to know*)

Some verbs can be both. *To win* is a classic example. You can *win a prize* (in
this case, it's transitive), but when *to win* means *to come first*, it is intransitive.
For example:

- *She won me in front of a large crowd. She always wins me when
  people are watching.*
  (Unless you're going to parties you'd rather not discuss (i.e. where
  you're the prize), then this is wrong.
  It should be: *She beat me in front of a large crowd. She always beats
  me when people are watching.*)

Indirect Object of a Verb. Some verbs have two objects: a direct object (see
above) and an indirect object. The indirect object is the person or thing for
whom the action was performed.

- *Jamie read the children a story.*
  (*a story* – direct object; *the children* – indirect object)
- *I will bake you all a cake.*
  (*a cake* – direct object; *you all* – indirect object)
- *Nearly all men can stand adversity, but if you want to test a man's
  character, give him power.* (Abraham Lincoln)
  (*adversity, a man's character, power* – direct objects;
  him – indirect object)

You can spot the indirect object by finding the verb and asking *for whom* or
to whom.

- *Jamie read a story* to whom? (*the children*)

- *I will bake a cake* for whom? (*you all*)
- *Give power* to whom? (*him*)

Passive Sentence. The subject of a sentence does not always do the action of the verb. Sometimes, the action is done to the subject. Such sentences are called *passive sentences*, because the subjects are being passive, i.e. not doing anything.

- *Carl was arrested.*
  (*Carl* is not doing anything, but he is the subject of the sentence. *Carl* is the subject of the verb *to be* (i.e. *was*).)

Passive verbs always have at least two words: *was* and *arrested* in this example. The person doing the action of the verb in a passive sentence is usually shown with the word *by*.

- *Carl was arrested by PC Adams.*

Passive sentences are useful.

Passive sentences are quite useful if you're trying not to apportion blame. Check this out:

- *The document had been released into the public domain.*
  (passive sentence – no blame)

Active Sentence. Active sentences are the opposite of passive sentences. In an active sentence, the subject of the verb performs the action.

- *Jackie released the document into the public domain.*
  (Jaaaaackiiieeeeeeeeeeeeeeee!)

Passive or Active? Many businesses encourage their staff to use active sentences. They consider passive sentences to be long-winded, less direct and less flowing. For this reason, the Microsoft Word grammar checker often suggests an active version of a passive sentence. For example:

- *The hook-shaped shoreline was eroded by time.*
  (passive sentence)
- *Time eroded the hook-shaped shoreline.*
  (active sentence)

If you prefer the passive version, stick with it. Here are some good reasons to use a passive sentence:

When you don't want to reveal who was responsible
- *The document had been released into the public domain.*
- *Bad advice was given.*
- *A serious failing in standing operating procedures had occurred.*

When the doer of the action is general, unknown or obvious
- *Pistachio nuts are grown in Iran.*
- *His parade uniform was stolen.*
- *English and German are spoken in many Cornish campsites.*
- *The windows must be secured.*
- *Divorces are made in heaven.* (Oscar Wilde)

To put something you want to emphasise at the start of your sentence
- *An estimated 258,000 people were injured in alcohol-related crashes.*

To use the same subject twice (e.g. once in an active clause and once in a passive one)
- *Martin crashed into the barrier and was tossed in the crowd.*

Conjugation of Verbs. A verb will change its form a little depending on the subject. For example:

- *I write. He writes.* (*write* and *writes*)
- *The camel laughs. The jackals laugh.* (*laughs* and *laugh*)

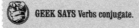 **GEEK SAYS** Verbs conjugate.

When verbs change in this way, it is known as *conjugation*. A verb conjugates according to the subject. The subject of a verb can be in one of six forms:

1. I
2. You
3. He / She / It
4. We
5. You
6. They

The first three are the singular forms (known as *first person singular*, *second person singular* and *third person singular*); whereas, the second three are the plural forms (known as *first person plural*, *second person plural* and *third person plural*). All subjects fit in one of these categories. *Camel* is like *he* (i.e. third person singular) and *jackals* is like *they* (i.e. third person plural). (This is the origin of the insurance term *third party*, i.e. insurance for them.)

This topic rarely causes problems for native English speakers, who conjugate verbs correctly without much thought. However, sometimes the subject of a verb can be "obscured" by other words (underlined in the example below) between it and the verb, and writers become distracted and choose the wrong conjugation. For example:

* *A list of <u>contributing factors</u> are being compiled.* ✖
  (*A list…are* – wrong. Should be: *A list…is*) (See Section 84.)

Participles. Participles are formed from verbs. There are two types: present participles and past participles. Present participles end … *ing*; whereas, past participles have various endings. Some examples:

Verb – Present Participle – Past Participle
* *to sing – singing – sung*
* *to drive – driving – driven*
* *to go – going – gone*
* *to rise – rising – risen*
* *to watch – watching – watched*
* *to be – being – been*

Participles are used as adjectives. For example:

* *Soaring prices affect the quality of the wool.*
  (*soaring* – present participle – used as an adjective to describe *prices*)
* *I am not the first to comment that prices are falling.*
  (*falling* – present participle – used as an adjective to describe *prices*)
  (Note: When an adjective is placed after the word it is describing, it is called a *predicate adjective*.)
* *He is a forgotten hero.*
  (*forgotten* – past participle – used as an adjective)
* *They were neglected.*
  (*neglected* – past participle – used as an adjective)
  (Note: This is a passive sentence (see above). In this role, *neglected* is known as a past passive participle. Why do you care? See *Lay, Laid and Lain* in Section 143.)

MISCELLANEOUS

56 ABBREVIATIONS – CONTRACTIONS

A contraction is a cut-down version of a word. Examples:

- *Mr (contraction of Mister)*
- *Revd (contraction of Reverend)*
- *para. (a contraction of paragraph)*

 GREAT TIP If the last letters are the same, don't use a period/full stop.

Here's the main point of this section:

If the last letter of a contraction is the same as the last letter of the whole word, then no period/full stop is required. Examples:

- *Mr* ✔ (contraction of *Mister*)
- *Revd* ✔ (contraction of *Reverend*)
- *Rev.* ✔ (This is also a contraction of *Reverend*. It's worth mentioning that some argue this is not a contraction but just an abbreviation. They claim a contraction must include the first and last letters of the original word. I can live with that. In fact, it helps make the point being made about whether to use a period/full stop at the end.)
- *Dr.* ✖
  (contraction of *Doctor*; r is the last letter of *Dr* and *Doctor* – no period/full stop required)
- *The theory is supported by Prof. Munro.* ✔
- *Para* ✖
  (contraction of *Paragraph*; last letters are different – period/full stop required)
- *Para. 1 and Paras 4–6* ✔
  (contraction of *Paragraph* and *Paragraphs*)

A great rule, but it's not well observed

I really like this rule. It is very logical, and it provides clear guidance on what to do. Unfortunately, it's not well observed, particularly in the US where all contractions tend to attract periods/full stops. It pains me to say it, but these days, you can pretty much do what you want at the end of a contraction, and no one will mark you down for it. That said, it's worth knowing the rule as it allows you to include or exclude periods/full stops with confidence. This rule needs reviving. I mean, writing "*Para. 1 and Paras 4–6*" and knowing precisely why – how great is that?

57 ABBREVIATIONS – E.G. AND I.E.

The abbreviation *e.g.* means *for example* (from the Latin *exempli gratia*) and *i.e.* means *in other words* or *that is* (from the Latin *id est*). *E.g.* and *i.e.* are often confused. This is because they are both used to introduce clarification of something previously mentioned.

E.g. *E.g.* is used to introduce an example. For example:

- *Although some fish (e.g. sharks) bear live young, most fish eggs are fertilised and hatch in water.* ✔ (e.g. = for example)
- *He was the school champion of many activities (e.g. chess, badminton and 110m hurdles).* ✔
  (e.g. = for example)

I.e. *I.e.* is used to restate an idea more clearly or to introduce more information. For example:

- *She kept repeating that his end-of-term results were surprisingly good; i.e. she was accusing him of cheating.* ✔
  (i.e. = in other words)
- *She kept repeating that his end-of-term results were surprisingly good; e.g. she was accusing him of cheating.* ✖
  (e.g. = for example)
- *Service charge is included in all prices, i.e. you don't have to leave a tip.* ✔
  (i.e. = in other words)

Getting Them Wrong. Often mixing *e.g.* and *i.e.* does not mean your sentence is grammatically incorrect. However, getting them wrong will change the meaning of your sentence. Examples:

- *All amphibians are thriving in the new pond, e.g. the two bullfrogs were being very active yesterday.* ✔
  (This sentence is fine grammatically. From it, we infer there are more than two bullfrogs in the pond.)

- *All amphibians are thriving in the new pond, i.e. the two bullfrogs were being very active yesterday.* ✔
  (This sentence is fine grammatically. We infer the only amphibians in the pond are two bullfrogs.)

Remembering Which Is Which. This may assist in remembering:

e.g. = example given
i.e. = in effect

A lot of leniency with formatting

The Format with e.g. and i.e. There is a lot of leniency on the syntax (commas etc.) surrounding *e.g.* and *i.e.* Simply pick the one you like and be consistent throughout your document.

Comma before is okay:
- *He directs a variety of genres, e.g. crime, disaster, fantasy.* ✔

Semicolon before is okay:
- *He directs a variety of genres; e.g. crime, disaster, fantasy.* ✔

Brackets are okay:
- *He directs a variety of genres (e.g. crime, disaster, fantasy).* ✔

Starting a sentence is okay:
- *He directs a variety of genres. E.g. he directs crime, disaster and fantasy.* ✔

Comma After in the US. In the US, it is usual to follow *e.g.* or *i.e.* with a comma. It is less common in the UK. There is leniency in all conventions. The golden rule is be consistent. Example:

- *He directs a variety of genres (e.g., crime, disaster, fantasy).*

Periods/Full Stops. It is usual to see periods/full stops with *e.g.* and *i.e.* However, you can write them without. Just be consistent. (They're not written in italics. I'm doing it, because I'm talking about them as opposed to using them.)

Don't Use etc. after e.g. The examples you offer after using *e.g.* are usually samples from a more complete list. Therefore, it is often inappropriate to use *etc.* with *e.g.* since it is understood that you are only offering a partial list by way of example. In the example below, the *etc.* is redundant:

- *Mark needs gloves to handle live fishing bait (e.g. rag worm, lug worm, crab, etc.)* ✖
  (The use of *e.g.* is correct, but the *etc.* is redundant.)

> **GREAT TIP** Delete the etc. from your list of examples. (But if you think the etc. is not redundant, have the confidence to leave it in.)

58 ABBREVIATIONS – FORMING PLURALS

The plural of an abbreviation is usually formed by adding *s* to the end. However, although not common practice, it is acceptable to use *'s* if it is deemed to assist the reader. (Using *'s* has a tendency to attract criticism – read this section carefully.) Examples:

- *Once I have finished this PC, I will only have three PCs to configure.* ✔
- *We have a dozen SUS's to collect from the station.* ✔
  (SUS = Soldier under Sentence)
  (The writer considers that SUS's is clearer than SUSs and has opted to use the 's version. This is acceptable.)
- *The fire fighters could not fully assist with three RTAs because their BA's were boxed up in the side panniers.* ✖
  (RTA = Road Traffic Accident / BA = Breathing Apparatus)
  (There is no good reason to write BA's – especially after showing how abbreviations are pluralised with RTAs.)

Pluralising Abbreviations with Periods/Full Stops. The rule above applies to abbreviations with periods/full stops too. Examples:

- *Once I have finished this P.C., I will only have three P.C.s to configure.* ✔
- *Not one of the S.O.S.'s was received by the coastguard.* ✔

A period/full stop is not required after the *s* when forming the plural. For example:

- *M.O.T.s* ✔
- *Anna was refused credit because of 3 C.C.J.s. and mortgage arrears.* ✖
  (C.C.J. = County Court Judgment)

Forming the plurals of letters and numbers (e.g. your S's look like 5's) is covered in Section 6.

59 ABBREVIATIONS – WITH OR WITHOUT PERIODS/FULL STOPS

It is considered untidy to mix abbreviations with periods/full stops and ones without in the same article. The first two examples below are both correct, because the writer has been consistent.

- *The band travelled around the UK and USA last year.* ✔
- *The band travelled around the U.K. and U.S.A. last year.* ✔
- *The M.D. insisted that his PA had left by 4 o'clock.* ✖
  (inconsistent – considered untidy)
- *It was only shown on ITV and not B.B.C.* ✖
  (inconsistent use of full stops/periods – considered untidy)

One period/full stop will suffice.

The last example has been marked wrong for inconsistency, but it does show us a good practice. There is no need to use another period/full stop at the end of your sentence if it already ends in one. In other words, the one at the end of B.B.C. counts twice. This is very common with *etc.* For example:

- *It is described as a database of information related to the geometry of triangles, squares, rhomboids, etc.* ✔

The Tendency. Abbreviations made up of capital letters tend not to have periods/full stops; whereas, abbreviations made up of lowercase letters tend to have them.

- *BBC / LRS (Linear Recursive Sequence) / ISAF*
  (This is a tendency not a rule.)
- *a.m. / i.e. / e.g. / p.m. / p.p.*
  (This is a tendency not a rule.)

Copy the official version.

In general, you have a choice whether to use periods/full stops or not. However, when an abbreviation is a company title, you should copy the version the company uses. If this means mixing conventions in your article, so be it.

60 ABBREVIATIONS – AD, BC, BCE AND CE

AD and BC are designations used to label years in the Julian and Gregorian calendars. The abbreviation AD (Anno Domini) denotes *of the Christian Era* and should be written before the year; whereas, BC (Before Christ) should be written after the year. Examples:

- *AD 2001* ✔
- *487 BC* ✔
- *Caesar reigned from 63 BC to AD 14.* ✔
- *The well was used for about 10 years but collapsed and was filled in by 71 AD.* ✖ (should be AD 71)

 OPPORTUNITY Show you know by putting AD before the year.

To be honest, I don't think many people would care whether AD is before or after the year. However, putting it before will notch up a tally mark for your credibility with your readers.

Cater for Religious Diversity. BCE (Before Common Era) equates to the time before Christ (BC). CE (Common Era) equates to the time after the birth of Christ (AD). They are often used to cater for religious diversity. Both are written after the date.

- *2001* CE ✔
- *487* BCE ✔

61 AN OR A

There is sometimes confusion whether to use *an* or *a* (particularly with abbreviations). The sound of a word's first letter determines which to use. If the word starts with a vowel sound, you should use *an*. If it starts with a consonant sound, you should use *a*. Examples:

- *Buy a house in an hour.* ✔
  (Although *house* and *hour* start with the same three letters (*hou*), one attracts *a* and the other *an*.)

- *An unknown goblin killed a unicorn.* ✔
  (Although *unknown* and *unicorn* start with the same two letters
  (*un*), one attracts *a* and the other *an*.)
- *An LRS...* ✔
  (*L* is a consonant, but it starts with a vowel sound (*el*).
  Incidentally, LRS = Linear Recursive Sequence)
- *It would be a honour.* ✖
  (*Honour* starts with an *o* sound – should be *an*)
- Send an US ambassador. ✖
  (*US* starts with a *y* sound – should be *a*)
- She was involved in a RTA. ✖
  (*RTA* starts with vowel sound (*ar*) should be *an*.
  Incidentally, RTA = Road Traffic Accident)

 BAD TIP Use an before a vowel, and use a before a consonant

To summarise, it's not about whether the word starts with a vowel or a
consonant. That's irrelevant. It's about how its first syllable is said. Here is a
quirky one:

- *Eventually, a SNCO will become an SRO.*
  (SNCO = Senior Non-Commissioned Officer. It is pronounced
  Senior EnSeeOh. SRO = Senior Reporting Officer. It is pronounced
  EssArOh.)

But, I hear you say, what if my audience reads SRO as *Senior Reporting Officer*
and not *EssArOh*? *An* would be wrong. Yep, it would. The answer? Know your
audience and be prepared to defend your choice of *an* or *a* to your proofreader. Does it matter? I think it does. I have actually seen two guys have a
proper fight over this. (I won.)

 CAPITAL LETTERS – WITH PROPER AND COMMON NOUNS

Use a capital letter for the names of people, places, planets, days of the week,
titles of rank or relationship (when joined to person's name), months, holidays,
departments, clubs, companies, institutions, bridges, buildings, monuments,
parks, ships, hotels, streets, historical events and documents. (These are known
as proper nouns.) Do not use a capital letter for common nouns.

Common Noun or Proper Noun? A common noun is the word for something (like *tower*). A proper noun is the name of something (like *the Eiffel Tower*). There is more on this in Section 48. Examples (proper nouns underlined):

- *The next lake the party visited was <u>Lake Michigan</u>.* ✔
  (The word *lake* is a common noun. It's just the word for an inland water feature. *Lake Michigan* is a proper noun – it's the name of the lake.)
- *<u>The Church</u> in London is not actually a church; it's a pub.* ✔
  (*The Church* – proper noun / *church* – common noun)
- *It was a rewarding day, and I intend to visit here again on <u>Armistice Day</u> next year.* ✔
  (*day* – common noun / *Armistice Day* – proper noun)
- *Ask <u>Sergeant Allan</u> or the other sergeant to arrange the patrol on Friday morning.* ✔
  (*Sergeant Allan* – proper noun / *sergeant* – common noun)

Oi, Stick to the Rules. Do not be tempted to give a word a capital letter just because it is an important word in your sentence.

- *I'm having the best day of my life, and I owe it all to not going to Church!* ✖ (Homer Simpson)
- *Lisa, Vampires are make-believe, like elves, gremlins and Eskimos.* ✖ (Homer Simpson)
  (*Vampires* is wrong. *Eskimos* is correct.)
- *We live in an age when Pizza gets to your home before the Police.* ✖
- *Place your order using the form in our latest Brochure.* ✖
- *We value our Clients' opinions.* ✖

 BEWARE The importance of a word does not determine whether it gets a capital letter.

In Business Writing. Grammar pedants will string me up for this, but it is acceptable to capitalise some common nouns, such as Company and Director – you have a choice.

- *The manager of your company confirmed the booking in writing on 15 August.* ✔
- *The Manager of your Company confirmed the booking in writing on 15 August.* ✔

In the main, this pertains to job titles and names of departments. For example:

- *Director, President, Office Manager, Commanding Officer, Division, Claims Department, Court, Regiment, Unit*

Many of these words sit on the blurry border of proper noun and common noun, which makes using capital letters a little easier to stomach. For example, is *Claims Department* the actual name of the claims department? I bet it is. What about the *Head of the Claims Department*? I bet that's his job title. There is another factor at play here: the need to be polite and respectful. I mean look at this:

- *The Manager of your Company confirmed the booking in writing on 15 August.* ✔

Right, let's take *Manager*. You can claim that's his job title. So, the capital *M* is justifiable. But what about Company? That won't be the name of the company. I am far less comfortable with this having a capital letter, but using a lowercase *c* seems a bit discourteous. If you don't think so, then crack on and write *company*.

> Using a lowercase letter on some words looks a bit discourteous.

This subject is a nightmare in military writing. The convention is to use capital letters for unit types (e.g. Regiment), ranks (e.g. Colonel), weapon systems (e.g. Multi-barrelled Rocket Launcher) and anything that can be abbreviated (e.g. Soldier Under Sentence (SUS)). Striking a balance between the real grammar rules and military convention is a challenge. I've tried applying strict capitalisation rules to a military document. I felt very uncomfortable with the result, and it got battered by my commanding officer… I mean Commanding Officer.

So, What's the Bottom Line? Only use capital letters for proper nouns. If you feel the need, use capital letters for generic job titles/types (e.g. *Manager*) and department titles/types (e.g. *Finance Section*). But, do not capitalise a word just because you think it's a key word in your sentence.

- *The Director will cast the final Vote.* ✖
  (I can live with *Director* but not *Vote*.)

63   CAPITAL LETTERS – IN ADVERTISEMENTS

Do what you want in adverts.

There are specific rules about when to use capital letters (see Section 62). But, as they attract the eye and make words look more important, they feature in advertisements more than they would under normal grammar rules. This is deemed acceptable.

After all, advertisements are meant to catch the eye. Don't try it anywhere else though – just in advertisements. Even then, you should consider the pros and cons of your deliberate grammar mistake. Some examples:

- *We offer independent Mortgage Advice.*
  (There is no reason for the *M* on *Mortgage* or the *A* on *Advice*, but I believe this is a more effective advertisement for those errors.)
- *Eat our Doughnuts and get Thinner!*
  (*D* and *T* acceptable in an advertisement)
- *Simply the Best Pies in town*
  (B and P acceptable in an advertisement)
- *Kids Eat FREE*
  (E and FREE acceptable in an advert)

64   CAPITAL LETTERS – AND THE POINTS OF THE COMPASS

The directions *north*, *east*, *south* and *west* should not be given capital letters, unless they form part of a name like *West Ham*, *West Sussex* and *South Africa*. That said, geographical areas known as *The North*, *The East*, *The South* and *The West* are usually written with capital letters. Examples:

- *I live in The North.* ✔
- *I travel north to Carolina at weekends.* ✔
- *There are no penguins at the North Pole.* ✔
- *Take 10 paces East and then dig.* ✘
- *Keep driving north on the M1 until you reach the M62 and then head west towards West Yorkshire.* ✔

To summarise, do not use a capital letter for north, east, south or west unless they're part of a name. This also applies to terms like north-east, north-eastern, etc.

65 CAPITAL LETTERS – AND THE FOUR SEASONS

As the days of the week and the months are written with capital letters, many writers automatically capitalise the seasons. However, the four seasons are not normally written with capital letters. Here's a cool rule though: if a season is given a human trait (i.e. personified), then it can be given a capital letter. Examples:

- *He was touched by Winter's icy breath.* ✔
  (*winter* given a human trait – capital letter okay)
- *One swallow does not make a summer.* ✔ (Aristotle)
  (no human trait – lowercase letter is correct)
- *The leaves had been subjected to Autumn's touch.* ✔
  (human trait – *A* is correct)
- *The coldest winter I ever spent was a summer in San Francisco.* ✔
  (Mark Twain)
  (no human traits – *w* and *s* are correct)
- *This is the second time I have been skiing this Winter.* ✘
  (no human trait – *W* should be *w*)

 OPPORTUNITY Look a real smarty pants by citing this rule when proofreading a peer's work.

The Personification Rule is under Change. I think this rule is really quaint, but I'm afraid it's going out of fashion, and actually there's no good reason for it to exist. Nowadays, it is acceptable to write the seasons without capital letters regardless of personification.

Of course, if a season name forms part of a name, then it is given a capital letter. For example:

- *I met her at the Summer Solstice Festival.* ✔
- *There were some incredible masks at the Rhine Winter Ball.* ✔

 GREAT TIP Play it safe. Only use a capital letter for a season when it forms part of a name.

66 CAPITAL LETTERS – WITH MOONS, STARS AND PLANETS

The Sun, the Sun, or the sun?

Like all proper nouns (see Section 62), the names of moons, stars and planets are written with capital letters. Confusion arises because the name of the moon orbiting Earth is called *The Moon*, and the sun of our solar system is called *The Sun*. Therefore, the words to denote our moon and our sun can be either proper nouns or common nouns depending on context. Examples:

- *The largest moon orbiting Jupiter is Ganymede.* ✔ (*moon* –
  common noun / *Ganymede* – proper noun, i.e. name of the moon)
- *The moon orbiting Earth is The Moon.* ✔
  (first *moon* – common noun / *The Moon* – proper noun,
  i.e. name of the moon)
- *Are all suns as hot as The Sun?* ✔
  (*suns* – common noun / *The Sun* – proper noun, i.e. name of the
  sun)

Capital T on The? When a name starts with *The*, it should be written with a capital letter (e.g. *The Sun, The Sex Pistols, The Ramones, The Great Gatsby*). However, there is a lot of leniency on this ruling, particularly with regard to *The Sun* and *The Moon*.

- *Does The Moon invoke romance?* ✔
- *Does the Moon invoke romance?* ✔
  (This version is more common.)

You have a couple of decisions to make if the word before such a proper noun is *the*. Do you use a capital T? Do you write *the The*? For example:

- *The songs in the film are taken from one of the The Sex Pistols
  albums.*
  (You could argue this is grammatically correct, but no one would
  say or write it. You should write: *The songs in the film are taken
  from one of the Sex Pistols albums.*)

Lots of proper nouns start with *The*. Grammar pedants will tell you that the *T* must be capital. I can't disagree, but this is one time when it is safe to let your instincts override the grammar rule. (Oh, I would never write *the The Sex Pistols* no matter how grammatically stringent I was being.)

67 CAPITAL LETTERS – TO START SENTENCES

At first look, this might seem a little basic for this book, but don't switch off just yet. This section is probably more useful than you think. We know a sentence starts with a capital letter. But, this also applies to sentences contained within speech marks and brackets as well as full sentences following colons. (There is a lot of leniency on this latter point.) Examples:

- *It was Homer who said: "Well, I'm tired of being a wannabe league bowler. I wanna be a league bowler!"* ✔
  (Capital *W* to start a sentence within speech marks)
- *This is the devilish thing about foreign affairs: they are foreign and will not always conform to our whim.* ✔ (James Reston)
  (When a full sentence follows a colon, it is usual to use a lowercase letter. However, if the second sentence is the main point (normally after a short introduction), a capital letter can be used.)
- *I follow Mark Twain's advice: Never put off until tomorrow what you can do the day after tomorrow.* ✔
  (Here, the sentence after the colon is the main point, and it follows a short introduction. The capital *N* on *Never* is correct.)
- *The human race is faced with a cruel choice: Work or daytime television.* ✖
  (If the words after the colon are not a full sentence, you have to use a lowercase letter.)

Here's the main point of this section:

Start a New Sentence. Once you have expressed a complete idea, you should put a period/full stop and end the sentence. You cannot insert a comma and continue writing. For example:

- *John sprang to his feet and ran to the shop, he needed to buy more beer before the second half started.* ✖ (This should be two sentences.)
- *The Loch Ness Monster was spotted eight times in the '60s on the loch's west bank, I camped there for a year and did not see a thing, I caught dozens of trout though.* ✖ (This should be three sentences.)

These are *run-on sentences*. A *run-on sentence* (or *run-on error*) is a common mistake. Occasionally, it may be appropriate to use a dash or a semicolon instead of a period/full stop and then continue writing – but never a comma. This is covered in Section 75.

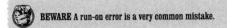
BEWARE A run-on error is a very common mistake.

Start a New Sentence with *However*. The majority of the time, the word *however* should start a new sentence. It is a common mistake to merge sentences using a comma and *however*. For example:

- *Do not feed the fish in this tank, however, you may feed the animals in the petting zoo.* ✖
- *The centre forward is very fast. However, he can only kick with his left foot.* ✔

Be aware that *however* does not always start a new sentence.

- *The chief weapon of sea pirates, however, was their capacity to astonish. Nobody else could believe, until it was too late, how heartless and greedy they were.* ✔ (Kurt Vonnegut)

68 CAPITAL LETTERS – AND TITLE CASE

Titles and names can be written in *title case*. This means only using capital letters for the principal words. Unless it's the first word in the title or name, do not use capital letters for:

- Prepositions (e.g. *at, under, near, upon, of, by*). See Section 49.
- Articles (This just means the words *a, an* and *the*.)
- Conjunctions (e.g. *and, or, but*). See Section 44.

The first word of the title is written with a capital letter regardless. For example:

- *The Last of the Mohicans* ✔
- *Have you seen About a Boy?* ✔
- *Snow White and the Seven Dwarfs* ✔
- *Newcastle upon Tyne / Brighton on Sea* ✔
- *The DiMaggio Line* ✔

Knowing title case removes the need to make decisions on capital letters.

Although title case looks neat, not everybody uses it. Many businesses use capital letters for all the words in their titles. When known, you should copy the official versions. Knowing title case is useful. It removes the need to make a decision on whether a word in a title or name should have a capital letter or not.

69 COMPARATIVES – AND SUPERLATIVES OF ADJECTIVES

Let's start with some definitions.

What's a Comparative? Words like *prettier* and *richer* (formed from the adjectives *pretty* and *rich*) are known as *comparatives*. A comparative is used to show who (or what) has a quality to the greater or lesser degree. (In the first example below, the quality being compared is height.)

- *You call that high? Blackpool Tower is higher.*
  (*higher*: comparative of *high*)
- *The male fish is more beautiful than the female.*
  (*more beautiful*: comparative of *beautiful*)

What's a Superlative? Words like *prettiest* and *richest* (formed from the adjectives *pretty* and *rich*) are known as *superlatives*. A superlative is used to show who (or what) has a quality to the greatest or least degree.

- *It is the most wonderful chocolate fudge I have ever tasted.*
  (*most wonderful*: superlative of *wonderful*)
- *Paul is good, but Adam is the best.*
  (*best*: superlative of *good*)

The rules for forming comparatives and superlatives from adjectives are varied. It's probably worth whipping over these quickly:

For one-syllable adjectives, add *er* (for the comparative) and *est* (for the superlative). Example:

- *Strong, stronger, strongest*

For adjectives of more than one syllable, add *less* or *more* (for the comparative) and *most* or *least* (for the superlative). Example:

- *Famous, less famous, most famous*

For adjectives of more than one syllable ending *y*, remove *y* and add *ier* (for the comparative) and remove *y* and add *iest* (for the superlative). Example:

- *Silly, sillier, silliest*

But, use *less* or *least* (if you mean to a lesser degree)

- *Silly, less silly, least silly*

There are no rules for the irregular ones:

- *Bad, worse, worst*
- *Good, better, best*
- *Many, more, most*

Here are some more examples of comparatives of adjectives:

- *Misty Blue is a stronger horse on the flat.*
  (*stronger*: comparative of *strong*)
- *The words that enlighten the soul are more precious than jewels.*
  (Hazrat Khan)
  (*more precious*: comparative of *precious*)
- *Peter is far clumsier.*
  (*clumsier*: comparative of *clumsy*)
- *Try this question. It is less difficult.*
  (*Less difficult* is the comparative of *difficult*. However, it is common practice to choose a word with the opposite meaning rather than use the *less* form; e.g. *less difficult = easier / less strong = weaker*.)

Here are some more examples of superlatives of adjectives:

- *Geoff is now officially the strongest man in the world.*
  (*strongest*: superlative of *strong*)
- *The bill is extortionate, and this is the noisiest place I have ever stayed.*
  (*noisiest*: superlative of *noisy*)
- *It is the least attractive offer, but we are obliged to take it.*
  (*least attractive*: superlative of *attractive*)
- *Last week, I stated that this woman was the ugliest woman I had ever seen. I have since been visited by her sister and now wish to withdraw that statement.* (Mark Twain)
  (*ugliest*: superlative of *ugly*)

Okay, that's the boring stuff out the way. Here are the important bits:

Only Do It Once. When forming a comparative or a superlative, be careful not to use a double comparative or a double superlative. This is a common mistake, particularly in speech (and "EastEnders").

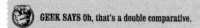 **GEEK SAYS** Oh, that's a double comparative.

- *Ann is more prettier than Carla.* ✖
  (This is a double comparative. The word *prettier* is the comparative of *pretty*. It is a mistake to use the word *more* as well.)
- *Ann is prettier than Carla.* ✔
- *He was the most best player.* ✖
  (This is a double superlative. The word *best* is the superlative of *good*. It is a mistake to use *most* as well. The word *bestest* is obviously wrong too.)
- *Geoff was most quickest in the trials.* ✖

Grammatical Howler. Using a double comparative or a double superlative is a grammatical howler. Your boss will think you're dense if use one. In truth, people make this mistake more when talking than writing, but even that is pretty unforgivable. In an argument, a girl once called me the "the most thickest person [she'd] ever met." Errr… [tongue-holding silence ensued].

More Single? Arguably, there are adjectives that should not have comparative or superlative forms, because their meanings already express the qualities to the highest possible degree. For example:

- *Instantaneous*
  (I mean, can something be more instantaneous?)

Other examples are:

- *single*, *unique* and *dead*.

I don't think it's a serious crime to say *more unique* or *more dead*, but just be aware there are pedants out there who will pick you up for these. It's worth avoiding them…the terms and the pedants.

70 COMPARATIVES – AND SUPERLATIVES OF ADVERBS

This section is closely related to the last, but this one is about adverbs as opposed to adjectives. To start, we need to cover some definitions.

What's a Comparative of an Adverb? An expression like *more slowly* (formed from the adverb *slowly*) is known as a comparative. It is used to show who (or what) has performed an action in a specific manner to the greater or lesser degree; i.e. it's used to compare two performances. For example:

- *Use Paul's version; he writes more diplomatically than Erika.*
  (In this example, *more diplomatically* compares Paul's performance with Erika's.)
- *Claire dances less elegantly.*
  (In this example, *less elegantly* is the comparative. It compares Claire's performance with somebody else's.)

What's a Superlative of an Adverb? An expression like *most carefully* (formed from the adverb *carefully*) is known as a superlative. It is used to show who (or what) has performed an action in a specific manner to the greatest or least degree. For example:

- *The chairman spoke most convincingly of all.*
  (*most convincingly*: superlative of *convincingly*)
- *Pete acted the least sociably.*
  (*least sociably*: superlative of *sociably*)

The rules for forming comparatives and superlatives from adverbs are varied. For one-syllable adverbs, add *er* (for the comparative) and *est* (for the superlative):

- *Fast, faster, fastest*

For adverbs of more than one syllable, add *less* or *more* (for the comparative) and *most* or *least* (for the superlative):

- *Carefully, less carefully, most carefully*

There are no rules for the irregular ones:

- *Badly, worse, worst*
- *Well, better, best*

Here are some examples of comparatives of adverbs:

- *That goat can see better than you think.*
  (*better*: comparative of *well*)
- *Try to paint the edges more carefully; it will save time later.*
  (*more carefully*: comparative of *carefully*)
- *The engine operates less efficiently with alcohol.*
  (*less efficiently*: comparative of *efficiently*)

Here are some examples of superlatives of adverbs:

- *The scientific theory I like best is that the rings of Saturn are composed entirely of lost airline luggage.* (Mark Russell)
  (*best*: superlative of *well*)
- *It was obvious they were not used to high heels, but Karen moved most gracefully of all.*
  (*most gracefully*: superlative of *gracefully*)
- *She answered least abruptly.*
  (*least abruptly*: superlative of *abruptly*)

Only Do It Once. In general, comparatives and superlatives of adverbs do not cause difficulties for native English speakers. However, the mistake of using a double comparative or a double superlative is fairly common in speech. This error is more common with the comparatives and superlatives of adjectives, but it is occasionally seen with adverbs.

- *Of all the fish in Europe, pike attack the most fastest.*
  (This is a double superlative. The word *fastest* is the superlative of *fast*. It is a mistake to use the word *most* as well.)
- *Charles completed the task more better.*
  (This is a double comparative.)

If you use a double comparative or superlative in writing, your readers will think you're a buffoon. They might be too polite to say it, but they'll be thinking it. Even saying one is pretty serious. The "best" I have ever heard is "much more betterer." Crikey, that's a triple comparative! On occasion, I commit this crime in speech. I have found the best recovery is to say, "Jeepers, did I just use a double superlative of an adverb?" and then follow up with the correct version. Your audience will think you're dull, but they won't think you're brainless. (So, it's only a partial recovery if the truth be known.)

71 AVOIDING DANGLING MODIFIERS

To keep your readers engaged, it's good practice to vary the structure of your sentences. One common practice is to say something about your subject before making the main point. For example:

- *With a keen eye for detail, Mark has fine project-management skills.* ✔
  (Here, the writer has said something about Mark before making the main point. In this sentence, Mark is the subject, and the words *with a keen eye for detail* are a modifier.)

 GEEK SAYS The words "With a keen eye for detail" modify the subject.

- *After being attacked by bulls in two separate incidents, the scout leader took off his red coat and put it in his rucksack.* ✔
  (*After being attacked by bulls in two separate incidents* modifies *the scout leader*.)
- *Packing my kit into three huge holdalls, I knew my little Jack Russell could sense I was leaving for a long time.* ✔
  (*Packing my kit into three huge holdalls* modifies *I*.)

Often, the modifying words (the modifier) and the thing being modified are separated by a comma. The modifier (to the left of the comma) must relate to whatever is on the right of the comma. If it doesn't, it's a *dangling modifier*, which is a grammar error. Here's the main point: The modifier must refer to the thing being modified. That seems pretty obvious. But, you'd be surprised how common dangling modifiers are. Here are some incorrect examples:

- *Vicious smelly creatures with huge tusks, the ship's crew were reluctant to drive the male walruses from the beach.* ✖
  (Nah, wrong – *the ship's crew* were not *vicious smelly creatures with huge tusks*.)
- *Having followed a strict high-protein diet, her weight dropped off rapidly.* ✖
  (*Her weight* didn't follow the diet. She did.)
- *Packing my kit into three huge holdalls, my little Jack Russell could sense I was leaving for a long time.* ✖
  (Jack Russells are smart dogs, but I doubt this one was packing kit into three holdalls.)

In my experience, dangling modifiers are really common in personnel appraisals. For example:

- *With a ferocious appetite for extra-curriculum activities, Sergeant Baker's work ethic is remarkable.* ✖
(This one is quite tricky. *Sergeant Baker* is the first thing after the comma, but he is not the subject. The subject is *work ethic*. Keep an eye out for "traps" like this.)

 GREAT TIP When proofreading: If a sentence starts with a modifier, assume it's modifying the wrong thing until you're happy it's not.

 OPPORTUNITY It's worth learning what a dangling modifier is just so you can tell your boss that his sentence contains a dangling modifier. For extra cool points, try to look nonchalant.

72 AVOIDING MISPLACED MODIFIERS

This section is about misplaced modifiers. If you thought *dangling modifier* (see the last section) was a cool term, you'll love this: *misplaced modifiers* might be *squinting modifiers*. I mean, it's worth learning what one is just so you can say "squinting modifier" in front of someone. There will be plenty of opportunities for that too. Misplaced modifiers are pretty common.

So, what is a misplaced modifier? A misplaced modifier is a badly placed word (or words) that could refer to more than one thing in the sentence. For example:

- *Lee claimed yesterday he saw a basking shark.* ✖
(So, did Lee see the shark *yesterday*, or did he make the claim *yesterday*? The word *yesterday* squints backwards at *claimed* and forwards at *saw*. It is a misplaced (or squinting) modifier.)
- *Cycling uphill quickly strengthens your calf muscles.* ✖
(*Cycling uphill quickly* or *quickly strengthens*? *Quickly* is a misplaced modifier.)
- *The gun crew were informed they had been replaced by the commanding officer.* ✖
(It's not clear whether the commanding officer replaced the gun crew himself or just informed them.)
- *Historians have been kept guessing over claims Dr James Barry, Inspector General of Military Hospitals, was in fact a woman for more than 140 years.* ✖ (Daily Telegraph)

Comedians often use misplaced modifiers:

- *"The other day, I shot an elephant in my pyjamas. How he got in my pyjamas, I'll never know."* (Groucho Marx)
  (This joke works because *in my pyjamas* is a misplaced modifier. Context tells you it modifies *I shot*, but the punch line tells you it modifies *an elephant*.)

More often than not, you can correct a misplaced modifier by changing its location in the sentence.

 GREAT TIP Keep your modifiers next to whatever they are modifying.

Here are corrections of the previous examples:

- *Lee claimed he saw a basking shark yesterday.* ✔
- *Cycling uphill strengthens your calf muscles quickly.* ✔
- *The gun crew were informed by the commanding officer they had been replaced.* ✔
- *Historians have been kept guessing for more than 140 years over claims Dr James Barry, Inspector General of Military Hospitals, was in fact a woman.* ✔

It's not squinting. It's just misplaced.

It's Wrong, but It's Not Squinting. Sometimes, a *misplaced modifier* is not ambiguous. It's just misplaced. (In such circumstances, a *misplaced modifier* can't be called *a squinting modifier*.) Let's imagine a chap called Mark went to Las Vegas and lost $14,800 on the roulette tables. In a postcard back to his wife (coz you're a good bloke like that), you could write either:

- *Mark nearly lost $15,000 in Vegas.*
- *Mark lost nearly $15,000 in Vegas.*

The first one gives him some wriggle room when he gets home. The second one doesn't. Can you see the difference? The word *nearly* in the first example is a *misplaced modifier*. It is modifying *lost* when it's supposed to be modifying *$15,000*.

Place your modifiers next to whatever they're modifying.

73 EITHER & NEITHER – DOUBLE NEGATIVE WITH NEITHER/NOR

You will be familiar with the pairings *either/or* and *neither/nor*. If you're interested, these are called *correlative conjunctions* (see Section 44). Here they are in use:

- *I could neither laugh nor cry.* ✔
- *Either the clerk or the secretary has the keys to the Rover.* ✔
  (Note: *has the keys* is correct / *have the keys* would be wrong –
  See Section 74)
- *The clerk or the secretary has the keys to the Rover.* ✔
  (You can often omit *either*.)
- *Adam did not find the key either on or under the mat.* ✔

Neither/nor plays a negative role.

Beware Double Negative. The pairing *neither/nor* plays a negative role in the sentence. Therefore, be careful not to use a double negative.

- *Adam did not find the key neither on nor under the mat.* ✖
  (This is a double negative.)
- *He did not mention neither the flooding nor the landslide.* ✖
  (This is a double negative.)
- *He mentioned neither the flooding nor the landslide.* ✔
  (A correct version of the example above)
- *He did not mention either the flooding or the landslide.* ✔
  (Another correct version)

More about Double Negatives. The two sentences below are also examples of double negatives:

- *David doesn't know nothing.* ✖
- *David did not see no car.* ✖

Remember, two negatives make a positive. (To quote Homer Simpson: "Lisa, two wrongs DO make a right." Obviously, they don't, but you get the point.) The previous examples marked ✖ are not grammatically incorrect, but they probably do not mean what the originator intended. Here is another example:

- *My kids don't believe in no Santa Claus.*
  (This means they do believe in Santa.)

Double negatives can be useful. Look at these two examples:

- *It wasn't uninteresting.* ✔
- *She is not unattractive.* ✔

The two examples above are fine. Sometimes, double negatives are useful for diplomacy. Look at this quote:

- *I cannot say that I do not disagree with you.* ✔ (Groucho Marx)
  (This brilliant quote is a triple negative. If you follow it through logically, you'll find it means *I disagree with you.*)

 GEEK SAYS Hey, that's a triple negative.

74 EITHER & NEITHER – SINGULAR OR PLURAL VERB

Is it singular or plural?

The big question with *either/or* and *neither/nor* is whether you write *neither A nor B <u>is</u>* or *neither A nor B <u>are</u>*.

The rule: If A and B (called the elements) are both singular, then use *is* (i.e. a singular verb). If one of them is plural, use *are* (i.e. a plural verb). For example:

- *Neither Mark nor Dawn is at the function.* ✔
  (*Mark* – singular / *Dawn* – singular / *is* – correct; i.e. not *are*)
- *Neither Dickens nor Thackeray was a panderer to the public taste.* ✔
  (*Dickens* – singular / *Thackeray* – singular / *was* – correct; i.e. not *were panderers*)
- *Either the clerk or the secretary has the keys to the Rover.* ✔
  (*clerk* – singular / *secretary* – singular / *has* – correct; i.e. not *have the keys*)
- *Neither Simon nor Gary does as he is told.* ✔
  (*Simon* – singular / Gary – singular / *does* – correct; i.e. not *do* / *he is* – correct; i.e. not *they are*)
- *Either a mouse or a rat eats the cable at night.* ✔
  (*Mouse* – singular / *rat* – singular / *eats* – correct; i.e. not *eat,* which is the plural version)

All the elements in the examples above were singular. But, if at least one of the elements is plural, then the verb must be plural too. For example:

- *Neither the lawyer nor the detectives are able to follow the sequence of events.* ✔
  (*lawyer* – singular / *detectives* – plural / *are* – correct)
- *There were neither cakes nor ice-cream at the party.* ✔
  (*cakes* – plural / ice-cream – singular / *were* – correct)
- *Neither the firemen nor the policemen know him.* ✔
  (*firemen* – plural / *policemen* – plural / *know* – *correct*;
  i.e. not knows, which is the singular version)
- *Either the budgies or the cat has to go.* ✘
  (*budgies* – plural / *cat* – singular / *has* – wrong; should be *have to go*)

The Proximity Rule

Proximity Rule. Not all grammar conventions agree with this ruling. When I first launched my website, my inbox was bombarded with emails telling me about an alternative convention called the proximity rule. Under the proximity rule, the verb is governed by the element nearest to it. For example:

- *Either crumpets or cake is sufficient.*
  (Under the standard convention, this should be *are sufficient* because *crumpets* is plural. However, under the proximity rule, the singular word *cake* takes precedence, because it is the nearest element to the verb.)
- *There was neither ice-cream nor chocolates at the party.*
  (Under the standard convention, this should be *There were neither* because *chocolates* is plural. However, under the proximity rule, the singular word *ice-cream* takes precedence, because it is the nearest element to the verb.)

Those who look at grammar through a mathematical prism (as I do) are more likely to take issue with the proximity rule. To my mind, it's like saying 3 x 1 = 1, because 1 is nearest to the equals sign. And, what about this:

- *Neither the lawyers nor I am going to be present.* ✔ (If you follow the proximity rule) (Should you put *am*, because *I* is the nearest element? Most of your readers will prefer *Neither the lawyers nor I are going…*)

That said, I can see why the proximity rule is so popular. Most sentences that follow the proximity rule grate less on the ear, and for this reason, people naturally follow this convention. And, that's how grammar rules change over time. Bottom line: Pick the convention you like and be prepared to defend it if your proofreader red pens it.

75 EXTEND A SENTENCE

The best way to write is to string clear, short sentences back to back. Start each with a capital letter and end each with a period/full stop. However, on occasion, there will be an opportunity to extend a sentence or merge two into one. This adds variety to your writing, and allows you to control flow of text and emphasis.

This section is about how to extend a sentence using a colon, a semicolon, three dots or a dash. These topics are repeated throughout the book. Your understanding of these techniques and the frequency with which you employ them will define your writing style and credibility.

Using a Colon. A sentence can be extended with a colon when the writer wishes to expand on something already mentioned in the sentence. (In other words, a colon is used to introduce more information about something mentioned before the colon.) Examples:

- *There were two pets in the house: a budgie and a cat.* ✔
  (*two pets*: *a budgie and a cat*)
- *He blamed his divorce on one thing: beer.* ✔
  (*one thing*: *beer*)
  This is covered more in Sections 10 and 67.

Using a Semicolon. A sentence can be extended with a semicolon when a slight break is preferable to a new sentence. Examples:

- *No one was hurt in the accident; the only real injury was a broken finger.* ✔
- *She did not approve of my design at all; she found it crass.* ✔

Quite often, there is a short phrase immediately after the semicolon which acts like a bridge between both halves of the sentence. Examples:

- *Everybody knows he is guilty; <u>however</u>, it will never be proven.* ✔
- *Her own guest was rejected; <u>as a result</u>, she left.* ✔
- *This business will collapse if you do not invest in the staff's well-being; <u>of course</u>, that is just my opinion.* ✔

This is covered more in Sections 31 and 32.

Using Three Dots. Mark Twain said: "The right word may be effective, but no word was ever as effective as a rightly timed pause." If you want to create pause for effect, use three dots. Examples:

- *I don't want to achieve immortality through my work…I want to achieve it through not dying.* ✔ (Woody Allen)
- *She had a bath once a year…whether she needed it or not.* ✔ (Mark Twain)
- *Bart, with $10,000, we'd be millionaires! We could buy all kinds of useful things like…love!* ✔ (Homer Simpson)
- *I've been looking for a girl like you…not you, but a girl like you.* ✔ (Groucho Marx)
- *A credit card stolen from a woman in Devon was used to buy a meal at a Chinese restaurant 18 hours later…in Hong Kong.* ✔

Using a Dash. Confused about colons, semicolons and three dots? Use a dash. The dash performs all the functions mentioned above. Examples:

- *He blamed his divorce on one thing – beer.* ✔
  (replaces a colon)
- *She did not approve of my design at all – she found it crass.* ✔
  (replaces a semicolon)
- *Everybody knows he is guilty – however, it will never be proven.* ✔
  (replaces a semicolon)
- *I've been looking for a girl like you – not you, but a girl like you.* ✔
  (Groucho Marx)
  (replaces three dots)
- *A credit card stolen from a woman in Devon was used to buy a meal at a Chinese restaurant 18 hours later – in Hong Kong.* ✔
  (replaces three dots)

Colons Different from Semicolons. A colon should only be used to extend a sentence when you are introducing words which expand on something previously mentioned. When a slight break is preferable to a new sentence, use a semicolon. For example:

- *The pilot's chances of landing safely were minimal: the elevators were packed with ice.* ✖

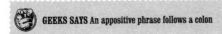

In Apposition. The words after the colon are known as an *appositive phrase*. (It just means an *equal phrase*.) You can also use the term *in apposition to*. For example:

- *There was only one fish in the vicinity: a great white shark.*
  (In this sentence, *great white shark* is in apposition to *fish*.)
- *This company has always had the same motto: Try it twice and then sack it.*
  (In this example, *Try it twice and then sack it* is in apposition to *motto*. Note the capital letter on *Try*. This is explained in Section 67.)

A Colon Is Like an Equals Sign. Many people like to think of a colon as an equals sign. Look back at the first two examples in this section.

- *two pets = a budgie and a cat*
- *one thing = beer*

Don't Rely Solely on Dashes. Although a dash covers the functions of a colon, a semicolon and three dots, it is worthwhile learning how all are used, so you can choose the one that looks best in your sentence. In the next example, there are already several hyphens and dashes. Therefore, using the three dots is preferable to another dash.

- *Mrs Thomas – the 64-year-old lady from Kent who swore she would never have a facelift – removed the bandages to find…a 40-year-old version of herself.* ✔

Another Use for Three Dots (Called Ellipsis). Three dots can also be used to show that words have been omitted. (This is covered more in Section 35.) For example:

- *The magazine claims: "The scene in the '70s was…controlled by The Ramones."* ✔

76 NUMBERS – WRITTEN IN FULL

When writing numbers in full, all numbers between 21 and 99 (except 30, 40, 50, 60, 70, 80 and 90) should be hyphenated regardless of where they appear within the whole number. Also, there are no commas in numbers written in full. For example:

- *51 (fifty-one)* ✔
- *234 (two hundred and thirty-four)* ✔
- *3,567 (three thousand five hundred and sixty-seven)* ✔
  (note: no comma in the full version)
- *44,120 (forty-four thousand one hundred and twenty)* ✔
- *25,223 (twenty five thousand two hundred and twenty three)* ✘
  (*twenty five* and *twenty three* should be hyphenated)
- *5,223 (five thousand, two hundred and twenty-three)* ✘
  (correctly spelt but comma not required)
- *23,237,897 (twenty-three million two hundred and thirty-seven thousand eight hundred and ninety-seven)* ✔

It is probably worth pointing out that 40 is spelt *forty* not *fourty*. This is a common mistake when a spellchecker can't assist.

This book isn't really about spelling, but while we're dabbling in that area, I want to talk about *misspelled/misspelt*. So, which is it? *Misspelled or misspelt*? Well, the internet's grammarians are still at war over this. Their arguments tend to focus on which is most widely used in Britain and America. The summary of that argument is: Use *misspelt* because it's more common in America and Britain than *misspelled*.

But, that's not really the point. You see, *misspelled* started out life as a transitive verb (see Section 55); e.g. *I misspelled three words in my letter. I misspelled her name. I misspelled forty. Misspelt*, on the other hand, was the participle (see Section 55); e.g. *Her name has been misspelt. This is a misspelt word*. If you want to be a grammar purist, adopt this position. But, if you just want a quick answer, use *misspelt*. The best solution is to make your sentence passive (see Section 55) and use *misspelt*. This way, you keep everybody happy, apart from those who claim *misspelled* is acceptable as a participle. But, they can sod off.

77 NUMBERS – AT THE START OF SENTENCES

Avoid starting sentences with numbers.

It is considered untidy to start sentences with figures. You should either reword your sentence or write the number in full (see Section 76). For example:

- *71 people were rescued from the ferry by the Latvian helicopter crew.* ✘
  (Saying this is wrong is a bit harsh, but it's certainly not easy on the eye.)
- *The Latvian helicopter crew rescued 71 people from the ferry.* ✔
  (This reworded version is tidier.)
- *Seventy-one people were rescued from the ferry by the Latvian helicopter crew.* ✔
  (Number written in full to avoid starting the sentence with *71*.)

How to Spell Per Cent. Sentences with numbers often include the words *per cent* or *percent*. For example:

- *Aw, people can come up with statistics to prove anything, Kent. Fourteen percent of all people know that.* ✔ (Homer Simpson)

per cent or percent?

So, is % spelt *percent* or *per cent*? At the outset, it was two words, but it morphed to one word in 1700s. More recently in the UK, it split again into two words, but in the US, it remained one word. I judge there is a lot of leniency on this subject in both the US and UK conventions. My advice: Pick the spelling you like and then be consistent.

If your sentence starts with a number that includes a decimal point, do not write it in full for the sake of a neat-looking sentence. Either live with it written as a figure or reword your sentence.

- *Forty-eight point three per cent of statistics are made up on the spot.* ✘
  (Way too messy)

78 NUMBERS – AS COMPOUND ADJECTIVES

Expressions like *three-and-a-half somethings* (e.g. *three-and-a-half ounces, two-and-a-quarter miles*) can be written with hyphens. For example:

- *Two-and-a-half-thousand people* ✔
- *Three-and-a-quarter million* ✔
- *One-and-a-half dozen* ✔
- *Three and a quarter million dollars (3,250,000)* ✖
  (technically, 3 and 250,000 equal 250,003)
- *One and a half dozen eggs (18)* ✖ (technically, 1 and 6 equal 7)

 GEEK SAYS By the way, "one-and-a-half" is a compound adjective.

Here's the geekery behind this ruling:

Numbers are a type of adjective (i.e. a describing word – see Section 40). An adjective made up of two or more words is called a *compound adjective* (see Section 41). The words in a compound adjective can be linked together by a hyphen (or hyphens) to show that they are part of the same adjective. (The use of hyphens is expected in the UK. Americans are more lenient.) For example:

- three-page document ✔
  (*three-page* is a compound adjective describing *document*)

This can get quite complicated with numbers. For example:

- *I gave him three and a quarter.* ✔
  (There are no adjectives in this sentence. No hyphens required.)
- *I gave him three-and-a-quarter million.* ✔
  (*three-and-a-quarter* is a compound adjective describing *million*.)
- *I gave him three-and-a-quarter-million dollars.* ✔
  (*three-and-a-quarter-million* is a compound adjective describing *dollars*.)
- *I gave him a three-and-a-quarter-million-dollar boat.* ✔
  (*three-and-a-quarter-million-dollar* is a compound adjective describing *boat*.)

79 ONE WORD OR TWO?

Occasionally writers get confused over words like *anyone, everyday, everyone, maybe, nobody, somebody, everybody, sometime* and *sometimes*. Each of these words is made up of two smaller words. When these smaller words coincidentally appear next to each other (and in the correct order), some writers are tempted to use the one-word version. For example:

- *I have some time on Tuesday after rugby practice.* ✔
  (Here, *some* and *time* appear next to each other by coincidence.)
- *I have sometime on Tuesday after rugby practice.* ✖
  (The writer has decided to go for the one-word version.
  Nope, that's wrong.)

Explaining the differences between the one-word and two-word versions would take up more of this book than the topic warrants. The underpinning grammar is a minefield. It's made worse by the fact that the meanings of the one-word and two-word versions can be close.

However, it is the meanings of these words which hold the key to determining which to use. The trick is to think clearly about what each of the one-word versions means.

anyone = any person
- *Always bear in mind that your own resolution to succeed is more important than <u>any one</u> thing.* ✔ (Abraham Lincoln)
  (Try the substitution: …*more important than <u>any person</u> thing.* ✖
  This is nonsense. Therefore, the two-word version is correct.)
- *I cannot teach you violence, as I do not myself believe in it. I can only teach you not to bow your heads before <u>any one</u> even at the cost of your life.* ✖ (Badly translated quote from Mahatma Gandhi)
  (Try the substitution: …*not to bow your heads before <u>any person</u> even at the cost of your life.* ✔ This works. Therefore, it should be the one-word version.)

everyday = normal
- *Computers dull the skills we use in <u>everyday</u> life.* ✔
  (Try the substitution: …*we use in <u>normal</u> life.* ✔ It works.
  Therefore, the one-word version must be correct.)

everyone = every person

● *Everyone is entitled to be stupid, but some abuse the privilege.* ✔
(Try the substitution: *Every person is entitled...* ✔ It works.
Therefore, the one-word version must be correct.)

maybe = perhaps

● *Maybe this world is another planet's hell.* ✔ (Aldous Huxley)
(Try the substitution: *Perhaps this world...* ✔ It works. Therefore,
the one-word version must be correct. For another *maybe/may be*
example, take a look at the *somebody* example below.)

somebody = an unknown person

● *Conscience is the inner voice that warns us somebody may be looking.* ✔
(H. L. Mencken)
(Try the substitution: *Conscience is the inner voice that warns us an
unknown person may be looking.* ✔ It works. Therefore, the one-
word version must be correct. Note: You can't flawlessly replace
may be with *perhaps*. Therefore, *may be* is correctly written as two
words in this example.)

Let's crack two in a oner:

nobody = no person
everybody = every person

● *A classic is something that everybody wants to have read and nobody
wants to read.* ✔ (Mark Twain)
(Try the substitutions: *A classic is something that every person
wants to have read and no person wants to read.* ✔ It works.
Therefore, the one-word versions must be correct.)

sometimes = occasionally

● *The squeaking wheel doesn't always get the grease. Sometimes it gets
replaced.* ✔ (Vic Gold)
(Try the substitution: *Occasionally it gets replaced.* It works.
Therefore, the one-word version must be correct.)

Another trick is to stick another word between the two smaller words. If your
sentence still works, then you've probably got the two-word version on your
hands. For example:

● *Conscience is the inner voice that warns us an unknown person may
possibly be looking.*

80 ONE WORD OR THREE?

This section is about *insofar* and *albeit*. I'll keep this short.

Write them as one word.
(Some grammarians claim *in so far* is British English. Okay, if you talk like that butler off "Magnum PI" or if you're an aide-de-camp to the Queen, you could think about writing *in so far*.)

81 PLURALS – FORMING PLURALS

In general, forming the plurals of words does not cause difficulties for native English speakers. I do not intend to go into how to form plurals here, because that's a little too basic for the intended readers of this book. I mean, we all know that *donkey* goes *donkeys*, *penny* goes *pennies* and dwarf goes *dwarfs* or *dwarves*. As we just touched upon though, the rules for forming plurals are varied. I would actually classify this as spelling as opposed to grammar, and your spellchecker will help you most of the time. However, there are some points about plurals that spellcheckers often miss.

Stolen Words. Some words that have been "stolen" from other languages form their plurals in an unusual way. The most obvious examples are:

- *stadium > stadia or stadiums*
  (Through common usage, the plural *stadiums* is acceptable too.)
- *criterion > criteria*
- *datum > data*
- *radius > radii or radiuses*
  (Through common usage, the plural *radiuses* is acceptable too.)
- *agendum > agenda*

Data is or data are?

Single or Plural? The biggest issue with these words is knowing whether the plural version is treated like a plural or a singular word in modern English. For example, *data* is a plural word (from *datum*), but nowadays, it is safe to treat it as singular. In fact, treating it as plural now seems wrong to many people.

Examples:

- *Today's agenda is pinned on the notice board.* ✔
- *Today's agenda are pinned on the notice board.* ✔
  (These days, *agenda is* grates less on the ear than *agenda are*.)

- *My data was corrupted by the power surge.* ✔
- *My data were corrupted by the power surge.* ✔
  (These days, *data was* grates less on the ear than *data were*.)

- *The criteria are non-negotiable.* ✔
- *The criteria is non-negotiable.* ✘
  (This is under change. For now though, treat *criteria* as a plural word.)

Not with an Apostrophe. Never use an apostrophe before the final *s* when forming a plural (except in the rare circumstances shown at the bottom).

- *Using the new cutter, the team can lay two patio's in a day.* ✘
  (should be *patios*)
- *As far as I am concerned, they are all hero's.* ✘
  (should be *heroes*)

The two examples above are grammatical howlers. This topic is also covered in Section 2.

 BEWARE Do not use 's to show a plural. Your credibility will take a punch in the kidneys.

Apostrophe in a Plural – Rare Circumstances. Using an apostrophe in a plural is the most common error regarding plurals. However, in some rare circumstances, it is possible to use an apostrophe:

- *Alan achieved two B's and three C's.* ✔
  (apostrophes not necessary, but acceptable)
- *Your 2's look like your 7's.* ✔
  (apostrophes not necessary, but acceptable)

This is also covered in Section 6.

82 PLURALS – OF COMPOUND NOUNS

What Are Compound Nouns? Compound nouns are nouns that consist of two or more words. For example:

- *Jack-in-the-box*

 GEEK SAYS Jack-in-the-box is a compound noun.

- *Knight Templar*
- *Court martial*
- *Forget-me-not*
- *Toothbrush*
- *Water bottle*
- *Ink-well*
- *Board of Education*

Some compound nouns are hyphenated. Some are not. (See Section 28.)

> *To form the plural, pluralise the principal word.*

The vast majority of compound nouns form their plurals by adding *s* to the principal in the compound. Examples:

- *He now has two mothers-in-law.* ✔
  (plural of *mother-in-law*)
- *They were visited by the Knights Templar.* ✔
  (plural of *Knight Templar*)
- *It was a sight to see four lieutenant generals fight it out at the table.* ✔
  (plural of *lieutenant general*)
- *Jerry had attended over a dozen courts martial.* ✔
  (plural of *court martial* / also, see third example below)

No Principal Word? When there is no obvious principal word, add *s* (or *es*) to the end of the compound.

- *Forget-me-nots make a wonderful present.* ✔
  (plural of *forget-me-not*)

- *Pack two toothbrushes.* ✔
  (plural of *toothbrush*)
- *Jerry had attended over a dozen court martials.* ✔
  (There is ambiguity about the principal word in *court martial*.
  Therefore, through common usage of both, *courts martial* and
  court martials are acceptable.)

Beware of 'Of.' When a compound noun is in the form *[word] of [word]*
(e.g. cup of tea), the first word is always the principal word.

- *I sold them four cup of teas, but they only drank one.* ✘
  (should be *cups of tea*)

Spoonfuls or Spoonsful? When a compound noun is in the form *[container]
ful* (e.g. *bucketful, cupful* and *handful*), an *s* is added to the end to form the
plural.

- *There were three spoonsful of honey left in the jar.* ✘
  (should be *spoonfuls*)
- *Please sprinkle two handfuls of corn on the porch for the chickens.* ✔

83 SINGULAR OR PLURAL – COLLECTIVE NOUNS

Collective Noun? A collective noun is a word that represents a group;
e.g. *committee, board, team, jury, family, choir, group.*

> **Q:** Is the **staff** singular or plural?
> **A:** It's both.

Collective Noun Singular or Plural? A collective noun can be singular or
plural depending on the sense of the sentence. In the first example below,
the shoal is considered as one unit. Therefore, *shoal* is considered singular.
However, in the second example, the *shoal* is considered as lots of individuals,
and *shoal* is considered plural. Examples:

- *The shoal was moving north.* ✔
  (singular – considered as one unit)
- *The shoal were darting in all directions.* ✔
  (plural – considered as individuals)
- *As far as I am concerned, Marylebone Cricket Club still has
  19th-century values and standards.* ✔

In the last example, *club* is treated as a singular noun; i.e. the writer uses *has* not *have*. But, if he had used *have*, I am sure 99% of his readers would not have given it a second thought. So, there is notable leniency on this. But, you should be as consistent as possible throughout your document. For example, if you decide *club* is singular, try to keep it singular throughout.

For example:

- *As far as I am concerned, Marylebone Cricket Club still has 19th-century values and standards. They still do not allow women to join.* ✖
  (*It still does not allow women to join* would be better…only grammatically speaking of course)

Add a Word to Avoid the Issue. To simplify matters, a word for the individuals within the group can be introduced. In the next example, it is necessary to decide whether the collective noun *jury* should be singular or plural. However, if you add *members of*, a plural verb must be used.

 GREAT TIP Use the construction "[members] of [collective noun]" to ensure it's plural.

Examples:

- *The jury is/are to convene at 4 o'clock.*
  (A decision is required: Is *jury* singular or plural?)
- *The members of the jury are to convene at 4 o'clock.* ✔
  (easy life – no decision required – the word *members* is plural)

84 SINGULAR OR PLURAL – PREPOSITIONAL PHRASES

When you have a construction like "A of B" (e.g. *box of tapes, nest of wasps, none of them*), it's always the first element (i.e. the A) that determines whether the construction is singular or plural. For example:

- *The evacuation of the offices is the floor manager's responsibility.* ✔
  (*evacuation* is singular – *is* and not *are*)
- *A box of tapes were discovered in his car.* ✖
  (The word *box* is singular. It should be *was* and not *were*.)
- *There are no need for meetings.* ✖
  (The word *need* is singular. It should be *is* and not *are*.)

- *A raft of factors <u>were</u> the cause of the crash.*
  (The word *raft* is singular, but it is a collective noun. I am reluctant
  to mark this as wrong. See Section 83.)
- *[Bernard Shaw] hasn't an enemy in the world, and none of his
  friends <u>like</u> him.* ✖ (Oscar Wilde)
  (The word *none* is treated as singular by many. (See explanation
  below.) Many would have preferred *none of his friends <u>likes</u> him*.)

A phrase like *of the offices, of tapes, of factors, of his friends* (called a *prepositional
phrase*) does not affect whether the main word is singular or plural.

 GEEK SAYS Prepositional phrases never affect the verb.

Beware of None. There is a growing misconception that the word *none* is
always singular. It's not. It can be singular or plural. However, this "rule" is
so well promulgated, many of your grammar-savvy readers will expect it to
be singular. If your *none* translates as *not one*, treat it as singular. If it better
translates as *not any*, treat it as plural. Your best bet is to remove the
prepositional phrase, and then play it by ear. Or, try your hardest to treat *none*
as singular, but, if you can't bear how it sounds, go plural.

- *None of them was present.* ✔
  (*of them* – prepositional phrase)
- *None of them were present.* ✔
  (If you can't bear the first one, use *were* and fight like a cornered rat
  against your proofreader.)
- *None of his friends is a lawyer.* ✔
- *None of his friends are lawyers.* ✔

 **VOCATIVE CASE**

 GEEK SAYS Hello, Chris. (Did you notice the comma? That puts Chris in the vocative case.)

Names that are being addressed directly are said to be in the *vocative case*.
(The word vocative is related to the word *vocal*.) You must separate words
in the vocative case from the rest of the sentence with a comma (or commas).
This is also covered in Section 23. Examples:

- *See you next Tuesday, Dan.* ✔
  (*Dan* is being addressed. His name must be separated from the rest of the sentence with a comma. The word *Dan* is said to be in the vocative case.)
- *To lose one parent, Mr Worthing, may be regarded as a misfortune; to lose both looks like carelessness.* ✔ (Oscar Wilde)
  (*Mr Worthing* being addressed directly – commas used)
- *Dammit, sir, it is your duty to get married. You can't be always living for pleasure.* ✔ (Oscar Wilde)
  (Someone being addressed directly as *sir* – commas used)
- *…and that was the end of the monster Dick.* ✖
  (*Dick* should be preceded by a comma as *Dick* is being addressed.)

Anything Can Be in the Vocative Case. Animals, even inanimate objects, can be addressed directly. They should also be separated from the rest of the sentence to show they are in the vocative case. Examples:

- *Ollie, fetch the stick like a good dog.* ✔
  (*Ollie* is being addressed – comma used)
- *You are my favourite car, you little beauty.* ✔
  (The car is being addressed directly as *you little beauty* – comma used.)

Could Be Important. President Clinton may have used the vocative case very cleverly in his claim:

> *…I did not have sexual relations with that woman, Miss Lewinski.*

 OPPORTUNITY At some point, you will get a chance to impress your mates with this perspective on the Lewinski scandal.

If you listen to how President Clinton speaks, he pauses after saying *that woman*. At this point, his audience would have been thinking, "He didn't say her name." However, he then satisfies their concerns by adding *Miss Lewinski*. This is genius. What he really did was put a comma between *that woman* and *Miss Lewinski*. This puts her name in the vocative case, meaning he could claim he was addressing her directly. Now, the identification of *that woman* was between him and Miss Lewinksi. If the law were based on the spirit of what is said, he would have been guilty. Luckily for him, it's not. The *letter of the law* is what counts. Later, on 17 August 1998, Clinton told the grand jury that his civil deposition had been "legally accurate." He was right. No one will be able to convince me this was about the definition of *sexual relations*.

Watch what he says again. It really looks like a deliberate pause to put *Miss Lewinski* in the vocative case, making his statement "legally accurate." It's simply genius.

Not in Formal Writing. It's unusual to use the vocative case in formal documents.

86 WHICH, THAT & WHO – AN OVERVIEW

What Are They? *Which*, *who* and *that* are used to add information to a sentence. (I suspect you're not that interested, but they are known as *relative pronouns*.) There are others, but these three are the most common (see Section 54). As you will instinctively know, *who* is used to add information about people, and *which* is used to add information about things. You can use *that* for people or things. Examples:

- *The man who swam the channel.* ✔
  (*who swam the channel* adds information about the man)
- *In Kent, a man who shot a swan was jailed for six months.* ✔
  (*who shot a swan* adds information about the man)
- *The PC which keeps freezing is under guarantee until May.* ✔
  (*which keeps freezing* adds information about the PC)
- *The vicar which was on BBC1 last night used to be our local vicar.* ✘
  (The vicar is a person. Therefore, *who* should be used and not *which*. *That* would have been okay.)
- *Please accept my resignation. I don't want to belong to any club that will accept me as a member.* ✔ (Groucho Marx)
  (*which will accept me as a member* would also have been okay.)

Not at the Start of a Sentence. Do not start a sentence with *which* or *who* (unless it is a question). For example:

- *Living in Scotland is cheaper than living in England. Which is lucky, because I live in Dumfries.* ✘

Starting a Sentence with That. Over the years, I have detected real disdain for the term *the fact that*. In military circles, if you use *the fact that*, senior officers nearly always restructure your sentence to get rid of it. I never use it these days. I have, however, noted a growing tendency to replace *the fact that* with just the word *that*. I am sure this is not a new practice, and it seems to survive proofreading by British officers every time. I've grown to like it. On the other hand, US officers are really not keen on it.

 OPPORTUNITY Replace "The fact that" with just "That". Some of your readers will love it. Some won't, but they'll respect your confidence.

For example:

- *The fact that some geniuses were laughed at does not imply all who are laughed at are geniuses.*
  (If you presented this to a senior British officer, he would probably reword it. But, the following might survive: *That some geniuses were laughed at does not imply all who are laughed at are geniuses.* I reckon an American would prefer the original.)
- *The fact that man knows right from wrong proves his intellectual superiority to other creatures.*
  (This would have more chance of surviving proofreading by a Brit if it were written: *That man knows right from wrong proves his intellectual superiority to other creatures.*)

Commas with Which and Who. The biggest issue for native English speakers is when to use a comma before *which* and *who*. Unfortunately, the ruling is not simple. It is covered in the next section.

 WHICH, THAT & WHO - WHEN TO USE COMMAS

*When do you put a comma before **which**?*
Oh, nasty subject...

There is often confusion over when to use a comma before *who* or *which*. Unfortunately, there is no simple rule. Sometimes there should be a comma, and sometimes there should not.

The rule is: When the clause is required for identification, there is no comma. The examples will make this clearer:

- *The boy who broke our window brought some flowers to the door.* ✔
  (The clause *who broke our window* is required to identify *the boy* – no commas.)

- *The driver <u>who stole indicator bulbs for his own car</u> was given a formal warning.* ✔
(The clause *who stole indicator bulbs for his own car* is required to identify the driver – no commas.)
- *Mr Jeremy Buxton of 16 High Street <u>who was born on the Isle of Wight</u> is the second person from the village to represent England at Cluedo.* ✘
(The clause *who was born on the Isle of Wight* is not required to identify *Mr Jeremy Buxton of 16 High Street*. This is just additional information. It should be offset with commas.)
- *His youngest daughter, <u>who was born on 16 June 1972</u>, swam the channel.* ✔
(The clause *who was born on 16 June 1972* is just additional information about *His youngest daughter* – commas required.)
- *James Baker's cat made its own way home after it was accidentally left on the beach at Scarborough. James, <u>who has lived in our village for 10 years</u>, has just won the lottery.* ✔
(The clause *who has lived in our village for 10 years* is just additional information about *James* – commas required.)

Sometimes, you have to think about it a bit harder. For example:

- *Sarah has always been close to her parents <u>who live in the same village as us</u>.* ✘
(The clause *who live in the same village as us* is not required to identify Sarah's parents. This is just additional information about them – it should be offset with commas. Well, one comma in this example.)
- *The man <u>who doesn't read good books</u> has no advantage over the man <u>who can't read them</u>.* ✔ (Mark Twain)
(Clauses required to identify *the man* – no commas)
- *The man <u>who can dominate a London dinner-table</u> can dominate the world.* ✔ (Oscar Wilde)
(Required to identify *the man* – no commas)

That – **Restrictive Clause**. When a clause is necessary for identification, it is called a *restrictive clause*. It is *restrictive* because you have to use it. There are never commas around a restrictive clause. When using a restrictive clause, the words *who* or *which* can be replaced with *that*. (Therefore, there are never commas around a clause which starts with *that*.)

- *The boy <u>who broke our window</u> bought me some flowers.* ✔
- *The boy <u>that broke our window</u> bought me some flowers.* ✔
- *The PC <u>which keeps breaking down</u> is under guarantee.* ✔
- *The PC <u>that keeps breaking down</u> is under guarantee.* ✔

Quite often with a restrictive clause, you can remove the *who*, *which* or *that* altogether.

- *The reprimand <u>which you received</u> was justified.* ✔
- *The reprimand <u>that you received</u> was justified.* ✔
- *The reprimand <u>you received</u> was justified.* ✔

watch for ambiguity.

Beware of Ambiguity. Compare the sentences below. Both are grammatically correct, but they are slightly different in meaning.

- *Sarah has always been close to her sister <u>who lives in the same village</u>.* ✔
- *Sarah has always been close to her sister, <u>who lives in the same village</u>.* ✔

In the first example, you can assume Sarah has more than one sister and Sarah is close to the one that lives in the same village. In the second example, you can assume Sarah has only one sister. As it happens, she lives in the same village as Sarah. Here's another:

- *Manx cats, <u>which live on the Isle of Man</u>, have a longer life expectancy than normal domestic cats.* ✔
- *Manx cats <u>which live on the Isle of Man</u> have a longer life expectancy than normal domestic cats.* ✔

The first example means all Manx cats have a longer life expectancy than normal cats. (The clause is simply additional information telling readers where Manx cats live.) The second example means only Manx cats living on the Isle of Man have a longer life expectancy (i.e. Manx cats that live elsewhere do not).

Alternatives to Commas. If a clause just adds additional information, then it should be separated from the rest of the sentence with commas. However, you could equally use brackets or dashes. (This is covered in detail in Sections 18 and 25.)

For example:

- *Manx cats, which live on the Isle of Man, have a longer life expectancy than normal domestic cats.* ✔
- *Manx cats (which live on the Isle of Man) have a longer life expectancy than normal domestic cats.* ✔
- *Manx cats – which live on the Isle of Man – have a longer life expectancy than normal domestic cats.* ✔

So, when do you use a comma before *which* and *who*? You can think of it like this:

 GREAT TIP If you'd be happy sticking it in brackets, it should be offset with commas.

Try the removal test.

Still Don't Get it? Try the Removal Test. A clause that just adds additional information can be removed without any loss of meaning to the main sentence.

- *Manx cats have a longer life expectancy than normal domestic cats.*

Therefore, if you can remove the information offered by *who* or *which* without destroying your sentence, then it should be offset with commas (or brackets or even dashes if you're feeling a bit flash).

EASILY CONFUSED WORDS

ACCEPT AND EXCEPT

The Quick Answer: *To accept most commonly means to receive willingly or to hold something as true. Except usually means apart from or excluding.*

>  **BEWARE** This is basic stuff. Confusing accept and except is a serious howler.

Accept. To *accept* has several meanings:

To receive something willingly
- *Please accept my resignation. I don't want to belong to any club that will accept me as a member.* ✔ (Groucho Marx)
- *I accept this award on behalf of the whole cast.* ✔
- *Do you accept dogs in your hotel?* ✔

To hold something as true
- *Where lipstick is concerned, the important thing is not color, but to accept God's final word on where your lips end.* ✔ (Jerry Seinfeld)
- *I accept she may have been tired, but that's still no excuse.* ✔

To answer 'yes' (especially to an invitation)
- *The minister would love to accept the invitation to your ball, but she has a prior engagement.* ✔

Except. *Except* has several meanings:

Apart from, not including or excluding
- *I can resist everything except temptation.* ✔ (Oscar Wilde)
- *I have nothing to declare except my genius.* ✔ (Oscar Wilde)
- *Weaseling out of things is important to learn. It's what separates us from the animals…except the weasel.* ✔ (Homer Simpson)
- *It has been said that democracy is the worst form of government except all those other forms that have been tried.* ✔ (Winston Churchill)

But or if not for the fact that
- *I would go swimming, except I am scared of big fish.* ✔

To exclude
- *You are excepted from the ruling.* ✔

89 ADOPTIVE AND ADOPTED

The Quick Answer: The difference between *adopted* and *adoptive* is best explained with a simple example:

> *Mr Smith says, "Sarah is my adopted daughter."*
> *Sarah says, "He is my adoptive father."*

 OPPORTUNITY Everyone avoids adoptive. Show you know the difference.

Over the years, I've noticed loads of people use *adopted* when they mean *adoptive*. I've come to the conclusion that everyone knows what *adoptive* means (i.e. they understand it when they read or hear it), but when it's their turn to use it, they play safe and use *adopted*. Well, that might be wrong.

Here's some legalese to help make the point: "Adoption is the act of legally placing a child with parents (or parent) who are not its natural parents. It has the effect of severing the parental responsibilities and rights of the birth parents and transferring them to the *adoptive* parents. The child is said to be *adopted*. The *adopted* child has two sets of parents: its natural parents and its *adoptive* parents."

Adopted. *Adopted* pertains to the person who has been adopted. Example:

- *Charles loved his adopted daughter as if she were his own.* ✔

Adoptive. *Adoptive* pertains to the person who has adopted. Example:

- *Rebecca loved her adoptive father as if he were her own.* ✔

It's easier with places. For example:

- *Malta is his adopted/adoptive country.* ✔
  (Pick any one – both are correct.)

90 ADVICE AND ADVISE

The Quick Answer: *Advice* means *a suggestion for a beneficial course of action.*
(*Advice* rhymes with *mice*. It is a noun – see Section 47.) *To advise* means *to
give advice.* (*Advise* rhymes with *surprise*. It is a verb – see Section 55.)

Advice. The word *advice* means a *suggestion for a beneficial course of action*. I
have noticed that native English speakers almost never write the wrong version
of *advice* or *advise* if they say it correctly. Therefore, it is worth knowing that
advice rhymes with *mice*. *Advice* is a noun. Examples:

- *Take my advice. I don't use it anyway.* ✔
- *He who can take advice is sometimes superior to him who can give it.* ✔
- *Many receive advice, but only the wise profit from it.* ✔

Advise. *To advise* means *to give advice*. (*Advise* rhymes with *surprise*. *Advises*
rhymes with *surprises*. *Advised* rhymes with *surprised*, etc.) *To advise* can also
mean *to notify* (e.g. *I advised him I was leaving.*) *To advise* is a verb.
Examples:

- *The rich are always advising the poor, but the poor seldom return the
  compliment.* ✔
- *Attach yourself to those who advise you rather than praise you.* ✔
- *Women will never be as successful as men because they have no wives
  to advise them.* ✔
- *I have found the best way to give advice to your children is to find out
  what they want and then advise them to do it.* ✔

 GREAT TIP Advise rhymes with surprise. Advice rhymes with mice. If you think about how
they're pronounced, you'll use the right one.

If the rhyming technique isn't working for you, here are some neat tricks to
spot which to use.

A Little Trick to Spot Advice. Try using the word *assistance* instead of *advice*.
If the sentence still makes sense, then *advice* is almost certainly correct. (This
trick works because *advice* is a noun, just like the word *assistance*.)

- *I offered my advice.* ✔
  (I offered my *assistance*.)

A Little Trick to Spot Advise. Try using *to assist* (in its various forms; e.g. *assisting, assisted, assists*) instead of *advise*. If the sentence still makes sense, then *advise* is almost certainly correct. However, if you find yourself trying to use *assistance*, then you should be using *advice*. (This trick works because *to advise* is a verb, just like *to assist*.) For example:

● *Are you trying to advise me?* ✔
  (Are you trying to *assist* me?)
● *I do not need your advise.* ✖
  (I do not need your *assistance*. This should be *advice*.)

91 ADVERSE AND AVERSE

The Quick Answer: *Adverse* means hostile. *Averse* means unwilling.

> **Averse** and **adverse** are good words to use. They are
> succinct and widely understood.

As you can see from the meanings below, there are lots of alternatives to *adverse* and *averse*, but both words are succinct, widely understood and look pretty smart in official correspondence. The danger, however, is if you use the wrong one, you'll look bit of a pecker for trying to use a posh word. I'd wager that most of your readers would spot the error.

Adverse. *Adverse* means antagonistic, opposing, harmful, hostile or unfavourable. Examples:

● *Adverse conditions including rain, snow, ice and fog affect your visibility.* ✔
● *He is not responsible for the adverse events in your life.* ✔

Averse. *Averse* means strongly disinclined, unwilling or loath. (Most often, it refers to people.) Examples:

● *Are you averse to hunting?* ✔
● *The company clerks are averse to change.* ✔

92 AFFECT AND EFFECT

The Quick Answer: *Effect* means outcome, consequence or appearance. *To affect* means *to transform* or *to change*. *Effect* is a noun, and *affect* is a verb.

Difference between Affect and Effect. There is often confusion over the words *effect* and *affect*. In order to understand which to use, you must know the difference between a noun and a verb. This is because *effect* is a noun, and *affect* is a verb. (See Sections 47 and 55.) However, if your brain really doesn't gel on this noun and verb stuff, there are some neat tricks to get around this.

> **BEWARE** If you don't know the difference between a noun and verb, now is the time to learn. You cannot afford to confuse affect and effect. Your credibility is at stake.

A Little Trick to Spot Effect. The word *effect* has several meanings. It can mean outcome, consequence or appearance. Try using one of these instead of *effect*. If the sentence still makes sense, then *effect* is almost certainly correct. (This trick works because *effect* is a noun, just like *outcome*, *consequence* and *appearance*.)

A Little Trick to Spot Affect. Try using *to transform* (in its various forms; e.g. *transforming*, *transformed*, *transforms*) instead of *affect*. If the sentence still makes sense, then *affect* is almost certainly correct. However, if you find yourself using *transformation*, then you should be using *effect*. (This trick works because *to transform* is a verb, just like *to affect*.)

Examples with both *effect* and *affect*:

- *What effect did foot-and-mouth disease have on your business?* ✔
  (Substitute: *What consequence did foot-and-mouth disease…*
  Sounds okay; *effect* is correct)
- *Did foot-and-mouth disease affect your business?*
  (Substitute: *Did foot-and-mouth disease transform your business?* ✔
  Sounds okay; *affect* is correct)
- *Shallow men believe in luck. Strong men believe in cause and effect.* ✔
  *(*Ralph Waldo Emerson, 1803–1882)
  (Substitute: *Strong men believe in cause and outcome…*
  Sounds okay; *effect* is correct)
- *Do not allow this incident to effect your decision.* ✖
  (Substitute: *…to outcome/consequence/appearance your decision.*
  Nonsense; *effect* is wrong.)

- *That spiral effect is effecting my eyes.* ✖
  (Substitute: *That spiral appearance is transforming my eyes.*
  (*Effect* is okay, but it should be *affecting* not *effecting*.)

No Confusion. There should be no confusion with *affecting* or *affected*. These are always from the verb *affect*. Well, nearly always (see below).

Be Aware. There is a verb *to effect*. It is quite rare, but useful in business writing. It means *to bring into being*. Example:

- *The new policy will be effected as soon as the paper is signed.*

Confusing *affect* and *effect* is a common mistake. It's almost reached the stage where you're impressed if the writer uses the correct one. You should expect your boss to know the difference, and his opinion of your abilities will be tainted if you mix them up. If you're relying on "what looks right" (which is what dozens of people have said to me over the years), then you need to spend 10 minutes learning the difference between a noun and a verb or practising the workarounds above. For some people, the acronym R.A.V.E.N. helps. It stands for "Remember, Affect Verb Effect Noun."

93 AID AND AIDE

An aide is a person.

The Quick Answer: *Aid* means help or assistance. (*To aid* means to help or to assist.) An *aide* is a person. *Aide* means helper or assistant.

Aid. *Aid* means help or assistance. It is commonly seen as an adjective, a noun and a verb. (As a verb, it means *to help* or *to assist*.) Examples:

- *Be bold and mighty powers will come to your aid.* ✔ (Basil King)
- *I have known sorrow and learned to aid the wretched.* ✔ (Virgil, 70–19 BC)

Aide. *Aide* means a helper or an assistant (usually a personal assistant). An aide is a person. Examples:

- *General McChrystal and his aides told the unvarnished truth.* ✔
- *The Libyan leader caused a scene at the African Heads of State Summit when he slapped one of his aides for taking him to a wrong venue.* ✔

When I was in Kabul, one of my mates (a US analyst) would have bet his life that Americans don't use *aide*. He was certain that *aid* was the only version used in the US. "That's another one of those half-English-half-French words that you're trying to impose on me," he contested. No, mate, it's not. *Aide* is an American word too. Now, think back to all the times you've incorrectly used *aid* and cringe.

94 A LOT, ALLOT AND ALOT

The Quick Answer: The word *alot* does not exist. *A lot* usually means *a large extent* or *to a large extent*. *To allot* means *to apportion something*.

> There's no such word as **alot**.

Alot. The word *alot* does not exist. It is often mistakenly written instead of *a lot*. For example:

- *After all is said and done, alot more will be said than done.* ✖

By far the most common mistake involving these three words is people writing *alot* instead of *a lot*.

A lot. The term *a lot* is the opposite of *a little*. *Lot* can mean *a large number*, *a large extent* or *a large amount*. It can also mean *to a great extent* or *to a great degree*. It nearly always appears in the form *a lot*. Examples:

- *A lot of fellows nowadays have a B.A., M.D., or Ph.D. Unfortunately, they don't have a J.O.B.* ✔ (Fats Domino)
- *You can observe a lot just by watching.* ✔ (Yogi Berra)

Allot. *To allot* means *to give out*, *to apportion*, *to divide* or *to distribute*. Examples:

- *You need to allot each syndicate sufficient time to question the presenter.* ✔
- *The state government on Wednesday agreed in principle to allot land for development of passenger and freight terminals around Hyderabad.* ✔
- *Justice is the constant and perpetual will to allot to every man his due.* ✔ (Domitus Ulpian, 100–228 AD)

95 ALLOWED AND ALOUD

The Quick Answer: *Aloud* means *out loud*. *Allowed* means *permitted*.

Native English speakers don't usually get this wrong.

I have never seen a native English speaker confuse *allowed* and *aloud*, but I have noticed that those with English as a second language are particularly prone to this error. It's included here for them.

Aloud. *Aloud* means *out loud* and refers to sound (almost always speech). Examples:

- *Please do not read aloud. You're disturbing everyone else in the library.* ✔
- *The public are not keen on lip-syncing; therefore, medal hopefuls must all learn to sing the national anthem aloud.* ✔

Allowed. *Allowed* is the past tense of *to allow*, which means *to permit*. *Allowed* is the same as *permitted*. Examples:

- *Democracy is being allowed to vote for the candidate you dislike least.* ✔ (Robert Byrne)
- *I am not aloud to go to the party on Saturday.* ✖ (should be *allowed*)

96 ALLUDE AND ELUDE

The Quick Answer: *To allude* means *to refer to indirectly*. *To elude* means *to avoid* or *to evade*.

Older versions of MS Word's grammar checker still wind me up on the "*allude elude*" issue. The older checkers simply offered the word you didn't type (i.e. *allude* if you put *elude*) in the hope you will spend a bit of time thinking about which one you want. MS recognised that writers often mix up *allude* and *elude*, but they relied on you knowing the difference yourself.

 OPPORTUNITY "Allude" can be a great word to use, because it proves you've spotted a hidden message.

Allude. *To allude* means *to refer to indirectly*. *To allude* and *to mention* are close in meaning, but *to allude* is less direct. It can be translated as *to hint at* or *to offer an indication about*. For example:

- *This Chinese saying alludes to nature's power: "A spark can start a fire that burns the entire prairie."* ✔ (The saying does not mention nature's power, but it offers a clue about nature's power. The saying alludes to nature's power.)
- *"Forewarned is forearmed" alludes to the importance of being in control.* ✔
(offers an indication about the importance of being in control)
- *The judge did not mention James's previous crimes specifically, but he alluded to them in his summary.* ✔ (hinted at previous crimes)

Elude. To elude means *to avoid*, *to evade* or *to escape from*.

- *Butch Cassidy and the Sundance Kid try to elude capture.* ✔
(try to avoid capture)
- *Peter Beardsley used to allude defenders with his trademark foot shuffle.* ✘
(*Peter Beardsley used to avoid defenders* – should be *elude*)

The word e*lude* starts with the same letter as e*scape*. This might help you remember which is which.

97 ALREADY AND ALL READY

The Quick Answer: *All ready* means *completely prepared*. *Already* means *prior to a specified or implied time*.

All Ready. The term *all ready* means *completely prepared*. It is slightly more emphatic than just *prepared*. Example:

- *Jillian is all ready. Mark is prepared to brief.* ✔
(Most readers would assume Jillian's state of preparedness to be higher than Mark's.)

Of course, it is possible for the word *all* to precede *ready* (in the same way that any word can precede another). Example:

- *Is the boat ready? Is Mark ready? Are you ready? Are you all ready?* ✔

Already. The word *already* means *prior to a specified or implied time* or *as early as now*. For example:

- *It is already illegal to culture human-animal embryos for more than 14 days.* ✔
  (*already* = since before now)
- *When they pulled the shark up in the net it was already dead.* ✔
  (*already* = since before then)
- *The wild Hepatica Nobilis flowers are already blooming – one month earlier than last year.* ✔
  (*already* = as early as now)

> Ready can replace **all ready** but not **already**.

All Ready = Ready. Here is a tip. The word *ready* can replace *all ready* but not *already*. Therefore, try to use just *ready*. If your sentence still makes sense, then you are safe to use *all ready*; otherwise, use *already*.

- *Jean is all ready.*
  (Try the substitution: Jean is *ready*. ✔)
  (Therefore, *all ready* is correct.)
- *There cannot be a crisis next week. My schedule is already full.*
  (Henry Kissinger)
  (Try the substitution: My schedule is *ready* full. ✘)
  (Therefore, *already* is correct.)

98 ALRIGHT OR ALL RIGHT

The Quick Answer: *Alright* is a nonstandard variant of *all right*. Even though *alright* is becoming more acceptable, it is best avoided.

Alright Is Not Widely Accepted. Many people use *alright* unaware that it is not widely accepted as a word. It should be written *all right*. However, the merger of *all right* to *alright* has been under way for over a century, and *alright* is becoming more acceptable. Mergers such as *altogether* and *already* are fully acceptable. (They are far older than *alright*.)

 GREAT TIP Play it safe. Only use all right.

It's Not Right and It's Not Wrong. Interestingly, the Microsoft Word spellchecker will not highlight *alright* as an error, but it will also not suggest *alright* if you spell it incorrectly. Therefore, Microsoft is sitting on the fence with regard to *alright* being accepted as standard.

Alright is Deemed More Modern by Some. Some would even argue that, through common usage, *alright* is becoming more acceptable than *all right*. The makers of the TV show *It'll Be Alright on the Night* are known to have considered *It'll be All Right on the Night*, but opted for the former as a more modern version.

Avoid It Altogether. Your readers will have different opinions on the use of *alright* and *all right*. Therefore, you could avoid both versions – especially in formal writing. This should not be difficult as they do not lend themselves to formal writing.

- *It is overdue all right.*
  (Here, *all right* reinforces an assertion. Delete *all right* or reword; e.g. *It is substantially overdue.*)
- *All right, it is time to discuss...*
  (Here, *all right* is an interjection that means *very well*. Delete *all right* or reword; e.g. *We agree that it is time to discuss...*)
- *Her work ethic was all right.*
  (Here, *all right* mean *okay or satisfactory*. Reword; e.g. *Her work ethic was satisfactory.*)

Use All Right in Formal Writing. If you cannot avoid *all right* or *alright*, then opt for *all right*. Using *alright*, especially in formal writing, runs a higher risk that your readers will view it as an error. It is far more difficult to justify *alright* than *all right*.

99 ALTAR AND ALTER

The Quick Answer: An *altar* is an area of religious worship. *To alter* means to change something.

Altar. The word *altar* is a noun. It denotes an area (usually a table) where religious worship or sacrifice occurs. Examples:

- *The ancient Britons used to sacrifice animals on elaborate stone altars.* ✔

- *We were married at the altar in St Paul's Cathedral.* ✔
- *Have you seen the water damage to the alter in St. John's Church?* ✖
  (should be altar)

Alter. *To alter* is a verb meaning to change something. Examples:

- *Will you alter this dress for Saturday's play?* ✔
- *Fashion is a form of ugliness so intolerable that we have to alter it every six months.* ✔ (Oscar Wilde)
- *Please altar your claim in Section 9.* ✖
  (should be *alter*; i.e. to amend or change)

100 ALTOGETHER AND ALL TOGETHER

The Quick Answer: *Altogether* means *with everything considered. All together* means *collectively.*

Altogether. *Altogether* means *wholly, to the full extent* or *with everything considered.* Examples:

- *I left him altogether convinced that the project will end on time.* ✔
- *Faith is, at one and the same time, absolutely necessary and altogether impossible.* ✔ (Stanislaw Lem)

All Together. *All together* is when a group acts or is acted upon collectively. (There can be other words between *all* and *together*.) Examples:

- *I want you to sing all together.* ✔
  (I want you all to sing together.)
- *The soldiers stood all together waiting for the plane.* ✔
  (The soldiers all stood together waiting for the plane.)
- *I would like to see you all together.* ✔
  (I would like to see all of you together.)

A Play on Words with Altogether and All Together. If I'm at the checkout and the assistant says something like "that'll be 12 dollars altogether," I have been known to break into song with a tuneful "That'll be 12 dollars." This is meant to be a play on words with *altogether* and *all together*. Usually nobody laughs. ("*All together*" is how a choirmaster might start his singers.) I'm pretty sure I stole this from "The Naked Gun" with Leslie Nielsen.

101 AMOUNT, QUANTITY AND NUMBER

The Quick Answer: Use *amount of* before singular things you cannot measure. Use *quantity of* before singular or plural things (especially inanimate things) you can measure. Use *number of* before plural things you can measure.

> **GEEK SAYS** Love is…a non-countable noun. (I'm not sure that would make a great T shirt.)

There are subtle differences between *amount of*, *quantity of* and *number of*. Most people I've asked don't know the differences and rely on instinct to choose the right one. Well, occasionally, their instincts let them down.

Amount Of. The term *amount of* is used for things you cannot count (or measure easily). It usually precedes a singular word. Examples:

- *I undertook an inordinate amount of work.* ✔
  (*work* – singular and cannot be measured or counted. You don't say, "I have three works.")
- *She had a certain amount of respect for the sales team, but she always dissented when they spoke at meetings.* ✔
  (*respect* – singular and cannot be measured or counted)
- *It is not difficult to see where that amount of hate derives.* ✔
  (hate – singular and cannot be measured or counted)

These types of words (more examples: *space*, *oxygen*, *love*) are called *non-countable nouns*.

Quantity Of. The term *quantity of* is used for things you can measure. (These are called *countable nouns*.) *Quantity of* is usually used for inanimate objects. Some grammar references advocate it can only precede a singular word; however, this view is now considered outdated. Examples:

- *I took control of a large quantity of money.* ✔
  (*money* – singular and can be measured or counted)
- *The ship was only carrying a large quantity of mangoes.* ✔
  (*mangoes* – plural and can be measured or counted)
  (*Number of* could also be used in this example. In fact, *number of* is preferable, because some of your readers might not like *quantity of* before a plural noun.)

Number Of. The term *number of* precedes a plural, countable noun. It can be applied to both animate and inanimate objects. Examples:

- *The disease affected a large number of camels in the town.* ✔
  (*camels* – plural, animate and can be counted)
- *The ship was only carrying a large number of mangoes.* ✔
  (mangoes – plural, inanimate and can be counted)
  (*Quantity of* could also be used in this example.)

 102 **APPRAISE AND APPRISE**

The Quick Answer: *To appraise* means to assess. *To apprise* means to inform.

I have noticed that dozens of really smart people use *appraise* when they mean *apprise*. I have never seen it the other way round (i.e. using *apprise* instead of *appraise*).

> **OPPORTUNITY** Apprise is a great word to use. Just don't confuse it with appraise.

Appraise. The verb *to appraise* means to assess or to evaluate. Examples:

- *Appraise war in terms of the fundamental factors. The first of these factors is moral influence.* ✔ (Sun-Tzu, c.400 BC)
  (assess/evaluate war)
- *Managers appraise their subordinates against objectives set in the terms of reference.* ✔
  (assess/evaluate their subordinates)

Apprise. The verb *to apprise* means to inform or to notify. Examples:

- *Please apprise the patient of the outcome of yesterday's meeting.* ✔
  (inform/notify/tell the patient)
- *Managers appraise their subordinates of objectives in the terms of reference.* ✖
  (should be *apprise their subordinates of objectives*, i.e. notify them)

This error is very common. Many are unaware that the verb *to apprise* even exists. Well, it does. In fact, in business writing, it's marginally more common than *to appraise*. At least it would be if people used it correctly.

103 BARE AND BEAR

The Quick Answer: *Bare* means exposed (e.g. without clothes). For everything else, use *bear*.

> **Bear** is a very versatile word. It's not just a big scary thing that kills hippies who get too close.

Trust the Bear. Writers are very familiar with *bear* as in *polar bear* or *grizzly bear*. However, the word *bear* is very versatile. It has many meanings. When they encounter these other meanings, some writers are attracted to *bare* because they know *bear* denotes the large mammal. Well, unless you mean *exposed* or *naked* (i.e. bare), then *bear* is correct:

- *This idea did not bear fruit.* ✔
- *This idea did not bare fruit.* ✖

Bear. The word bear has many meanings:

To carry (in many senses of the word)
- *We come bearing gifts for your chief.* ✔
- *Our camels do not mate regularly, but we are expecting Tsu Tsu to bear her first baby next season.* ✔
- *This small tree bears hundreds of apples every year.* ✔
- *Who will bear the responsibility for this vandalism?* ✔
- *My auntie is the tall lady bearing the green hat.* ✔
- *He bears himself with utmost dignity.* ✔

Bear also means *to carry* in an even looser sense (i.e. to have)
- *You bear a resemblance to your mother.* ✔
- *Does this document bear your signature?* ✔
- *I bear bad news, I'm afraid.* ✔

To endure or to tolerate
- *Mrs Taylor cannot bear the constant drone of the generator.* ✔
- *Human kind cannot bear much reality.* ✔ (T. S. Eliot)
- *It is very easy to endure the difficulties of one's enemies. It is the successes of one's friends that are hard to bear.* ✔ (Oscar Wilde)

To maintain a direction
- *Bear left at the next two Y junctions.* ✔
- *This track bears north for the next 10 miles and then bears east as far as the lake.* ✔

A large mammal
- *Yogi Bear* ✔

Bare. *Bare* means uncovered, naked or exposed (i.e. without cover, clothing or cladding). Examples:

- *Don't go out in bare feet. You'll catch a cold.* ✔
- *Was the protestor totally bare when he ran in the meeting room?* ✔
- *You need to cover those pipes. Bare pipes will freeze this winter.* ✔
- *Peter ploughed those fields with his bear hands?* ✘
  (should be *bare hands* – unless he's got hands like a bear)

Bore, Borne, Born. The past tense of *to bear* is *bore*. For example:

- *They bore gifts for the chief.* ✔
- *You bore a remarkable resemblance to your mother when you were younger.* ✔

 GREAT TIP Don't use born with has/had/have. Use borne.

Occasionally, you may need to write *borne* or *born*. An explanation of which to use would require us to delve into some nasty grammar, but the following ruling covers it well: Use *borne* every time, but if you're talking about birth, use *born*. But, if you mean *has/have given birth to*, use *borne*. For example:

- *The burden borne by the managerial team was simply too heavy.* ✔
  (This has nothing to do with birth – *borne* is correct.)
- *She has borne two children since moving to India.* ✔
  (This is about birth and it means *has given birth to* –
  borne is correct.)
- *She was born in Manchester.* ✔
  (This is about birth and it does not mean *has given birth to* –
  born is correct.)

104 BEING OR BEEN

The Quick Answer: Use *been* after *to have (*in all its forms – *has, had, will have, etc.)* Use *being* after *to be (*in all its forms – *am, is, are, was, were, will be, etc.)*

> Don't use **being** after **had/has/have**. Use **been**.

Being and Been. Writers occasionally confuse *being* and *been*. As a rule, *been* is always used after *to have* (in any form; e.g. *has, had, will have, having*); whereas, *being* is never used after *have*. *Being* is used after *to be* (in any form; e.g. *is, was, were*). Examples:

- *Income tax returns are the most imaginative fiction being written today.* ✔
  (*...are...being written*)
- *Arithmetic is being able to count up to 20 without taking off your shoes.* ✔
  (*...is being able*)
- *Fools rush in where fools have been before.* ✔
  (*have been*)
- *It has been said that man is a rational animal. All my life, I have been searching for evidence which could support this.* ✔
  (Bertrand Russell)
  (*has been...have been*)
- *Terry has being taking the stores to the shelter.* ✘
  (*being* cannot follow *has* or *have*)

Living Being. The word *being* can denote a *person* or *creature*. Examples:

- *I am not an animal. I am a human being.* ✔
- *A strange being stepped out of the space ship.* ✔

Being an Idiot. The word *being* can also mean *acting, behaving* or *existing*. Examples:

- *Do you like being so ignorant?* ✔
- *The accident was caused by his being so clumsy.* ✔
- *I live in terror of not being misunderstood.* ✔ (Oscar Wilde)

105 BESIDE AND BESIDES

The Quick Answer: *Beside* means *next to*. *Besides* means *apart from* or *and another thing*.

I have noticed some writers use *beside* when they mean *besides*. I wouldn't call this a common error, but I've seen it enough to include it in this book.

Beside. *Beside* means *close to* or *next to*. (It is a preposition. See Section 49.) Examples:

- *Come and sit beside me.* ✔
- *She is beside herself.* ✔
  (The term *beside oneself* expresses extreme emotion, usually joy. It denotes being out of one's mind or soul due to emotion; i.e. being next to one's mind or soul.)

Besides. *Besides* means *in addition to* or *apart from*. (In this role, it is a preposition.) *Besides* can also mean *furthermore* or *and another thing*. (In this role, it is an adverb. See Section 40) Examples:

- *Besides Craig, who else caught a bass?* ✔
  (*Besides* is a preposition here. *Apart from Craig, who else…*)
- *Besides, it's not just about determination.* ✔
  (*Besides* is an adverb in this example. *Furthermore, it's not just…*)

106 BREATHE AND BREATH

The Quick Answer: *Breath* (rhymes with *death*) denotes the air inhaled or exhaled during breathing. *To breathe* (rhymes with *seethe*) means to inhale and expel air from the lungs.

Breath. The word *breath* is a noun. It denotes the air either inhaled or exhaled during breathing. Colloquially, it can also mean a short pause (e.g. Take a breath and try again.) *Breath* rhymes with *death*. Examples:

- *Paul pinched his nose, took a breath and jumped off the boat.* ✔
- *He would fight until his last breath.* ✔

Breathe. The word *breathe* is a verb. It rhymes with *seethe*. It has the following closely related meanings:

To inhale and expel air from the lungs

- *Is she breathing?* ✔
  (Note: *Breathe* drops the *e* when *ing* is added.)
- *Virtually all fish breathe through gills.* ✔

To allow gas or moisture to pass through

- *The new synthetic material can breathe to prevent moisture building up against the skin.* ✔

To impart (often used figuratively)

- *He breathed new life into the project.* ✔
- *He breathed a sigh of relief.* ✔

GREAT TIP Breeeeathe. Native English speakers only confuse breath and breathe in writing. If you use the e at the end of breathe to remind you that breathe rhymes with seethe, you will eliminate this error.

---

 107 CAPITAL AND CAPITOL

The Quick Answer: (Only relevant for non-Americans) *Capitol* is not a typo of *capital*. It is the building where the US Congress meets.

Many non-Americans who see the word *Capitol* assume it is a typo of *capital*. It isn't.

Oi, Brits, **Capitol** *is not a spelling mistake.*

Capitol. *The Capitol* is the building that serves as the seat of government for the United States Congress. It is located in Washington on top of Capitol Hill. It should always be written with a large C.

Capital. The word *capital* has numerous meanings.

The seat of the government for a country or state

- *Around AD 1000, London was the most prosperous city in England, but the official capital was still Winchester.* ✔

An amount of money or property

- *Do you have any capital invested in her business?* ✔

An uppercase letter

- *In German, all nouns start with a capital letter.* ✔
  (Ich habe eine **K**atze = I have a cat.)
- *Always spell Capitol with a capital C.* ✔

First rate or excellent

- *That was a capital speech, old boy.* ✔

Main or principal

- *Our capital concern is that everyone gets fed during the electricity failure.* ✔
  (*Capital* and *principal* mean the same, and they both end *al*.
  So what? Use this to remember the difference between *principal*
  and *principle*. See Section 155.)

108 CAN AND MAY

The Quick Answer: *May* relates to permission. *Can* relates to ability. These days, however, they are pretty much interchangeable.

Don't expend too many calories worrying about **can** *and* **may**. *These days, they're interchangeable.*

Many writers do not know the difference between *can* and *may*. I don't consider this a serious flaw. I reckon they're largely interchangeable these days. Knowing the difference will allow you to make an informed decision on which to use. For example, if you opt for *can* because *may* sounds a bit pretentious, at least you can defend your decision against a snotty proofreader.

Can. The word *can* relates to ability.

- *I can swim.* ✔ (I have the ability to swim.)
- *Dan, can you even grow a beard?* ✔
  (Dan, do you have the ability to grow a beard?)

May. The word *may* is used to denote permission.

- *You may swim in this river.* ✔
  (You are allowed to swim in this river.)
- *May I have a biscuit?* ✔
  (Am I permitted to have a biscuit?)

Can for Permission (Informal Setting). These days, the word *can* is used for both ability and permission, particularly in an informal setting.

- *You can swim in this river.* ✔
  (You are allowed to swim in this river.)
- *Can I have a biscuit?* ✔
  (Am I permitted to have a biscuit?)

Always May for Permission in a Formal Setting. In a formal setting or in polite company, you will score some points if you use *may* when seeking permission.

- *May I leave the table?* ✔
  (Am I permitted to leave the table?)

You should be aware that grammar purists (and your grandparents) would probably argue that *may* and *can* are not interchangeable.

"Can I go outside, grandma?"
"You can. You're just not allowed."
"Whatever."

109 CANVAS AND CANVASS

The Quick Answer: *Canvas* is heavy cloth. *To canvass* means *to survey opinion* or *to solicit votes*.

The words *canvas* and *canvass* sound identical, but their meanings are very different. Using the wrong one is bit of a grammatical howler, which your boss would probably notice. If you don't get this one right, your credibility will take a little punch in the kidneys.

Canvas. *Canvas* (with one *s* at the end) refers to a heavy-woven cloth of hemp, flax or cotton. It is used for sails, tents and paintings (including figuratively; e.g. *She was a blank canvas*). It is also used to denote the floor of a boxing or wrestling ring. (Quite often, they are not made of canvas.)

Canvass. *To canvass* has several closely related meanings. (It is a verb. See Section 55.) It can mean:

To collect opinions

- *Can you canvass the local area to determine the support for the bypass?* ✔

To electioneer (i.e. to collect votes through persuasion of voters in a political campaign)

- *Mr Millar will arrange for Joan's team to canvass High Street and Bond Street on Saturday. We need as much support from the west side of town as possible.* ✔

To examine closely

- *Penny canvassed every shop in Wigan before she found the right shoes.* ✔

To ask around

- *The investigation team will canvass the neighbourhood to see whether there were any witnesses to the crash.* ✔

Canvass Used as a Noun. For grammarians, the most obvious difference between the two is that *canvas* is a noun (see Section 47), and *canvass* is a verb. However, nowadays, *canvass* is also used as a noun to denote the processes above. Examples:

- *Did your canvass of the local area succeed in determining the support for the bypass?* ✔
- *I heard Joan's canvass was postponed because of the storm.* ✔

(The noun *canvassing* is more common than the noun *canvass*. It can be substituted in both examples above.)

110 CENSOR, CENSURE AND SENSOR

The Quick Answer: *To censor* means to forbid. A *sensor* is a detector. *Censure* is displeasure.

Censor. *To censor* means *to forbid public distribution of something* (usually a film or a newspaper). A *censor* is a person who performs censorship. Example:

- *How did that statement end up on the streets? I censored the article myself.* ✔

- *Assassination is the extreme form of censorship.* ✔ (G. Bernard Shaw)

Sensor. *Sensor* denotes a detector of a stimulus (such as heat, light, motion, pressure). Example:

- *An infrared sensor designed to detect movement triggered the roadside bomb.* ✔

Censure. *Censure* denotes a formal rebuke or official displeasure. Examples:

- *He has received two letters of censure from the commandant.* ✔
- *You do ill if you praise, but worse if you censure what you do not understand.* ✔ (Leonardo da Vinci)

111 CITE, SIGHT AND SITE

The Quick Answer: *Cite* means to mention or to quote. *Sight* relates to vision. *Site* means *a piece of land* or *to assign a position to*.

Sight. Sight relates to vision (i.e. perception by the eyes). It can also be something that is seen (e.g. What a beautiful sight.)
Examples:

- *The newborn foal was an emotional sight for all of us.* ✔
- *After the laser treatment, her sight was perfect.* ✔

Site. *Site* denotes a place (e.g. a website, building site). *To site* means *to position in a place* (e.g. I will site the slide near the swings.) More examples:

- *According to this website, there are three landfill sites nearby.* ✔
- *Mr Dodds claimed his tools had been stolen from the archaeological site.* ✔

Cite. *Cite* means *to quote, to refer to, to summon to appear before a court of law* or simply *to mention*.
Examples:

- *The lecturer cited several instances of illegal behaviour.* ✔
- *The young inspector was cited for his outstanding achievements.* ✔
- *Remember to cite expert opinion to support your points.* ✔

The Culprit Is Site. The word *site* (meaning *a piece of land*) is the one that causes problems. The most common error is writing *sight* instead of *site*. Here's a half-decent tip:

A site usually houses a building or construction work. You can remember the definition of site using the *te* to remind you of **t**radesman's **e**ntrance. (A site is likely to have a tradesman's entrance.)

112 CLIMACTIC AND CLIMATIC

The Quick Answer: *Climactic* pertains to the highest point. *Climatic* pertains to the weather.

Climactic. *Climactic* derives from *climax*. It pertains to a peak, a decisive moment or the point of greatest tension.
Examples:

- *In the climactic scene of the movie, the aliens emerge from the capsule and start zapping the onlookers.* ✔
- *Who would have thought that the season would have ended in such a climactic way?* ✔

Climatic. *Climatic* derives from *climate*. It pertains to the weather. Examples:

- *His assessment on the eco-climatic system over Africa is based solely on satellite data.* ✔

> Climactic comes from climax. Climatic comes from climate.

It's worth knowing the difference between *climactic* and *climatic* because of the sexual connotations of *climax*, which have the potential to attract more attention to an error than it probably deserves.

- *From the outset, she has been struggling to cope with the climactic conditions, and I have taken the decision to send her back to base camp.* ✖

113 COARSE AND COURSE

The Quick Answer: *Coarse* means rough or crude. Most commonly, *course* means: (1) a series of educational lessons; e.g. a French course (2) A direction; e.g. That's an odd course to take.

Coarse. *Coarse* means rough, crude, of low quality or not fine in texture. Examples:

- *coarse sand* ✔
- *coarse manners* ✔
- *Perch – a type of coarse fish* ✔
  (not as refined as trout or salmon, which are classified as game fish)

Course. The word course has many meanings:

Education delivered in a series of lessons
- *English course* ✔
  (It's also the students who attend. E.g. *You have been an excellent course.*)
- *I took a speed-reading course and read 'War and Peace' in 20 minutes. It involves Russia.* ✔ (Woody Allen)

A direction
- *A southerly course* ✔
- *The river changed course.* ✔

A series of events
- *The government took an unexpected course.* ✔
- *A mind troubled by doubt cannot focus on the course to victory.* ✔
  (Arthur Golden)

To move (of liquids and ships)
- *The German ships coursed the Baltic.* ✔
- *The stream coursed through the peat bog.* ✔

Part of a meal
- *We're having a three-course meal. The first course is whitebait or mussels.* ✔

To hunt with dogs
- *Hare coursing / to course after hares.* ✔

Naturally
- *Of course* ✔

Area of land (or water) for sport
- *Golf course and skiing course* ✔

 COMPLEMENT AND COMPLIMENT

The Quick Answer: *Compliment* is associated with praise. *Complement* is associated with enhancement.

> **BEWARE** Writing compliment instead of complement is a very common mistake. Your readers will know the difference.

Compliment. A *compliment* (with an *i*) is an expression of praise. Examples:

- *My compliments to the chef for such a wonderful starter.* ✔
  (my praise to the chef)
- *When she said your eyes looked misty, she meant that as a compliment.* ✔
  (meant that as praise)
- *Tell the cook of this restaurant with my compliments that these are the very worst sandwiches in the whole world, and that, when I ask for a watercress sandwich, I do not mean a loaf with a field in the middle of it.* ✔ (Oscar Wilde)
  (*compliments* can also mean good wishes, regards or respect)

Complement. A *complement* (with an *e*) is something that enhances something else or goes well with it. (For example, cranberry sauce is a complement for turkey.) It is not common, but *complement* can also mean composition or make-up. (When used, it is often seen in the term *full complement*, meaning *the whole number*.)

- *The cashew nuts were an excellent complement for the soup.* ✔
  (cashew nuts went well with the soup)
- *The drums were a perfect complement to their dancing style.* ✔
  (drums enhanced their dancing style)

To Compliment and To Complement. Both words exist as verbs too. *To compliment* means *to praise*, and *to complement* means *to enhance*. Examples:

- *I want to compliment the pilot on such a smooth landing.* ✔
  (to pass praise to the pilot)
- *The jade and silver cufflinks complement the green tie.* ✔
  (go well with the green tie)

 GREAT TIP To compliment has an i in it – just like to praise. To complement has two e's in it – just like to enhance.

Complimentary and Complementary. *Complimentary* is used to describe something *given as a courtesy*; i.e. it's free. *Complementary* describes something that *forms a complement*; i.e. it goes well with something else. So, you will have to pay for *complementary drink* but not a *complimentary drink*.

115 COMPOSE AND COMPRISE ('COMPRISE OF' AND 'IS COMPRISED OF')

The Quick Answer: *Compose* means *to make up* (e.g. Four slices compose the cake.) *Comprise* means *to consist of* (e.g. The cake comprises four slices.) Some quirks with comprise:

1 No *of* with comprise (e.g. It comprises of… ✖).
2 Avoid the construction *is comprised of*.
3 Don't name the constituent parts first (e.g. Four slices comprise the cake.)

There is often confusion over *comprise* and *compose*. If you stick to the guidelines below, you'll be on safe ground.

Comprise. *To comprise* means *to consist of* or *to be made up of*. It is used to denote that something is made up of smaller parts. Do not use the word *of* with comprise. Jeepers, this nearly caused a war between the British and US staff officers in Kabul. The US chaps – to a man – wanted to write *comprises of*. Well, that's wrong – even under US grammar conventions. (I have used *made up of* throughout this book, because I know many will think the omitted *of* is a typo.)

 GREAT TIP If you're uncomfortable with omitting the *of* with *to comprise*, then use a different construction. Don't stick the *of* in.

Examples:

- *The water molecule comprises two atoms of hydrogen and one atom of oxygen.* ✔
  (The whole comprises the smaller parts.)
- *The water molecule comprises of two atoms of hydrogen and one atom of oxygen.* ✖
  (Do not use the word *of* with comprise.)
- *Two atoms of hydrogen and one atom of oxygen comprise the water molecule.*✖
  (This is one of the areas under debate. Many advocate that *comprise* cannot be used to denote that the smaller parts make up the whole. They believe this is when *compose* should be used. If you adhere to this ruling too, you will never be wrong.)
- *The three wise monkeys comprise Mizaru (see no evil), Kikazaru (hear no evil) and Iwazaru (speak no evil).* ✔
- *The quadriceps femoris comprise the rectus femoris, the vastus medialis, the vastus intermedius and the vastus lateralis.* ✔

Is Comprised Of. The construction *is comprised of* (note: it correctly includes the word *of*) is considered by many to be non-standard English. To avert criticism, reword your sentence to avoid this construction. Examples:

- *The water molecule is comprised of two atoms of hydrogen and one atom of oxygen.* ✖ (Contentious version. Some of your readers might frown at this.)
- *The water molecule consists of two atoms of hydrogen and one atom of oxygen.* ✔ (Reworded, non-contentious version)

 GEEK SAYS Many consider *comprised of* to be non-standard English.

Compose. *To compose* means *to make up* or *to make*. It is used to denote that parts make up the whole (i.e. the opposite of *comprise*). Do not use the word *of* with compose. Examples:

- *Mercury, Venus, Earth and Mars compose the inner planets.* ✔
- *The rectus femoris, the vastus medialis, the vastus intermedius and the vastus lateralis compose the quadriceps femoris.* ✔
- *Two atoms of hydrogen and one atom of oxygen compose the water molecule.* ✔

Is Composed Of. The construction *is composed of* (note: it correctly includes the word *of*) does not attract the same criticism as *is comprised of*. Examples:

- *The USA is composed of 50 states.* ✔
- *The water molecule is composed of two atoms of hydrogen and one atom of oxygen.* ✔
- *The scientific theory I like best is that the rings of Saturn are composed entirely of lost airline luggage.* ✔ (Mark Russell)

Name All the Constituent Parts. Make sure you name all the constituent parts when using *comprise* or *compose*. Example:

- *Since 2006 when the International Astronomical Union declassified Pluto as a planet, only eight planets compose our solar system.* ✖ (Space-gazers will tell you that our solar system also includes the Sun, an asteroid belt and a number of dwarf planets. Therefore, from their perspective, *compose* is incorrect in this example.)

Beware 'Include.' It is worth pointing out that some grammarians shudder if you name all the constituent parts when using *include*. For example:

- *The water molecule includes two atoms of hydrogen and one atom of oxygen.* ✖
  (oooh [shudder])
- *The water molecule includes one atom of oxygen.* ✔

116 CONFIDENT, CONFIDANT AND CONFIDANTE

The Quick Answer: A *confidant* is someone to whom private matters are confided. (The words *confidant* and *confidante* are interchangeable, but strict grammarians reserve *confidant* for males and *confidante* for females.) *Confident* relates to having self-belief or being certain.

Confident. Someone with confidence (i.e. not shy and with self-belief) is described as being *confident*. Being *confident* also means to be assured or certain of something that is pending. Examples:

- *My theory is that if you look confident you can pull off anything – even if you have no clue what you're doing.* ✔ (Jessica Alba)
- *No matter what a woman looks like, if she's confident, she's sexy.* ✔ (Paris Hilton)

- *And in rejecting an atheistic other world, I am confident that the Almighty God will be with us.* ✔ (President Herbert Hoover)

confidant = man / confidante = woman

Confidant and Confidante. A *confidant/confidante* is a trusted person. It is someone to whom private or personal matters are confided. Most people consider the word *confidante* to be an alternative spelling of *confidant*. However, some claim *confidante* is the female version of *confidant*, which they reserve for males. If you know a person is a female, I would advise using *confidante*. Examples:

- *Finding a confidant can be difficult if you have a hard time placing trust in others.* ✔
- *An Egyptian believed to be a close confidant of Bin Laden has been killed in a drone strike.* ✔

The words *confidant* and *confidante* are quite rare, but *confident* is very common. The most common mistake is writers using *confidant* when they mean *confident*. This is a grammatical howler. Your readers will notice if you make this mistake, and they will think less of you if you do. (A related story: One of my mates ditched his new girlfriend, because she described him as "extremely confidant" in a letter. She also wrote "langauge" in the same letter – so, it's probably a fair one.)

117 COUNCIL AND COUNSEL

The Quick Answer: A *council* is a committee elected to lead or govern. *Counsel* is advice (usually legal advice). *To counsel* is to advise.

Council. *Council* denotes an assembly of people who serve in an administrative capacity. For example, a committee elected to lead or govern could be described as a council (e.g. a church council, a town council and student council). Examples:

- *The emergency session was convened due to the failure of the United Nations Security Council to resolve the instability at the Suez Canal.* ✔
- *In December 1046, Holy Roman Emperor Henry III established a church council to reform the papacy.* ✔
- *She yelled: "It's not the council's job to sift through your bins for glass."* ✔

Counsel. *To counsel* means *to give advice*. In this role, it is a verb (see Section 55). It can also be a noun (Section 47) meaning advice (usually legal assistance) or opinion. *Counsel* can also refer to a body of people set up to offer advice (usually legal advice); e.g. the Queen's Counsel, the General Counsel of the Army. More examples:

- *We are seeking staff who can counsel the homeless on where to attain social services.* ✔
  (*Counsel* is a verb in this example.)
- *The litigation team offers excellent counsel on a range of subjects.* ✔
  (*Counsel* is a noun in this example.)
- *After bereavement, who counsels the counsellor?* ✔

> **OPPORTUNITY** To counsel is a good verb to use. It means more than to advise. It has a connotation of mentoring too.

 118 DEPENDANT AND DEPENDENT

The Quick Answer: For Brits, *dependent* means reliant on. *Dependant* is a person (usually a child or a spouse). Americans, don't worry about *dependant*, you can use *dependent* for both.

Only Brits have to worry about this one.

In British English, there is often confusion over the words *dependent* and *dependant*. The most common mistake is writing *dependant* instead of *dependent*. For example:

- *Dependant on the weather.* ✖

A fair wedge of your readers will know that's a mistake, and your halo will slip a bit if you make this error. It's worth learning the difference.

Dependant. A *dependant* is person who is dependent on someone else. (For example, a child is dependent on its parents. Therefore, a child is a dependant of its parents.) Example:

- *All embassy staff and their dependants must be at the airport by 6 o'clock.* ✔
  (Here, the word *dependants* means spouses and children.)

Dependent. The word *dependent* means contingent on, reliant on, supported by or addicted to. Examples:

- *The result is dependent on Mark's contribution, I'm afraid.* ✔
  (contingent on *Mark's contribution*)
- *The man least dependent upon the morrow goes to meet the morrow most cheerfully.* ✔ (Epicurus, 341–270 BC)
  (least reliant on *the morrow*)

119 DECENT, DESCENT AND DISSENT

The Quick Answer: *Descent* means going downwards, a downward slope or ancestry. *Decent* means civilised, good or adequate. *Dissent* means to argue or a difference of opinion.

Descent. Descent has a few meanings:

The action of descending (i.e. going downwards)
- *The Boeing 737 started its descent from 20,000 feet.* ✔

A downhill incline
- *It features a long, steep descent that is ideal for advanced skiers.* ✔

Family origin
- *She is of Indian descent.* ✔

Decent. *Decent* means civilised, good or adequate. (It rhymes with *recent*.) Examples:

- *Ninety-eight percent of the adults in this country are decent, hardworking citizens.* ✔
- *That's a decent plate of food.* ✔

Dissent. *Dissent* means *difference of opinion* or *to disagree*. Examples:

- *The referee has given him a red card for dissent.* ✔
- *Acceptance of dissent is the fundamental requirement of a free society.* ✔
- *I will dissent if you continue with this course of action.* ✔

BEWARE If you confuse descent (meaning origin) with decent or dissent, expect the person you're describing to be unforgiving.

Decent Rhymes with Recent. Native English speakers always pronounce these words correctly. Confusion only occurs in writing. Therefore, if you remember that *decent* rhymes with *recent* (which is logical considering they share the same last five letters), you will succeed in differentiating between *decent* and *descent*.

Diss = Dissent. The street word *diss* (deriving from *disrespect*) has connotations of disagreement and arguing. Therefore, the first four letters of *dissent* can remind you of its meaning.

 **120 DEFUSE AND DIFFUSE**

The Quick Answer: *To defuse* means to remove the fuse. *Diffuse* means spread out.

Defuse. *To defuse* refers to the act of deactivating a bomb. (Defuse literally means *to remove the fuse*.) It is often used figuratively to mean *to disarm* or *to pacify*. Examples:

- *Paul, go back in the meeting and defuse all the arguing.* ✔
- *How long did it take you to defuse the bomb?* ✔

Diffuse. *Diffuse* means *spread out* or *not concentrated in one place*. *To diffuse* means *to circulate* or *to spread*.

 OPPORTUNITY Diffuse is a great word to use. It's fresh and widely known. But, confusing it with defuse looks like you're writing above your level.

Examples:

- *She is the CEO of a large diffuse company.* ✔
- *I need speakers that will diffuse my music around the whole arena.* ✔

121 DEFINITE AND DEFINITIVE

The Quick Answer: *Definite* means *known for certain*. *Definitive* means *conclusive*.

Definite. *Definite* means *known for certain* or *precise*. Examples:

- *Is it definite that the plane has left?* ✔
- *There was a definite process by which one made people into friends, and it involved talking to them and listening to them for hours at a time.* ✔ (Rebecca West)

Definitive. *Definitive* means conclusive or authoritative. Examples:

- *This is the definitive paper on the company's holdings.* ✔
- *Was that the judge's definitive verdict?* ✔

Definitely Not Definate. There is no such word as *definate*, which is a very common misspelling of *definite*. *Definately* does not exist either. No, really, it doesn't.

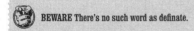 **BEWARE** There's no such word as definate.

Please help me get the message out there that *definitely* is not spelt *definately*. I know at least two people who have added it to their spellchecker's dictionary, because they were so sure it was correct.

> *"No 'a' in definitely? Are you sure? My spellchecker didn't pick it up."*
> *"We had this conversation last year, and you told me you added definately to your spellchecker."*
> *"Oh, yeah. It still looks right."*
> *"It isn't."*

122 DESERT AND DESSERT

The Quick Answer: *Desert* means *arid land* or *to abandon*. *Dessert* is the sweet course at the end of a meal. I've lost count how many restaurants and messes (UK) / chow halls (US) I've been in that offer a *desert menu* instead of a *dessert menu*. (Actually, one in Iraq did it on purpose, which I thought was mildly amusing – although *mildly amusing* is probably way too strong.)

Desert. The word *desert* has the following meanings:

Arid land with little or no vegetation
- *The Sahara Desert* ✔
- *The plants and animals possess special features which allow them to cope with the desert conditions.* ✔
- *When my new cactus died, I got depressed. I am less nurturing than a desert.* ✔

To abandon or to defect or to leave in the lurch
- *If disturbed too often, the adult birds will desert the fledglings.* ✔
- *If you desert, you will be shot when you're caught.* ✔

To leave behind
- *As soon as the bell went, the kids deserted the building.* ✔

Things deserved (usually in the plural: *deserts*)
- *He got his just deserts* ✔
  (*Deserts* is pronounced like *desserts*, which contributes to why some people wrongly use *desserts* to mean *things deserved*.)

Dessert. A *dessert* is typically the final course of a meal. It is usually sweet (e.g. ice-cream, cake, pudding).

- *Would you like to see the dessert menu?* ✔

I was proofreading a senior US officer's work in Kabul, Afghanistan. I was a little surprised to see he'd written *dessert conditions* instead of *desert conditions*. I underlined it. Looking over my shoulder, he said:

"*Dessert* is twice as good as *desert*, and *dessert* equals *strawberry shortcake*."
"Yes, sir. Quite."

123 DISCREET AND DISCRETE

The Quick Answer: *Discrete* means *individually distinct*. *Discreet* means *inconspicuous*.

Discreet is far more common than *discrete*. It's worth learning the difference, because *discrete* is a cool word to use in official correspondence. (No one will have to look it up in a dictionary – its meaning is widely known. And, it shows confidence. "Hey, I know the difference between *discrete* and *discreet*.")

Discrete. *Discrete* means *individually distinct* or *separate* (i.e. something that is not part of something else). Examples:

- *There is a rack on the bench that contains all the discrete electronic components.* ✔
- *Our club has three discrete membership categories.* ✔

 GREAT TIP Discrete – the e's are individually distinct. Discreet – the e's look like shifty eyes.

Discreet. *Discreet* means *respecting secrecy*, *inconspicuous* or *diplomatic*. Examples:

- *You can trust my aide – he is very discreet.* ✔
- *The painting was won by a discreet telephone bidder.* ✔

When I'm not near a PC (when I could use MS Word's synonyms), to remember *discrete*, I think of the two *e*'s being separated by the *t*. They are *individually distinct*. To remember *discreet*, I think of the two *e*'s looking like shifty eyes, which remind me of secrecy. (On an unrelated issue, if you've got a problem with my use of an apostrophe in *e*'s, please read Section 6.)

(124) DISINTERESTED AND UNINTERESTED

The Quick Answer: *Disinterested* means impartial. *Uninterested* means not interested.

Many people use *disinterested* and *uninterested* interchangeably, but they do not mean the same thing. If it were always used correctly, the word *disinterested* would be far less common. (After all, *bored* is a more common word than *impartial*.)

Uninterested. *Uninterested* means *not interested*. It is the consequence of something being uninteresting (i.e. boring, uneventful or arousing no interest). Examples:

- *Paul, I am quickly becoming uninterested in your ideas.* ✔
  (Paul's ideas arouse no interest.)
- *I used to collect stamps, but I am uninterested these days.* ✔
  (not interested / find it boring)

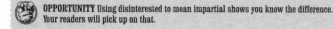
OPPORTUNITY Using disinterested to mean impartial shows you know the difference. Your readers will pick up on that.

Disinterested. *Disinterested* means *not taking sides* or *impartial*. It denotes that there is no personal benefit at stake. Examples:

- *We are struggling to identify 12 disinterested people for the jury.* ✔
  (12 impartial people)
- *An investigation into the penalty decision has reportedly uncovered that the referee was not disinterested in the outcome of the match.* ✔
  (the referee had a personal interest in one particular side winning)

125 ECONOMIC AND ECONOMICAL

The Quick Answer: *Economic* pertains to the economy. *Economical* means not wasteful.

Economic. *Economic* pertains to the economy, finances or wealth. Examples:

- *The economic deceleration will likely cause a further fall in unemployment.* ✔
- *The host will interview the winners and losers of the current economic situation.* ✔
- *It's not about money – he is fine from an economic perspective.* ✔

Economical. *Economical* denotes that something saves money or resources or is not wasteful of money or resources. Examples:

- *It has a powerful yet economical engine that is suitable for high-mileage drivers.* ✔
- *The most practical and economical way to see Brazil is by air.* ✔

Don't get this wrong if you're a high flyer.

This is one of those words you don't want to get wrong if you're on the up. You see, if you show that you don't know the difference between *economic* and *economical*, then you obviously don't understand the economy. If you don't understand the economy, you probably don't understand finances… politics… management… leadership. In fact, you're probably bit of a lager lout. You get the message. Hey, there is some good news. You can use *economically* for both.

126 ELICIT AND ILLICIT

The Quick Answer: *To elicit* means *to draw out* or *to obtain* (usually information). *Illicit* means illegal.

Elicit. *To elicit* means to obtain. However, it has the connotation of actively obtaining something (usually information). It can often be translated as *to draw out*, *to extract*, *to deduce* or *to construe*.

For example:

- *His questioning sought to elicit the conclusion he had reached even before the hearing began.* ✔
- *Fog always seems to elicit strong feelings of melancholy.* ✔

Illicit. The word *illicit* means *illegal* or *contrary to accepted morality* (i.e. *naughty*). Examples:

- *The act seeks to prevent the illicit trafficking of narcotics.* ✔
- *We have been told to expect a purge on illicit file-sharing websites.* ✔

 BEWARE Elicit and illicit are a little bit pompous. Don't get them wrong.

Elicit and *illicit* are great words, but I think they are at the pompous end of the spectrum of similar-meaning words (e.g. to extract, illegal). There is a danger with words of this ilk: If you confuse them, your reader will think you are using words above your writing ability.

 GREAT TIP Elicit = Extract. Let the first letter of elicit remind you it means extract.
Illicit = Illegal. Let first three letters of illicit remind you it means illegal.

127 ENVELOP AND ENVELOPE

The Quick Answer: *Envelop* (without an *e* on the end) means *to surround* or *to enclose*. *Envelope* most commonly refers to *a flat rectangular paper container for a letter*.

Envelop. *Envelop* can mean *to surround, to enclose, to cover up, to conceal* or – in military circles – *to conduct a flanking manoeuvre*. It used to be spelt with an *e* on the end, and this likely contributes to people confusing it with *envelope*. In the past tense, the *e* reappears (e.g. The German division enveloped the town.) Examples:

- *The bridge was enveloped by fog.* ✔
- *Every year, an eerie mist envelops the hotel on the anniversary of his gruesome murder.* ✔

Envelope. An *envelope* holds a letter. *Envelope* is also used to describe the limits of a system's operating capability (e.g. An altitude of 10,000 feet is the top of the aircraft's envelope.) Examples:

- *Q: What word starts with e, ends in e, but only has one letter in it?*
  A: Envelope. ✔
- *In June's test flights, the speed and altitude envelope was progressively expanded from the previously flown 170 knots and 12,000 feet.* ✔

128 ENQUIRY AND INQUIRY

The Quick Answer: *Inquiry* and *enquiry* are interchangeable in the US and the UK. However, in the UK, it is becoming preferable to use *inquiry* to denote *an investigation* and *enquiry* to denote *a question*.

> Americans, please note that **enquiry** is not a spelling mistake.

Enquiry and Inquiry. *Enquiry* and *inquiry* can mean question, inquest or investigation. They can be used interchangeably, but in the US, *inquiry* is the more widely accepted. The words *enquiry* and *inquiry* derive from *to enquire* and *to inquire*.

Not So Simple in the UK. In the UK, a distinction between *enquiry* and *inquiry* is developing. *Inquiry* is being used in relation to a formal inquest (i.e. an investigation); whereas, *enquiry* is being used to denote the act of questioning. However, there is still notable leniency on this distinction. Of note, many in the US will consider *enquiry* a spelling mistake of *inquiry*. Examples (UK convention):

- *I would like to enquire about the toilet facilities in the hotel.* ✔
  (*enquire* = to ask)
- *The judge has suspended the inquiry into the police shooting of the escaped mental patient.* ✔
  (*inquiry* = inquest or investigation)

129 FEWER OR LESS

The Quick Answer: Use *less* when referring to a single item. Use *fewer* when referring to more than one item.

Writers often misuse the words *less* and *fewer*. The word *less* should be used for a single item (e.g. less time, less space); whereas, *fewer* should be used when there is more than one item (e.g. fewer mice, fewer omissions). Some more examples:

- *There is less cheese on this plate.* ✔
  (cheese – singular)
- *There are fewer pieces of cheese on this plate.* ✔
  (pieces – plural)
- *There are less pigeons in Trafalgar Square than there used to be.* ✖
  (should be *fewer* pigeons)
- *In the future, there will be less coins in circulation.* ✖
  (should be fewer coins)
- *Fewer people will vote in the forthcoming elections.* ✔

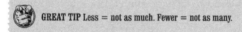

GREAT TIP Less = not as much. Fewer = not as many.

Adopt the Rule. Many people consider this rule outdated. It is certainly not well observed by some large reputable companies.
For example:

- *We're using less bags* ✖
  (Asda poster)
- *Less napkins. More plants.* ✖
  (Starbucks)
- *Less emissions, not less style.* ✖
  (Volvo)

I can guarantee all these companies will have considered the "correct" version. In my view, these slogans are more *effective* with the word *less* than with *fewer*. However, I advise that you play it safe and adopt the rule. Using *less* incorrectly may irk your readers. Using *fewer* correctly will showcase your grammar skills.

130 FOURTH AND FORTH

The Quick Answer: *Fourth* relates to the number four (e.g. fourth place). *Forth* usually means forward or onward.

Forth. *Forth* means forward or onward (e.g. from this day forth, bring forth, go forth). It can also mean *come out into view* (e.g. Come forth from the crowd). More examples:

- *Put a cherry on the first cake, then the second, and so forth.* ✔ (*and so forth* = more of the same)
- *I need to be present at the meeting to put my ideas forth.* ✔ (to make the ideas apparent; i.e. to bring them into view figuratively)

Fourth. *Fourth* relates to the number four. It can be a noun (e.g. one fourth, i.e. a quarter), an adjective (e.g. the fourth car) or an adverb (e.g. the new driver came fourth).

Forty. The word *forty*, which obviously relates to the number four, is not spelt with a *u*. (This is a common spelling mistake, particularly in handwritten text.)

131 GETAWAY AND GET AWAY

The Quick Answer: *Getaway* means: (1) a location for respite (2) an escape. *Get away* means: (1) to escape (2) Unbelievable!

Getaway. *Getaway* has two meanings:

A location visited to escape daily routine
- *Alison is going to a little getaway in the hills for a week.* ✔
- *This is my little getaway. I come here every Friday night.* ✔

An escape
- *The robbers made their getaway in a silver Mondeo.* ✔
- *Fingers, you can be the getaway driver.* ✔

Get Away. *Get away* has two meanings:

To escape or to keep away

- *Tonight, the prisoners will attempt to get away.* ✔
  (*get away* = to escape)
- *Get away from my apples, you pesky kids.* ✔
  (*get away* = keep away)

Never or unbelievable

- *Get away, a 4-pound bass? Are you sure, Lee?* ✔
  (*Get away* = never or unbelievable)

132 GRISLY AND GRIZZLY

The Quick Answer: *Grisly* means horrible. *Grizzly* is a bear from North America.

Grisly. *Grisly* means *horrible, shockingly repellent, terrifying* or *gruesome*.

- *In the grisly climax to the South Park episode, the kids try to rescue Chef, but he falls off a bridge into a ravine, where he is impaled on a tree trunk and mauled by wild animals.* ✔
- *A convicted killer was today found guilty of a second murder, betrayed by his grisly habit of cutting off his victims' breasts.* ✔
- *The police spokesman told the reporters that they had uncovered some grisly clues in the missing-girl case.* ✔

Grizzly. *Grizzly* refers to a powerful brownish-yellow bear found in the uplands of western North America. It can be called either a *grizzly* (plural: *grizzlies*) or a *grizzly bear*.

- *Avoid grizzly bears. If you get caught off guard by a grizzly, and it decides to attack you, shoot it in the heart and the face. If you do not have a gun and you cannot get away, tuck into a tight ball or play dead. However, if the grizzly is intent on you being its next meal, fight back with everything you've got.* ✔
- *If attacked by a grizzly bear and you haven't got a gun, run away. It'll give you something to do before you're killed.* ✔

I know the advice on how to act if attacked by a grizzly is contradictory in these two examples, but apparently that's normal. Opinions are varied on what to do. I once asked a guide whether you should climb a tree. He answered: "Only if you want to die up a tree." Oh, joy.

133 HISTORIC AND HISTORICAL

The Quick Answer: *Historic* means *having importance in history*. *Historical* means *from the past* or *relating to history*.

The words *historic* and *historical* are close in meaning, but their uses are quite different.

Historic. *Historic* means *having importance in history* or *having influence on history*.

Historical. Historical means *having taken place in history, from the past* or *pertaining to history*. Here are some examples that highlight the difference:

- *This is a historical event.* ✔
  (one that happened in the past)
- *This is a historic event.* ✔
  (one that is important in history, e.g. landing on the moon)
- *He was a historical scholar.* ✔
  (A scholar who studied history)
- *He was a historic scholar.* ✔
  (A scholar who was important in history, e.g. Dr Johnson)
- *The bones were of historical significance.* ✔
  (significant from a perspective of history, i.e. possibly worthless but important to study history)
- *The bones were of historic significance.* ✔
  (very significant, i.e. important in history)

 GREAT TIP You can say *an historical* or *a historical*. You have a choice. Don't want a choice? Use *a historical*.

An Historical or a Historical? With *historic* and *historical*, the stress falls on the second syllable, and many pronounce these words as starting with a vowel (i.e. they say "istorical").

For those people, it is appropriate to use *an* before *historic* and *historical*. But, in actual fact, you have a choice depending on what sounds best for you. There is a lot of leniency on this issue. If you're still unsure, opt for *a historical* and *a historic* as these remain preferable – especially in formal writing.

134 IF OR WHETHER

The Quick Answer: Use *if* to introduce a condition. In all other circumstances, use *whether*. (This ruling will see you right, but there are other options.)

Keep It Simple. Before we dive into this fairly tortuous subject, let's look at "The Quick Answer" again. It is a simple rule that will keep you right:

Always use *whether* unless you are introducing a condition. (A condition is something that must be satisfied before something else occurs.)

For example:

- *If it rains, bring in the tables.* ✔
  (*If it rains* = condition)
- *Add a point if I get the right answer.* ✔
  (*if I get the right answer* = condition)

 GREAT TIP Always use whether unless you're introducing a condition.

If you're a native English speaker, you can rely on your instincts to detect a condition. That means you are probably safe to use *whether* in every single case without giving it much thought. However, if your brain starts screaming that *whether* is wrong, then you've probably tried to use *whether* to introduce a condition. Try replacing the *if* with *whether* in the previous examples. Is your brain screaming at you?

Whether and If (Interchangeable). The words *if* and *whether* are sometimes interchangeable. But, this is not always the case. They can be used interchangeably in the following circumstances:

When reporting yes/no questions
- *I am unsure whether I will be attending the party.* ✔
- *I am unsure if I will be attending the party.* ✔
  (In this example, the yes/no question is "Am I attending the party?")
- *Janice wondered whether she had unplugged the iron.* ✔
- *Janice wondered if she had unplugged the iron.* ✔
  (In this example, the yes/no question is "Did Janice unplug the iron?")

In whether/if...or...constructions
- *I would like to know whether it is a true story or fabricated.* ✔
- *I would like to know if it is a true story or fabricated.* ✔

Note: Using *whether* is far more common. It is certainly more formal.

Whether. In the following circumstances, *whether* should be used:

To present two alternatives (neither of which is a condition)

- *Inform the clerk whether Mark needs a seat.* ✔
  (In this example, the two alternatives are *Mark needs a seat* and *Mark does not need a seat*. The clerk is to be informed in either case.)
- *Inform the clerk if Mark needs a seat.*
  (This sentence is not grammatically wrong, but it does not mean the same as the first example. Here, the clerk is only to be informed if Mark needs a seat. Therefore, Mark needing a seat is a condition. This is a conditional sentence. See *If* on the next page.)
- *Let Sarah know whether the boss is able to go to Crowborough.* ✔
  (In this example, the two alternatives are *going* and *not going*. Sarah needs to know the answer regardless of which is chosen.)
- *Let Sarah know if the boss is able to go to Crowborough.*
  (This sentence is not grammatically wrong, but it does not mean the same as the one above. Here, Sarah needs only to be told if the boss is going to Crowborough.)

After prepositions (see Section 49)
- *I want to talk about whether you are going to California.* ✔
  (The word *about* is a preposition.)
- *At this point, the flight attendant makes the decision on whether the passenger stays on the aircraft.* ✔
  (The word *on* is a preposition.)

Before infinitive verbs starting to (e.g. whether to ask...)
- *I have been thinking whether to grow my own tomatoes this year.* ✔
  (*To grow* is an infinitive verb.)

When whether is the first word of the idea
- *Whether you sink or swim is not my concern.* ✔
  (*Whether you sink or swim* is the subject of this sentence.)
- *I don't care whether you sink or swim.* ✔
  (*Whether you sink or swim* is the complement of *to care*.)

In formal writing. (When *if* and *whether* are interchangeable, choose *whether* in formal writing.)

- *Please establish a committee to determine whether the proposed funding lines are appropriate.* ✔

If. Use *if* to introduce a condition (i.e. use *if* in a conditional sentence). In a conditional sentence, a condition has to be satisfied before something occurs. Examples:

- *If you sing, I'll pay you £10.* ✔
- *Peter will catch you if you fall.* ✔

Time to Reiterate the Easy Rule. How hideous was all that? My advice? Use *whether* every time until your brain tells you it's wrong. It's very unusual, but this is one time when you can rely on your instincts.

Whether or Not. Very often, the *or not* after *whether* is superfluous (i.e. not required). However, when *whether or not* means *regardless of whether*, the *or not* part is required. Examples:

- *Reprimand Chris whether or not he is on time today.* ✔
  (...*regardless of whether* he is on time today. The *or not* is required.)
- *The parade will go ahead whether it rains or not.* ✔
  (...*regardless of whether* it rains. The *or not* is required.)
- *Please establish a committee to determine whether or not the proposed funding lines are appropriate.* ✘
  (It's not wrong, but the *or not* is superfluous.)

There is leniency on where the *or not* is placed. It does not have to follow immediately after *whether*.

135 ILLUSION AND ALLUSION

The Quick Answer: An *allusion* is an indirect reference to something. An *illusion* is deception.

Allusion. An *allusion* is a subtle or indirect reference to something (i.e. a hint at something). It derives from *to allude* (see Section 96). Examples:

- *The Simpsons is full of allusions to well-known films.* ✔
- *His consistent allusions to being so poor as a child are not in keeping with his brother's version of their childhood.* ✔

Illusion. An *illusion* is a false impression or deception. Examples:

- *It's not an oasis – it is an illusion.* ✔
- *I am under no illusion how much work is required.* ✔

136 IMMORAL AND AMORAL

The Quick Answer: *Immoral* means morally wrong. *Amoral* means *not related to morality*.

Immoral. *Immoral* means *not adhering to moral principles* (i.e. deliberately breaking the rules of right and wrong). Example:

- *Stop looking at Peter's answers. Your conduct is immoral.* ✔

 GEEK SAYS In my experience, there's a 97% chance you mean immoral not amoral.

Amoral. *Amoral* is very technical and rare. It means *not related to morality*. It's from *amorality*. *Amorality* is a state in which the concept of right and wrong is invalid. Examples:

- *Deciding which scent you like best is an amoral decision.* ✔
- *The scientists try not to consider whether their research is right or wrong. They are encouraged to adopt a totally amoral attitude.* ✔

137 IMPLY AND INFER

The Quick Answer: *To imply* means to state indirectly. *To infer* means to deduce.

> **GREAT TIP** The reader infers what the writer implies.

Imply. *To imply* means to state indirectly (i.e. to include a suggestion in a message). Examples:

- *His speech on transitioning to today's needs strongly implies that the typist pool will be made redundant.* ✔
- *Would I like a pack of mints? What are you implying? I don't have bad breath, do I?* ✔

Infer. To infer means to deduce (i.e. to extract a suggestion from a message). Examples:

- *The reader can easily infer that Sarah needs the money but is too proud to ask for charity.* ✔
- *Am I right to infer you think my team removed the safety valve? Is that what you're implying?* ✔

Transmitters and Receivers. When you imply, you transmit an indirect message. When you infer, you receive the indirect message. What's an indirect message? An indirect message is the one said to be *between the lines*. For example:

- *Reading between the lines, I infer the MD is content with our performance, but he clearly implies the marketing section needs an overhaul.* ✔

> **OPPORTUNITY** People ask "What are you inferring?" all the time. The overwhelming majority of the time, this is wrong. If they're being stroppy, you can slam them with: "Inferring? I don't understand. Oh, I see. I was implying…."

138 INCIDENCE AND INCIDENTS

The Quick Answer: An *incident* is an event. The plural is *incidents*. *Incidence* is a rare word. It means *a proportion* (usually of society in relation to a disease).

Incidents. *Incidents* is the plural of *incident*, which means an occurrence or an event. Examples:

- *There is no evidence to link the two incidents at this time.* ✔
- *The police are investigating two incidents of shooting.* ✔

Unless you study diseases, you probably mean **incidents**.

Incidence. *Incidence* is very technical and quite rare (unless you study the spread of disease). It relates to the chance of developing some new condition (usually a disease) within a specified time period. Examples:

- *The chart 'Incidence of Flu by Area' shows the number of people with flu and flu-like illnesses who visited their doctor last week.* ✔
- *They suffer a higher incidence of measles as they did not invest in health-care systems to deliver vaccinations effectively.* ✔

139 INCITE AND INSIGHT

The Quick Answer: *Insight* means *an understanding*. *To incite* means *to stimulate action*.

Insight. *Insight* means *an understanding of something*. It often carries the connotation of *a clear understanding with an insider's perspective*. Examples:

- *The film offers a useful insight into sharks' behaviour.* ✔
- *She has a good insight into the company's strategy.* ✔

Incite is like **excite**.

Incite. *To incite* means *to stimulate action, to rouse, to stir up* or *to excite*. Examples:

- *A 29-year-old man from Dover was arrested for trying to incite a riot.* ✔
- *The event is seeking to incite enthusiasm in young people.* ✔

140 INSTANCE AND INSTANTS

The Quick Answer: An *instance* is an example. An *instant* is a moment of time.

Instance. *Instance* means an example or an occurrence. Examples:

- *This is another instance of Mark's poor behaviour.* ✔
- *Take a look at his latest project for instance.* ✔

Instants. The word *instants* is the plural of *instant*, which means a moment of time. Examples:

- *The light bulb lasted no longer than a few instants.* ✔
- *A couple of instants after the lightning, a deafening thunder roared above our heads.* ✔

141 INTO, ONTO AND UP TO

The Quick Answer: *Into* is one word. But, if *in* and *to* coincidentally appear side by side in your sentence, you must write them as two words. This usually happens with words like *drive in* and *put in*. The same applies to *onto* and *on to*. *Upto* is a never one word – it's a spelling mistake.

This subject has some nasty quirks and is bit of a nightmare. Prepare to have your brain fried a little.

In To and Into. The secret to differentiating between *into* and *in to* is to spot when *in* and *to* just happen to be next to each other in a sentence. When this happens, *in* and *to* should be written as separate words. (This usually happens with verbs that include the word *in*; e.g. *hand in*, *step in*, *turn in*.) For example:

- *Paul wanted to hand the purse in to see if there was a reward.* ✔
  (In this example, *in* comes from *hand in* and *to* is from *to see*.)
- *Paul wanted to hand the purse in to the police.* ✔
  (Here, *in* comes from *hand in* and *to* is from *to the police*.)

The word *into* is used when *in* and *to* are not coincidentally side by side.
- *She turned everything she touched into gold.* ✔
  (*into* comes from *turn into*)

Turn in and **turn into** are both valid verbs.

Unfortunately, the situation is complicated with verbs like *turn in*, *drive in* and *put in*, because these are valid verbs just like *turn into*, *drive into* and *put into*. Look at these examples:

- *Put the fruit in the basket.* ✔
  (*put in* – okay)
- *Put the fruit into the basket.* ✔
  (*put into* – okay)
- *Put the fruit in to the basket.* ✘
- *Dive in the water.* ✔
- *Dive into the water.* ✔
  (alternative to above)
- *Dive in to the water.* ✘
- *Dive in to test the water.* ✔

Is It Magic? Writers should be particularly wary of *turn into*, because it has two meanings. Example:

- *The car turned into a garage.* ✔
  (Was the car transformed into a garage or did the car drive into a garage?)

To avoid ambiguity, it is normal to write:

- *Turn in to* for drive into, walk into, etc.
- *Turn into* for transform into

For example:

- *He turned the car in to the cul-de-sac.* ✔
  (With *turn in to*, it is acceptable to write *in to* as two words. Of course, using *turn into* would not be wrong. You just run the risk of the ambiguity.)
- *He turned his mum's car into a stockcar.* ✔

On To and Onto. The guidelines above also apply to *onto*.

- *They had to push on to reach the summit before dark.* ✔
- *The crowd got onto the cars.* ✔
- *The crowd got on to the cars.* ✘

Be aware that when *onto* means *on top of*, this sense can override your intended meaning. When this causes a problem, use *on to*. For example:

- *After seeing the sheep, the judges moved onto the cows.* ✔
  (Not wrong, but it conjures up a humorous image.)
- *After seeing the sheep, the judges moved on to the cows.* ✔

Up To and Upto. Finally, the easy one. *Up to* is never written as one word. Examples:

- *I can afford upto £400.* ✘
  (should be *up to*)
- *It takes up to four hours to hard-boil an ostrich egg.* ✔

142 ITS AND IT'S

The Quick Answer: *It's* is short for *it is* or *it has*. *Its* is the possessive form of *it*. (In other words, *its* is to *it* as *his* is to *he*, and *her* is to *she*.)

 BEWARE Getting this wrong is a grammar howler. There are no points for getting it right. You're supposed to know the difference.

There is too much confusion between *its* and *it's*. If you delve into this issue (and we'll touch on it later), you will see there is good reason for the confusion. However, if you just want to know what is right, it is very simple.

It's. *It's* is short for *it is* or *it has*. This is a 100% rule. It cannot be used for anything else. If you cannot expand *it's* to *it is* or *it has*, then it is wrong.

Its. *Its* is like *his* and *her*. Here's how:

His is used for things owned by a male. (e.g. *These are his pies.*)
Her is used for things owned by a female. (e.g. *These are her flowers.*)
Its is for things owned by something neuter. (e.g. *These are its footprints.*)

His, *her* and *its* are called *possessive adjectives*. That's logical – they're used to show possession. Some examples of *it's* and *its*:

- *I'm astounded by people who want to "know" the universe when it's so hard to find your way around Chinatown.* ✔ (Woody Allen)

- *It's one of the hardest courses in it's history.* ✖
  (The first *it's* is correct. The second should be *its*.)
- *I think the company wants to have its cake and eat it.* ✔
  (*its* – possessive adjective. This is correct.)
- *The reef shark chases it's prey through the coral.* ✖
  (should be *its*, i.e. the possessive adjective. You cannot expand this
  to *it is* or *it has*.)
- *A lie gets halfway around the world before the truth has a chance to
  get its pants on.* ✔ (Winston Churchill)
- *There is nothing in the world like the devotion of a married woman.
  It's a thing no married man knows anything about.* ✔ (Oscar Wilde)
- *Whenever cannibals are on the brink of starvation, Heaven, in its
  infinite mercy, sends them a fat missionary.* ✔ (Oscar Wilde)
- *A frog can't empty its stomach by vomiting. To empty its stomach, a
  frog throws up its stomach first, so the stomach is dangling out of its
  mouth. Then the frog uses its forearms to dig out all of the stomach's
  contents and then swallows the stomach back down again.* ✔
- *A completely blind chameleon will still take on the colours of its
  environment.* ✔

Here's a very cool tip: <u>Never ever</u> write *it's*. It's a bit draconian, but this is
the easiest way to get it right. Instead of writing *it's*, write the full version (i.e.
it is or *it has*). If your sentence does not make sense, use *its*. This works
well, because *it's* is a contraction (see Section 4), and it is normal not to use
contractions in formal writing (see more guidance in Section 52). In 25 years
of report writing, I have never used *it's*...not once.

The Confusion. Apostrophes are used to show possession (See Section 3).
For example, the possessive form of *dog* is *dog's* (e.g. *the dog's teeth*). Therefore,
somewhat understandably, many think that the possessive form of *it* should be
it's. It seems to fit the pattern. To make matters worse, there is some evidence
that the possessive form of *it* used to be *it's*. The word *it's* is used erroneously
(by today's conventions) throughout the American Constitution.

Some big players still get this wrong.

Some very prominent companies still get this wrong. For example:

- *"...A secure home for your money, from the bank rooted in it's
  principles."* ✖ (Cooperative Bank advertisement)

Oh, and *its'* is never ever correct. It doesn't exist.

(143) LAY AND LIE

The Quick Answer: *To lay* means *to place in a horizontal position*. *To lie* means *to be in a horizontal position* (beware, the past tense is *lay*) or *to speak an untruth*.

This is a nasty subject (especially with *lay* being the past tense of *to lie*). *Laid* and *lain* add even more confusion to the whole saga. Prepare to have your brain fried. (It's so complicated, I've put a table at the end of the section.)

Lay and Laid. *To lay* means *to put something in a position (especially a horizontal position)*. Examples:

- *The maids lay the table for dinner at 7 o'clock.* ✔
- *Sudan urges rebels to lay down arms.* ✔
- *Put your hands up, and lie down your weapons.* ✘
  (should be *lay down*)
- *In April, our white spotted bamboo shark began to lay eggs.* ✔

For the past tense, use *laid*. Examples:

- *Annabelle laid the puppy in the basket.* ✔
- *They laid the body on the bank and notified the coroner.* ✔
- *According to the pamphlet, we should have laid old sheets on the floor to prevent paint splashes landing on the decking.* ✔
- *A teenager killed by a shark in northern New South Wales has been laid to rest.* ✔

Lie, Lied, Lay and Lain. *To lie* has two unrelated meanings:

To say something which is untrue in order to deceive. (For the past tense, use *lied*.)

- *Did you lie about your age to join the Army?* ✔
- *Your eyes betray you when you lie.* ✔
- *My reflexologist says I am lying about my health. He says that my feet, however, do not lie.* ✔
  (The *ing* version is *lying*. This is called the *present participle*.)
- *Malcolm lied his way past the doormen.* ✔
- *Billy lied so often about his boxing achievements, he forgot the truth.* ✔
- *Malcolm had lied his way past the doormen.* ✔

To be in, or move into, a horizontal position. (There are two versions used for the past tense: *lay* and *lain*.) Examples:

- *The lion and the calf shall lie down together, but the calf won't get much sleep.* ✔ (Woody Allen)
- *An alibi? I just lay on the sofa all night, watching The Simpsons.* ✔ (*lay* – past tense of *to lie*)
- *The snow lay on the field all week.* ✔
- *Mark had lain at the foot of the knoll for hours.* ✔ (Use *lain* for the past tense if it is partnered with the word *have* (in its various forms; i.e. *has, had, have, will have, having*). The word *lain* is the past participle of *to lie*.)
- *Adversity has the effect of eliciting talents, which in prosperous circumstances would have lain dormant.* ✔ (Horace, 65–8 BC)

Main Problem. The most common mistake is to use *lie* instead of *lay*. If you remember you cannot *lie something*, you will eliminate this error.

- *To lay your head on the pillow.* ✔
- *To lie your head on the pillow.* ✘ (Remember, you cannot *lie something*. So, you cannot *lie your head*.)
- *My chicken lays eggs.* ✔
- *My chicken lies eggs.* ✘ (It is very obvious in this example. You cannot *lie something*. So, a chicken cannot *lie eggs*.)

Laid Sounds Right But Often Isn't. *Lay* is past tense of *to lie*. For many people, *laid* sounds okay:

- The crocodile laid still for hours. ✘ (should be *lay*)

Lain is not a common word. Therefore, for many people, *laid* sounds correct. Remember, *lain* is usually partnered with the word *have* (in its various forms).

- *The snow had laid on the field all week.* ✘ (This should be *lain*. Here, it is partnered with the word *had*.)

Nightmare. I told you it was a nightmare. Here's a table to clarify things a tad:

Present Tense	Past Tense	The Participles
To lay (to place something in a horizontal position)		
He lays (something)	He laid (something)	is laying (something) (something) was laid the laid (something)
To lie (to tell an untruth)		
He lies	He lied	is lying has lied
To lie (to be in a horizontal position)		
He lies	He lay	is lying has lain

 144 LEAD AND LED

The Quick Answer: *To lead* (rhymes with seed) means *being in charge* or *being in front*. The past tense of *to lead* is *led*. Confusion arises because *lead* (a soft toxic metal) is pronounced *led*.

Lead. *Lead* (rhymes with seed) is a versatile word. It can be an adjective, noun or verb (see Sections 40, 47 or 55). It is associated with *being in charge* or *being in front*. Examples:

- *Lead the team back to the tents.* ✔ (*lead* as a verb)
- *You can take your dog off the lead.* ✔ (*lead* as a noun)
- *Keep this pace up. You are in the lead.* ✔ (*lead* as a noun)
- *You have been selected to be the lead tenor.* ✔ (*lead* as an adjective)

Led. *Led* is the past tense of *to lead*. Examples:

- *He led the cavalry over the hill.* ✔
- *He has led the cavalry over the hill.* ✔

The Other Lead. *Lead* that rhymes with *bed* is a soft heavy toxic metallic element.

- *In the UK, it is illegal to use lead in fresh-water fishing.* ✔
- *Someone has stolen the lead off the church roof again.* ✔

145 LICENCE AND LICENSE

The Quick Answer: If you're following UK convention, then *licence* is a noun, and *license* is a verb. If you're following US convention, ignore the word *licence* completely.

For those not following US convention, there is often confusion over *licence* and *license*. Unfortunately, to understand which to use, you must know the difference between a noun and a verb (see Sections 47 and 55). This is because *licence* is a noun, but *license* is a verb. If you don't have time to learn the grammar behind it, here are a couple of tricks to help.

A Little Trick to Spot Licence. Try using the word *card* (or *papers*) instead of *licence*. If the sentence still makes sense, then *licence* is almost certainly correct. (This trick works because *licence* is a noun, just like *card* and *papers*.)

A Little Trick to Spot License. Try using *to allow* (in its various forms; e.g. allowing, allowed, allows) instead of *license*. If the sentence still makes sense, then *license* is almost certainly correct. However, if you find yourself using *allowance*, you should be using *licence*. (This trick works because *to license* is a verb, just like *to allow*.) Examples:

- *This restaurant is licensed to sell alcohol.* ✔
  (This restaurant *is allowed* to sell alcohol.
  Sounds okay; *licensed* is correct.)
- *Can I see your driving licence please?* ✔ (UK)
  (Can I see your driving *card/papers*?
  Sounds okay; *licence* is correct)
- *I am unable to give you a license because of your history.* ✖ (UK)
  ("…to give you an *allow/allowing/allowed*…" Nonsense; *license* is wrong. "…to give you a *card/allowance/papers*…" Sounds okay; should be *licence*)

Licencing and *licenced* are always wrong.

Cut Down the Confusion. There should be no confusion with *licensing* or *licensed*. The endings *ing* and *ed* mean these are always from the verb.

License in America. In American English, *license* is both noun and verb. In other words, it's safe to ignore the word *licence*. However, I should point out there is growing tendency in the US to observe the difference between the noun and verb. This is also true for *practice* and *practise* (see Section 153).

146 LOATH AND LOATHE

The Quick Answer: *To loathe* means to hate. *Loath* means unwilling.

Confused in writing and speech

I have noticed a lot of people confuse *loath* and *loathe* – not only in writing but in speech. The meanings of *loath* and *loathe* are related as they both relate to not liking something.

Loathe. *Loathe* means to hate. In fact, it is stronger than *to hate*. It can also be translated as *to hate intensely*. Examples:

- *She will eat just about anything, but she loathes celery.* ✔
- *He loved the Army as an institution and loathed every single thing it required him to do.* ✔

Loath. *Loath* means unwilling. Examples:

- *She is loath to join, because her friends play for a rival team.* ✔
- *Magazines and newspapers are loath to discuss these types of deals publicly.* ✔
- *At daybreak, when loathe to rise, have this thought in thy mind: I am rising for a man's work.* ✖
  (should be loath)

This Might Help. *Loathe* ends in a soft *th* sound. It rhymes with *betroth*. *Loath* ends in a hard *th* sound. It rhymes with *oath* or *both*. *Loathe* takes much longer to say. It's so long, there's plenty of time to emphasise the hatred. When you say *loathe*, you can almost feeling your eyes narrowing as your face acts out the hate. That's how I remember it.

147 LOOSE AND LOSE

The Quick Answer: *Loose* means *not tight* or *free from constraint*. *To lose* means to fail to (1) keep (2) win or (3) make money.

The confusion over the words *loose* and *lose* is due to the lack of consistency in pronouncing words that end *oose* and *ose*. For example, *loose* rhymes with *noose* but not *choose*.

Lose. *Lose* rhymes with *snooze*. It has the following meanings:

Fail to keep (either physically or in an abstract sense), to misplace, fail to make money
- *If I lose my glasses once more this week, I am going to glue them to my head.* ✔
- *Terry had already lost one family member to the cult. He did not want to lose another.* ✔
- *The surveillance team will lose their target if he enters the park.* ✔
- *"Here, geezer, if you don't shift those clock radios, I'll lose 300 sovs."* ✔
  (UK slang: *shift* = sell / *sovs* = sovereigns = pounds)

Fail to win
- *Back in 2002, our pub landlord bet £10,000 on Brazil to lose against Germany in the World Cup final.* ✔
- *If you do not train during the week, you will lose on Saturday.* ✔

Loose. *Loose*, which rhymes with *moose*, means *not tight*, *not dense* or *free from constraint*. Although very rare, it can also mean *to unleash* (e.g. to loose plagues upon humanity). Examples:

- *Watch your footing on this loose gravel.* ✔
  (not dense / not compact)
- *Travellers are advised to wear a lightweight shirt that is lose fitting. This is important for air circulation.* ✖
  (should be *loose fitting*)
- *There is a dangerous dog loose on the street.* ✔
  (free from constraint)

Moose on the Loose. People make mistakes with *loose* and *lose* because of the confusion over pronunciation. If you remember that *loose* rhymes with *moose*, you will eliminate this error.

(148) NO-ONE AND NO ONE

The Quick Answer: Spell *no one* without a hyphen.

No Hyphen. The formal spelling of *no one* is without a hyphen. However, more recently, the *no-one* version has become more popular. Some grammarians condone the hyphenated version, claiming it eliminates ambiguity with *no one* as in "*No one person can overcome her power*." However, the times when there would be true ambiguity are very rare. Here is one example:

- *No one can will work.*
  (This could mean: *None of the cans will work* or *No person is able to incite work.*)

'No One' Is Always Right. There is notable leniency on how to write *no one* – using a hyphen does not constitute a grammatical howler. However, let's be clear on this, the correct spelling is *no one*.

'Noone' Is Never Right. *Nobody* and *nowhere* have become single words. However, *no one* has not. *Noone* is wrong.

(149) NOTABLE AND NOTICEABLE

The Quick Answer: *Notable* means worthy of comment. *Noticeable* means detectable.

Notable. *Notable* means *worthy of comment, worthy of distinction, celebrated, widely known* or *esteemed*. It can also mean *a person of note*. Examples:

- *The award is for the volunteer who has made the most notable contribution to the development of netball at a local level.* ✔
- *I would like to discuss some notable omissions from the text I gave you.* ✔
- *Be respectful. He is a notable.* ✔

Noticeable. *Noticeable* means *detectable* (i.e. sufficient to be noticed). Examples:

- *The blue sheen in your hair is hardly noticeable.* ✔
- *The difference in processing speed is very noticeable.* ✔

(150) PAST AND PASSED

The Quick Answer: *Passed* is the past tense of *to pass*. For everything else, use *past*.

Passed. *Passed* is the past tense of *to pass*, e.g. *I pass* (present tense), *I passed* and *I have passed* (both past tense), and *I will pass* (future tense). Examples:

- *She passed the exam with distinction.* ✔
  (In this example, to pass = to be successful in a test)
- *The operator has already passed the note to the typist.* ✔
  (In this example, to pass = to hand over)
- *The lion passed the zebra without so much as a glance.* ✔
  (In this example, to pass = to move past)

Note: *To pass* often means *to move past*, and this is where confusion can arise. (Obviously, *to pass* can also mean *to sail past, to fly past, to run past, to hop past*, etc. – the method of moving is irrelevant.) So, all words denoting movement are partnered with *past* and not *passed*. Remember, *passed* is the past tense of *to pass*. This is a 100% rule.

- *The lion passed the zebra without so much as a glance.* ✔
- *The lion wandered past the zebra without so much as a glance.* ✔
- *The Harrier passed at an altitude of 100 feet.* ✔
- *The Harrier flew past at an altitude of 100 feet.* ✔

Past. *Past* has several meanings (usually related to *time before the present* or to indicate movement *from one side of a reference point to the other side*.) *Past* can be used as an adjective (see Section 40), an adverb (see Section 42), a noun (see Section 47) or a preposition (see Section 49). Here's a tip:

Substitute with 'Went Past'. When referring to movement (i.e. not passing tests or handing stuff over), only use *passed* when it is the past tense of the verb *to pass*. To test whether *passed* is correct, replace it with *went past*. If your sentence still makes sense, then *passed* is the correct version.

- *He passed the shop.* ✔ (Substitute: *He <u>went past</u> the shop.* ✔
  Still makes sense – *passed* is correct)
- *He skipped passed the shop.* ✘
  (Substitute: *He skipped <u>went past</u> the shop.* ✘
  Not correct – *passed* is wrong – should be *past*)

Substitute with 'Gone Past'. I won't bore you with the grammar, but on occasion, it may be necessary to use *gone past* to test whether *passed* is correct.

- *He has passed the dockyard.* ✔
  (Substitute: *He has <u>gone past</u> the dockyard.* ✔
  Still makes sense – *passed* is correct)
- *He has driven passed the dockyard.* ✘
  (Substitute: *He has driven <u>gone past</u> the dockyard.* ✘
  Not correct – *passed* is wrong – should be *past*)

Confused? Let's go back to "The Quick Answer" at the start of this section: *Passed* is the past tense of *to pass*. For everything else, use *past*.

151 PLAIN AND PLANE

The Quick Answer: *Plane* usually means *an airplane, a flat surface* or *a tool for shaving wood*. *Plain* usually means *simple* or *an expanse of lowland*.

The words *plane* and *plain* have several meanings. Unfortunately, both have a meaning relating to flatness, and this is often the source of confusion.

Plain. *Plain* has several meanings:

Simple (i.e. not elaborate)
- *a plain girl* ✔
- *a plain cake* ✔
- *a plain colour* ✔

Simple (i.e. apparent)
- *It is plain to see.* ✔
- *It seems quite plain to me.* ✔

An expanse of level and low land
- *The Russian Plain.* ✔
- *I joined the Chinese farmers as they attempted to drive the yaks across the plain in western China.* ✔

Plane. *Plane* has several meanings:

An airplane
- *I feel about planes the way I feel about diets. They are wonderful things for other people to go on.* (Jean Kerr) ✔

A flat surface (especially in mathematics) or a level (usually figurative)

- *In a 3D space, a plane can be defined by specifying a point and a normal vector to the plane.* ✔
- *I was hoping for a conversation on a higher plane.* ✔
  (In Afghanistan, I once heard a British general "wound" one his colonels with this sentence. To me, it was apparent from the colonel's eyes that his brain was considering a smart-arse retort that played on *plane* also meaning *airplane* – something like "Yeah? Well, there's one leaving in two hours." As you'd expect, discipline won the moment, and nothing was said. However, it was too late for me. I'd already "heard" the retort. The next two minutes were the longest of my life as I fought to stifle a laugh that was brewing uncontrollably. I left the room with teeth marks inside my cheeks and memories of dead pets that I'd rekindled to keep the laugh at bay)

To shape wood, or a tool for smoothing or shaping wood

- *Can you plane a few inches off the top of the door?* ✔

To travel on the surface of water

- *The car hit the puddle and planed straight into the back of the lorry.* ✔
  (also known as *to aquaplane*)

152 PORE, POUR AND POOR

The Quick Answer: *To pour* means *to tip a liquid out of a container. To pore* means *to examine closely.* A *pore* is a *small opening in the skin. Poor* usually means impoverished or inadequate.

Pour. *To pour* means *to transfer a liquid from a container* (usually by tipping).

- *Shall I pour the gravy?* ✔
- *Happiness is a perfume which you cannot pour on someone without getting some on yourself.* (Ralph Waldo Emerson) ✔

You can **pore over** or **pore through** a document.

Pore. The word *pore* has two unrelated meanings:

To examine closely

- *He pored through the documents for hours looking for a loop hole.* ✔

- *I need to pore over these files before tomorrow.* ✔
(Note: You can pore over something or pore through something.)

A small opening in the skin
- *The dust clogs your pores.* ✔
- *The sweat was leaking from my pores.* ✔

Poor. *Poor* means impoverished (i.e. having little money or few possessions), or low quality (e.g. poor crop) or unfortunate (e.g. that poor cat). Examples:

- *Religion keeps the poor man from murdering the rich.* ✔
- *The exam results are poor.* ✔
- *Will you take that poor animal to the vets?* ✔

(153) PRACTICE AND PRACTISE

The Quick Answer: If you're following British conventions, then *practice* is a noun, and *practise* is a verb. If you're following US convention, ignore the word *practise*.

If you're a Brit, **practice** is a noun and **practise** is a verb.

For those not following US convention, there is often confusion over *practice* and *practise*. Unfortunately, to understand which to use, you must know the difference between a noun and a verb (see Sections 47 and 55). This is because *practice* is a noun, but *practise* is a verb. If you don't have time to learn the grammar, here are a couple of tricks to help.

A Little Trick to Spot Practice. Try using the word *preparation* (or *lessons*) instead of *practice*. If the sentence still makes sense, then *practice* is almost certainly correct. (This trick works because, like *preparation* and *lessons*, *practice* is a noun.)

- *You need more practice.* ✔
(Substitute: *You need more preparation/lessons.* ✔
Sounds okay; *practice* is correct)

A Little Trick to Spot Practise. Try using *to prepare* (in its various forms; e.g. preparing, prepared, prepares) instead of *practise*. If the sentence still makes sense, then *practise* is almost certainly correct. However, if you find yourself using *preparation,* you should be using *practice.* (This trick works because *to practise* is a verb, just like *to prepare.*)

- *You should practise more.* ✔
  (Substitute: *You should prepare more.* ✔
  Sounds okay; *practise* is correct)
- *They practice in the office for 10 weeks and are then sent out.* ✘
  (Substitute: *They lessons/preparation in the office for 10 weeks...* ✘
  This is nonsense; *practice* is wrong.
  Substitute: *They prepare in the office...* ✔
  Sounds okay; *practise* is correct)

Cut Down the Confusion in the UK. There is no confusion with *practising* and *practised*. The endings *ing* and *ed* mean these are always from the verb; i.e. there are no such words as *practicing* and *practiced* in British English.

Practice in America. Although many in the US have adopted *practise* as the verb and *practice* as the noun, it is acceptable to use *practice* for both noun and verb in American English.

- *I must keep practising/practicing that accent.* ✔
  (both versions acceptable in American English)

154 PRECEDENCE AND PRECEDENT

The Quick Answer: *Precedence* pertains to ranking. A *precedent* is *a previous example used to guide a decision.*

Precedence. *Precedence* pertains to *ranking* or *status in order of importance or urgency*. Examples:

- *The medics treated them in order of precedence according to their injuries.* ✔
- *The rules that govern the precedence of members of the Royal Family are complex.* ✔

Precedent. *Precedent* means *an example from the past that provides evidence for an argument*. It is most commonly used in legal circles and, more specifically, can be described as *a previously decided case that guides the decision of a future case*.

GEEK SAYS If you hear someone say: "There is past precedence/precedents," it is wrong. Precedence is wrong, because it's the wrong word. Precedents is wrong, because it's plural; therefore, they should have said: "There are past precedents."

Examples:

- *Having discovered a similar case in the past, the prosecution team used this precedent to support their argument.* ✔
- *There is precedent with last year's Smith versus Jones case.* ✔

155 PRINCIPAL AND PRINCIPLE

The Quick Answer: *Principal* means main. *A principal* is the head (of a department). *Principle* means *general law* or *code of conduct*.

Confusing **principal** and **principle** is a common mistake. Expect your readers to spot the error.

What is it about these words? In my experience, writers confuse these two words in formal writing more than any other pairing (although it's a close-run thing with *affect* and *effect*). Expect your audience to know the difference between *principle* and *principal*. This mistake is so common that readers tend to pause momentarily on these words to ensure you've used the right one. If you haven't, it's a kidney punch in the credibility.

Principal. In its most common role, *principal* means main or key. Examples:

- *The principal objective is to make a profit.* ✔
- *The inspector highlighted my principal concern in his opening sentence.* ✔

Principal also means head or chief. (In the US, it means *head teacher*.)

- *"I hate the teachers and the principal*
  Don't wanna be taught to be no fool
  Rock, rock, rock, rock, rock'n'roll high school" ✔
  (Lyrics from Ramones' Rock and Roll High School. Oh, and thank you, America, for the Ramones – they were top notch.)
- *The allegations against the former principal were that he not only allowed the cage fights to take place, but he also egged on the participants.* ✔

Principle. *Principle* has a range of meanings, including rule, belief, tenet and theory. In general, *principle* offers the idea of *general law* or *code of conduct*.

- *No! It is against my principles!* ✔
- *Those are my principles. If you don't like them, I have others.* ✔
  (Groucho Marx)
- *He applied the Aufbau principal to determine the electron configuration of the silicon.* ✖
  (should be *principle | principle* = theory or general law)

Think of A1. If you imagine that the *l* on the end of *principal* looks like a *1*, then the last two "letters" become *A1*. Use this to help you remember that *principal* denotes *the most important* or *main*. For example:

- *My principal concern is the safety of the dove.* ✔
  (my A1 concern; i.e. main concern)

Even General Stanley McChrystal's proofreaders let one slip in the General's initial assessment on the war in Afghanistan in August 2009:

- *Addressing the external actors will enable success; however, insufficiently addressing either principle threat will result in failure.* ✖

Principal and Money. It's not a common use of *principal*, but it's probably worth adding that when referring to a loan, the *principal* (or *principal sum*) is the original amount of a debt or investment on which interest is calculated.

156 PRECEDE AND PROCEED

The Quick Answer: *To precede* means *to come before* (usually in time). *To proceed* means *to go forwards* or *to continue*.

The words *precede* and *proceed* sound quite similar, and writers sometimes confuse them. In particular, people use *precede* when the mean *proceed*. (E.g. Okay, let's precede. ✖) It almost never happens the other way around.

Precede. *To precede* means *to come before* (usually in time). Examples:

- *King George VI preceded Queen Elizabeth II.* ✔
  (in time)

- *The professor will precede the lecture with his opening remarks.* ✔
- *The flight simulator is unable to replicate the airframe shudder that precedes the stall.* ✔

Precede Can Mean Outrank. Occasionally, *precede* can mean *to come before in rank*. Example:

- *Within the noble ranks, each peer is graded according to the date of receiving the peerage, but peers of England (prior to 1707) precede peers of Scotland (prior to 1707).* ✔
  (The word *precedence* derives from *precede* in this meaning.)

Proceed. *To proceed* means *to go forwards* or *to continue*. The noun *proceeds* (always in the plural) means *the profit arising from an event or sale*. Examples:

- *As soon as security has removed the protesters, I shall proceed.* ✔
  (*proceed* = continue)
- *We are proceeding at pace.* ✔
  (*proceeding* = moving forward / moving on / progressing)
- *Have you spent the proceeds from the disco already?* ✔
  (*proceeds* = profit)

157 PROPHECY AND PROPHESY

The Quick Answer: A *prophecy* is *knowledge of the future* (from a divine source). *To prophesy* means *to predict the future* (with divine inspiration).

Prophecy. *Prophecy* is a noun (See Section 47). The last syllable is pronounced *see*. (You will understand why that's important later on.) Examples:

- *On the second day of the course, we will study the prophecies of Nostradamus.* ✔
- *The prophet has revealed his latest prophecy in which three cities are razed to the ground.* ✔

Prophesy. *Prophesy* is a verb (See Section 54). The last syllable is pronounced *sigh*. Examples:

- *He prophesies a great war between East and West.* ✔
  (last syllable pronounced *sighs*)

- *He prophesied that a flood would cover the Earth.* ✔
  (last syllable pronounced *sighed*)

Not Prophesize or Prophesise. There is no need for Americans and Brits to have a fight over *ize* or *ise* endings – both are wrong in this case. *To prophesy* goes like this:

I prophesy
You prophesy
He prophesies
We prophesy
You prophesy
They prophesy ✔

Just to reiterate, there is no such word as *prophesize* or *prophesise*. This is most commonly seen as: He prophesizes ✖ (should be *prophesies*)

158 PROSCRIBE AND PRESCRIBE

The Quick Answer: *To prescribe* means *to recommend* or *to authorise*. *To proscribe* means *to forbid*.

Prescribe. *To prescribe* means to recommend or authorise. Examples:

- *I have prescribed you a course of antibiotics.* ✔
- *The law prescribes a minimum of 10 years' incarceration for your offence.* ✔

Proscribe. *To proscribe* means to forbid, to limit or to banish. Examples:

- *These photos are worthless. Such images are proscribed by law.* ✔
- *Police have been tracking three members of the group, which was proscribed in the 80s.* ✔
- *Name one country that does not proscribe theft.* ✔

Proscribe looks like it should have positive connotations.

Pro is Bad? Really? The explanations seem simple enough. So, why do people get this wrong? Well, *proscribe* causes confusion because people do not expect a word that starts with *pro* to have such negative connotations. (*Pro* often means *for* or *supportive of*.)

159 PROVIDED AND PROVIDING

The Quick Answer: The words *provided* and *providing* are interchangeable when used to mean *on condition that*.

Provided and Providing. Through common usage, the words *provided* and *providing* are interchangeable when used to mean *on condition that*. (Back in the early 1900s, when used in this way, *providing* was considered a grammar error.) Examples:

- *Provided that the weather is fine, we'll have a picnic on Saturday.* ✔
- *Providing that the weather is fine, we'll have a picnic on Saturday.* ✔
- *Tony will attend provided that Sarah is not chairing the meeting.* ✔

No Need for That. The word *that* can usually be omitted. Examples:

- *Provided the weather is fine, we'll have a picnic on Saturday.* ✔
- *Providing the weather is fine, we'll have a picnic on Saturday.* ✔

Do you need **that**?

When I was in Kabul in 2010, a senior US Navy officer who proofread one of my papers made no corrections or suggestions other than removing every single *that* from my paper. He did this the next time I asked him to check my paper too. Actually, he won me over. I have really cut down my use of *that*. Most of the time, you don't need the word *that* at all. I would recommend asking yourself whether it's necessary every time you use it.

Provided Is More Formal. Some writers maintain *provided* is preferable to *providing* as a conjunction (see Section 44) meaning *on condition that*. Both are acceptable. However, as some of your readers may prefer *provided*, it is safer to choose this option. If you get picked up for using *providing* as opposed to *provided*, you've probably got a real grammar pedant on your hands.

 GREAT TIP When you mean on condition that, use provided instead of providing.

160 RAISE, RISE AND RAZE

The Quick Answer: *Raise* means *to lift something upwards* (it's not always literal, e.g. to raise a question). *Rise* means *to ascend*. *Raze* means *to destroy*.

The words *raise* and *rise* cause confusion, because they are so close in meaning.

Raise and Rise. The word *raise* means *to lift* or *to elevate*. *Rise* means to move from a lower position to a higher position. It has the same meaning as *to ascend*. The past tense of *rise* is *rose*. (There is no such word as *rised*.)

- *He is raising the blue ball.* ✔
  (With *raise*, there is usually something lifting something else.)
- *The blue ball is rising.* ✔
  (With *rise*, the thing ascends itself.)

Remember, *raise* is not always about lifting – you can raise a question and raise children. The point is that one thing raises another thing. Examples with both *raise* and *rise*:

- *"How to Raise Your I.Q. by Eating Gifted Children"*
  (Book by Lewis B. Frumkes) ✔
- *It would be too expensive to rise the remnants of the Titanic.* ✘
  (should be *raise the remnants of the Titanic*)

Yeah, that's all pretty simple. But, what about these two examples:

- *The sheer skirt made eyebrows rise.* ✔
  (Here, the eyebrows rise themselves. The sheer skirt is the cause.)
- *The sheer skirt will rise a few eyebrows.* ✘
  (This should be *raise*. Grammatically speaking, the skirt is doing the raising. You would be very unlucky to come across an example as nasty as this.)

The Letter 'a' in Raise. Let the letter '*a*' in *raise* remind you that *to raise* acts on something.

- *I raised my eyebrows.* ✔
  (In this example, it is acting on *my eyebrows*.)
- *She raised a question.* ✔
  (In this example, it is acting on *a question*.)

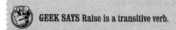

GEEK SAYS Raise is a transitive verb.

Verbs that act on things are known as *transitive verbs*. This is important because *to raise* is a transitive verb, but *to rise* is not. It is *intransitive*. It does not act on anything. This is the most notable difference between *raise* and *rise*. (See Section 55.)

- *I will rise my eyebrows.* ✖
  (*To rise* is intransitive. You cannot rise something. This is wrong.)
- *My eyebrows rose.* ✔
  (Here, *rose* is not acting on anything. Remember, *rose* is the past tense of *to rise*.)
- *Watch the moon rise.* ✔
- *Watch the moon raise.* ✖
  (Watch the moon raise what? This sentence either isn't complete or it's wrong.)

Wait for one of your colleagues to get this wrong. While underlining the error, say something like (and don't forget the condescending voice): "*I think you'll find the verb 'to rise' is intransitive.*"

Raze. *Raze* is a less common word than *raise* and *rise*. It means to demolish completely or to delete. (It can also be written *rase*. This is not a UK convention. It is simply an alternative spelling.)

- *The arsonist razed the forest to the ground.* ✔
- *The plough will raze the ice from the road surface.* ✔

Raze and *raise* sound identical, but they are close to being opposites (consider: *raise a block of flats* and *raze a block of flats*). If you think of *raze* as being like *erase*, your brain will be more comfortable with *razing something to the ground*.

161 ROLE AND ROLL

The Quick Answer: A *role* is an actor's portrayal of a character, a job or function. A *roll* is a list (of names) or a piece of bread. *To roll* usually means to move by rotating.

Role. *Role* means an actor's portrayal of a character, a job or function (of a person or thing). Examples:

- *Teddy was totally convincing in the role of Shylock.* ✔
- *The thermostat's role is to keep the temperature below 200 degrees so the casing does not melt.* ✔

Roll. The word *roll* has several meanings:

To move by rotating or gather by rolling
- *Roll the hay bale down the hill.* ✔
- *Roll over a bit. You're hogging the bed.* ✔
- *Roll your sleeves up and roll me the best cigar ever.* ✔

To move on wheels
- *The skateboarders rolled past the park attendant, and he did not say a word.* ✔

 BEWARE A role is not a list. A roll is a list. (Remember, roLL = Long List.)

A list
- *Please check the nominal roll to ensure we're all present.* ✔

To start
- *Roll the cameras* ✔

A small round piece of bread
- *Would you like butter on your roll?* ✔

The word *roll* usually has a circular, spherical or cylindrical connotation. (For example, roll a cigar, roll the film, roll away.) The most obvious exception to this is when *roll* means *list*. In this case, let the last two letters of *roll* remind you of *long list*. Alternatively, think of a *scroll*.

162 STATIONARY AND STATIONERY

The Quick Answer: *Stationary* means not moving. *Stationery* is office supplies (e.g. paper, pens).

 GREAT TIP Let the e in stationery remind you of envelope.

The words *stationary* and *stationery* are both very common. At least, they would be if people used *stationery* correctly. I've lost count how many times I've seen store rooms with *Stationary* on the door or seen emails asking workers to reduce *stationary costs*. In these examples, the word should have been *stationery*. It's pretty simple:

Stationary. The word *stationary* means not moving or still. Examples:

- *We had to wait stationary for the school shop to open.* ✔
- *The hostages were ordered to remain stationary.* ✔

Stationery. *Stationery* (with an *e*) means office supplies (e.g. writing paper, envelopes, pens). Examples:

- *The office junior is in charge of ordering our stationery.* ✔
- *The office junior is in charge of filling the stationery cupboard.* ✔
- *Save 50% on all office stationery.* ✔

163 STORY AND STOREY

The Quick Answer: *Story* means narrative. It also means *level of a building* in the US. However, in British English, the *level of a building* is written *storey*.

There's no such word as **storey** in American English.

Story and Storey. If you're following US conventions, you can ignore the word *storey*. This is because in American English, *story* is used for *narrative* and *level of a building*. In British English, *level of a building* is written *storey*. The plural of *story* is *stories*. The plural of *storey* is *storeys*. Examples:

- *Did you hear the story about the bungee jumper who died because he miscalculated the height of each storey before diving off a building?* ✔ (UK) ✘ (US)
- *Beowulf is an epic traditional good-versus-evil story. Beowulf battles three monsters throughout the story.* ✔
- *With 160 storeys, the Burj Khalifa in Dubai is the tallest building in the world.* ✔ (UK) ✘ (US)
  (US version would be *With 160 stories*)

First Floor or Ground Floor? While we're talking about *storeys* and *stories*, it's worth pointing out that Americans call the ground-level floor of a building the *first floor*, but the British call it the *ground floor*. Therefore, the second floor in the US is the first floor in the UK. These little differences wouldn't be so annoying if Americans didn't gloat about chucking our tea in Boston Harbor in 1773…I mean Boston Harbour.

⓹ THEIR, THERE AND THEY'RE

The Quick Answer: *They're* is short for *they are*. *Their* shows that something belongs to *them*. *There* is a place.

If you use the wrong version of *they're*, *their* or *there* and your reader does not think you had a moment of absentmindedness, he/she will think you're poorly educated. Fact! A mistake involving these is a serious grammatical howler. Living in a constant frenzy, I make mistakes with these all the time – almost exclusively in email. I tend to spot them the instant I press the send button. Thankfully, I've grown confident enough not to send an email straight afterwards pointing out the error. I always consider it though.

 BEWARE Getting these wrong will seriously damage your credibility.

They're. *They're* is a shortened version of *they are*. (The apostrophe replaces the letter *a*.) Only use *they're* if you can substitute it with *they are*. Examples:

- *My doctor gave me two weeks to live. I hope they're in August.* ✔
  (Ronnie Shakes)
- *Things are only impossible until they're not.* ✔ (Jean-Luc Picard)
- *Why do you listen to them? They're unqualified.* ✔
- *More than 20 people left they're coats in the cloakroom.* ✘
  ("…20 people left *they are* coats in the cloakroom" – nonsense)

- *"The coffee facility will be removed if staff do not keep it tidy. Staff are reminded to put they're cups away after use."* ✖
  (I saw this sign in a staff rest area. It makes you want to smash the place up a bit, doesn't it? No? Err, no, me neither.)

Quick Tip. Never use *they're* in a formal document. Always expand it to *they are*. (See Section 52 for more guidance.)

Their. *Their* is used to show possession. It is just like *my*, *your*, *his*, *her*, *its* and *our*. (These are all called *possessive adjectives*.) If the grammar sends you to sleep, here's a little trick.

A Trick to Spot Their. Use the word *our* instead of *their*. If your sentence still makes sense, then *their* is almost certainly correct. This trick works because *our* and *their* are both possessive adjectives used to represent plurals. Examples:

- *Can you show the guests to their cabins?* ✔ ("…show the guests to *our* cabins" – sounds ok; *their* is correct)
- *I have seen their footprints before.* ✔ ("I have seen *our* footprints before." – sounds ok; *their* is correct)
- *Their all leaving.* ✖ ("*Our* all leaving." This is nonsense. *Their* is wrong. It should be *They're*.)
- *Their less likely to cause offence.* ✖
- *Experience is the name every one gives to their mistakes.* ✔
  (Oscar Wilde)

There. The word *there* is similar to the word *here* – both represent places. *There* has two main uses: (1) It is a specified place (like in the first example below) and an unspecified place (like in the second example) (2) Like in the second and third examples, the word *there* can be used to show that something exists. Examples:

- *The Germans are over there.* ✔
  (specified place)
- *There are two apples.* ✔
  (unspecified place – two apples exist)
- *There used to be a real me, but I had it surgically removed.* ✔
  (Peter Sellers)
  (*a real me* used to exist)
- *If you don't know where you're going, any road will take you there.* ✔
  (Lewis Carroll)
  (Remember, *there* is a place.)

(165) THEN AND THAN

The Quick Answer: *Then* relates to time. *Than* is used to introduce a comparison.

Then. The word *then* usually relates to time. It is most commonly used as an adverb – see Section 42. It has the following meanings:

Subsequently or afterwards
● *Get your facts first, and then you can distort them as much as you please.* ✔ (Mark Twain)
● *A cucumber should be well-sliced, dressed with pepper and vinegar, and then thrown out.* ✔ (Samuel Johnson)

As a consequence or in that case
● *If you had cleaned your teeth properly, then you wouldn't be in this predicament.* ✔
● *If there are no stupid questions, then what kind of questions do stupid people ask? Do they get smart just in time to ask questions?* ✔ (Scott Adams)

At that time or that time
● *She used to holiday in Ceylon as it was then known.* ✔
● *Happiness just wasn't part of the job description back then. You tried to find a helpmate to keep the cold wind and dogs at bay. Happiness just wasn't part of the equation. Survival was.* ✔ (Robin Green)

Than. The word *than* introduces a comparison. It is most often seen with comparatives (see Sections 69 and 70) and words like *more, less* and *fewer*.

● *When you hire people smarter than you are, you prove you are smarter than they are.* ✔ (R. H. Grant)
  (*Smarter* is a comparative.)
● *Money is better than poverty, if only for financial reasons.* ✔ (Woody Allen)
  (*Better* is a comparative.)
● *Never eat more than you can lift.* ✔ (Miss Piggy)

Beware comparisons involving time.

Comparisons Involving Time. Comparisons involving time add to the confusion between *than* and *then*. Remember, use *than* for comparisons, including those involving time.

For example:

- *Nature is earlier then man, but man is earlier than natural science.* ✖ (should be *than man*)
- *Summer is earlier than autumn.* ✔

Those with English as a second language are particularly prone to confusing *than* and *then*. A native English speaker confusing these words constitutes a grammatical howler.

166 TOO OR TO

The Quick Answer: *Too* means *as well* or conveys the idea of *in excess*. *To* is a preposition (e.g. Give it to her.) or is used to show the infinitive form of a verb (e.g. I want to run).

Both words have two uses, and that confuses the matter.

You really can't afford to mix up *too* and *to*. Your credibility will take an uppercut to the chin if you reveal that you don't know the difference. Luckily, *too* and *to* are so common that even those who can't fully explain the grammar have tuned themselves to get it right. In my experience that's how lots of people operate, and – if it works – it's good enough.

As we'll see, the harder to explain is *to*. *Too* is relatively simple. But, those who get this wrong tend to write *to* when they mean *too*. It's not common the other way around, which seems a little counterintuitive to me. Anyway...

Too. *Too* has two uses:

1 ***Too* means *as well* or *also*.**
- *I can do it too.* ✔
- *Did you think that too?* ✔
- *The gods too are fond of a joke.* ✔ (Aristotle, 384– 322 BC)

2 *Too* **portrays the idea of** *in excess* **or** *more than it should be.*

- *This cat is too chubby.* ✔
- *The shoes were too expensive.* ✔
- *You can fool too many of the people too much of the time.* ✔
  (James Thurber)
- *Progress might have been all right once, but it has gone on too long.* ✔
  (Ogden Nash)
- *I'm glad to hear you smoke. A man should always have an occupation of some kind. There are far **too** many idle men in London as it is.* ✔
  (Oscar Wilde)

To. *To* has two uses:

1 *To* **is used in expressions like** *to walk, to run, to paint,* **etc.**
These are all verbs in their infinitive forms. There's a bit more on this below, but it's also covered in Section 55.

- *Did you tell her what to think?* ✔
- *The only way to entertain some folks is to listen to them.* ✔
  (Kin Hubbard)
- *I'm glad **to** hear you smoke. A man should always have an occupation of some kind. There are far too many idle men in London as it is.* ✔ (Oscar Wilde)
  (See the same quote in the section above.)

A Bit on the Grammar – Infinitive Form. Verbs are doing words (e.g. *to dance, to sit, to fly, to think*) When *to* is in front of a verb, the verb is said to be in its *infinitive form.* For example:

- *She likes to dance.* (This is the verb *to dance* in its infinitive form.)
- *She dances.* (This is the verb *to dance* not in its infinitive form.)

2 *To* **is used in expressions like** *to the park, to the postman, agree to a proposal.* **The word** *to* **in these examples is a preposition.**
There's more on this below, but it's also covered in Section 49.

- *She handed the parcel to the stranger.* ✔
- *Experience is the name everyone gives to their mistakes.* ✔
  (Oscar Wilde)
- *The chief obstacle to the progress of the human race is the human race.* ✔ (Don Marquis)
- *A diplomat is a person who can [send you] to hell in such a way that you actually look forward to the trip.* ✔ (Caskie Stinnett)

A Bit on the Grammar – Preposition. Prepositions show the relationship between at least two words in a sentence. *Preposition* literally means *positioned before* (pre = before). A *preposition* sits before a word to show its relationship to another word in the sentence. Words like *on*, *in* and *by* are also prepositions. There are lots of others. (See Section 49.)

- *He agreed to the proposal.*
  (*To* sits before *proposal* to show its relationship with *agreed*.)
- *David ran to the park.*
  (*To* sits before *park* to show its relationship with *ran*.)

This example has all versions of *to* and *too*:

- *Like Charles de Gaulle, I too have come to the conclusion that politics are too serious a matter to be left to the politicians.* ✔
- *I too have come…* (*too* meaning also)
- *…too serious a matter…* (*too* meaning in excess)
- *…come to the conclusion…left to the politicians* (*to* as a preposition)
- *…to be left* (*to* showing a verb in its infinitive form)

167 VAIN, VEIN AND VANE

The Quick Answer: A *vein* is a blood vessel or a distinctive style. *Vain* means *self admiring* or *futile*. The term *in vain* means *without success*. A *vane* is a stabilising fin or blade.

Vein. *Vein* has several meanings:

A blood vessel that carries blood from the capillaries towards the heart
- *As long as I am an American citizen and American blood runs in these veins, I shall hold myself at liberty to speak, to write, and to publish whatever I please on any subject.* ✔ (Elija Lovejoy)

A distinctive style or manner
- *Mr Mellor continued in the same vein despite several reprimands.* ✔

A layer of ore or mineral between layers of rock
- *The mineral contents of a vein depend chiefly upon the chemical composition of the waters from which its minerals have crystallised.* ✔

The ribs that support an insect's wing
- *The non-contact laser scanning produced high-quality images which finally allowed us to interpret vein relief in fossil insect wings.* ✔

Vain. *Vain* means *conceited* or *self admiring*. *Vain* can also mean *fruitless*. In this meaning, it is often seen as *in vain* meaning *without success* or *in a futile manner*. Examples:

- *Carly Simon promised that in the newly recorded version of "You're So Vain," the name of the vain man in question would be revealed when the song was played backwards.* ✔
- *Liberty without learning is always in peril; learning without liberty is always in vain.* ✔ (John F. Kennedy)

Vane. A vane is a blade or a fin usually used to stabilise an object in the air or in water. It is most commonly seen in the word *weathervane*. Examples:

- *The stabilising vane has come loose.* ✔
- *The steel casing protects the vane from damage in the event that the vessel hits the rocks.* ✔

I Know What Vain Means. The term *in vain* is the one that causes the most problems. Knowing that *vain* means *self admiring*, some believe that the term *in vain* must be spelt *in vein*. Well, it isn't. The word *vein* attracts a similar but less common mistake. Knowing a *vein* is a blood vessel, people believe the term *in the same vein*, must be spelt *in the same vain*. Well, it isn't.

168 WAIST AND WASTE

The Quick Answer: *Waist* is the middle part of the body. *Waste* means rubbish or garbage. *To waste* most commonly means *to expend without reason*.

Native English speakers tend not to get this wrong.

I have never seen a native English speaker confuse *waist* and *waste*. However, those learning English as a second language are often tripped up.

Waist. *Waist* is the part of the body between the ribs and hips. A section of clothing that fits the waist may also be called the *waist* (e.g. The *waist* on this suit is too tight.) Similarly, midsections of airplanes and ships can also be referred to as *waists*.

Waste. *Waste* has several meanings:

"Useless" materials left over from another activity (i.e. rubbish/garbage)
- *Originally, soya milk was a waste product of tofu.* ✔
- *The new concept encourages producers to leave no municipal waste for landfill.* ✔

To expend materials or resources without reason
- *Youth is a wonderful thing. What a crime to waste it on children.* ✔ (George Bernard Shaw)
- *Junk mail invades our homes and wastes our time.* ✔

To wear away, to weaken or to tire
- *Her quadriceps have wasted badly since the injury.* ✔
- *I am wasted after that run.* ✔
  (I am tired...)

Uninhabited or uncultivated (usually of land)
- *This area has turned to wasteland since the flood.* ✔

To kill (slang)
- *I am going to waste that little punk.* ✔

169 WEATHER, WHETHER AND WETHER

The Quick Answer: *Whether* is similar to *if* (e.g. I wonder whether it will rain.) *Weather* refers to temperature, wind, clouds, rain, etc. A *wether* is a castrated ram (male sheep).

What's a wether?

Whether. The word *whether* is a conjunction (see Section 44). It is similar to *if.* (The difference between *if* and *whether* is in Section 134.) *Whether* is most often used to introduce an indirect question. Examples:

- *It matters not whether you win or lose; what matters is whether I win or lose.* ✔ (Darrin Weinberg)
- *When they call the roll in the Senate, the Senators do not know whether to answer "Present" or "Not guilty."* ✔ (Theodore Roosevelt)

Weather. *Weather* means the *atmosphere in terms of temperature, wind and clouds and precipitation*. *To weather* can mean *to withstand* or *to endure* (e.g. to weather an onslaught) or *to erode over time* (e.g. to weather the surface rock). Examples:

- *Don't knock the weather. If it didn't change once in a while, nine out of ten people couldn't start a conversation.* ✔ (Kin Hubbard)
- *We'll anchor up, weather the storm and then head back to land.* ✔ (*weather* meaning to endure)
- *The sea will weather that rope in less than a week.* ✔ (*weather* meaning to erode)

Wether. A *wether* is a male sheep, especially a castrated ram.

Did the Wether Survive? If you can follow this sentence, you have a good grasp of *weather, whether* and *wether*:

> *The farmer wondered whether the wether would weather the weather or whether the weather would kill the wether.*

 **WHO OR WHOM**

The Quick Answer: *Who* is like *he* and *they* – they are always the subjects of verbs. *Whom* is like *him* and *them* – they are never the subjects of verbs.

You would never say "Him is very tall" or "Them are very tall." Well, it's the same deal with the word *whom*. You can't say "Whom is that?" It's no coincidence that *him, them* and *whom* all end in the letter *m*. It's because, from a grammatical perspective, they are very similar words. Likewise, *who* is similar to *he* and *they*. To get to the bottom of this, we need to delve into some grammar geekery. More specifically, you need to understand what is meant by *the subject of a verb* (see Section 55). If you can't be bothered to learn this, there are some neat tricks at the bottom of this section that will help.

 BEWARE Using whom when it should be who looks like you're trying to be clever – and failing.

Who. The word *who* can only be used when it is the subject of a verb. Examples:

- *Who paid for the meal?* ✔ (*Who* is the subject of the verb *to pay*.)

- *I have not seen the man who lives in the hut by the beach for a week.* ✔
  (*Who* is the subject of the verb *to live*.)
- *I wonder who is in charge.* ✔
  (*Who* is the subject of the verb *to be* – *is* in this case.)
- *Sarah gave the tickets to who?* ✘
  (*Sarah* is the subject of *to give*, but *who* is not the subject of any verb. Therefore, you cannot use *who*. It should be *whom*.)

Whom. *Whom* is never the subject of a verb. Examples:

- *You sat by whom all night?* ✔
  (*Whom* is not the subject of any verb. *You* is the subject of *to sit*.)
- *She is a wistful recluse whom lives near the river.* ✘
  (*Whom* cannot be the subject of the verb *to live*. It should be *who*.)
- *Claire saw whom yesterday?* ✔
  (*Whom* is not the subject of any verb. *Claire* is the subject of *to see*.)

 OPPORTUNITY Using whom correctly confirms to your readers that you know your onions.

Whom after Prepositions. Always use *whom* after prepositions. (Prepositions are words like *to*, *with*, *by*, *on*, *in*, *near* – see Section 49.) For example:

- *You have a child by whom?* ✔ (*by* – preposition)
- *With whom did you see Janice?* ✔
  (*with* – preposition)
- *That is the lady to whom I made the promise.* ✔
  (*to* – preposition)
- *That is the lady whom I made the promise to.* ✔
  (This is similar to the example above. Ideally, you should not end a sentence in a preposition (like *to*), but sometimes it sounds better. The word *to* still governs *whom* even though it is not directly before it.)

Grammatically Incorrect Joke. Here's a joke I heard on the radio:

> *There are two owls playing pool. One accidentally nudges the cue ball. The first owl says, "That's two hits." The second responds, "Two hits? Two hits to who?"*

Funny? No, not really. Call me a pedant, but it should be "*Two hits to whom?*" You can't have *who* after a preposition.

Who = He (a Neat Trick). Replace *who* with the word *he*. If that part of the sentence still makes sense, then *who* is almost certainly correct.

- *Who paid for the meal?* ✔
  (Substitute: *He paid for the meal.* Sounds okay; *who* is correct.)
- *I have not seen the man who lives in the hut by the beach for a week.* ✔
  (Substitute: *...he lives in the hut...* Sounds okay; *who* is correct.)
- *Sarah gave the tickets to who?* ✘
  (Substitute: *...gave the tickets to he.* Sounds wrong; should be *whom*.)

To perform this trick for plurals, you will have to replace *who* with the word *they*.

- *I met the people who were on the plane.* ✔
  (Substitute: *...they were on the plan...*
  Sounds okay; *who* is correct.)

This trick works because *who*, *he* and *they* are always the subjects of verbs.

Whom = Him (A Neat Trick). Replace *whom* with the word *him* (or *them* for plurals). If that part of the sentence still makes sense, then *whom* is almost certainly correct.

- *Sarah gave the tickets to whom?* ✔
  (Substitute: *Sarah gave the tickets to him.*
  Sounds okay; *whom* is correct.)

This trick works because *whom*, *him* and *them* are never the subjects of verbs.

Still Don't Get It? Use Who. If you're in a hurry and still unsure which to use, use *who*. Firstly, it is much more common than *whom*. Secondly, the use of *whom* is starting to be considered old fashioned in some circles. (Of course, I do not condone this practice, but if you don't have time to learn the difference, this advice will do for now.) Example:

- *Who are you going to believe, me or your own eyes?* ✘
  (Groucho Marx)
  (Unfortunately, this great quote by Groucho Marx is grammatically incorrect. It should start with *Whom*, because *you* is the subject of the sentence. However, as *whom* sounds a bit contrived, we'll let Groucho off this time.)

171 WHO'S AND WHOSE

The Quick Answer: *Who's* is short for *who is* or *who has*. *Whose* is used to show possession or to ask who owns something.

> **BEWARE** Writing who's instead of whose is a serious error.

Who's. *Who's* is short for *who is* or *who has*. It has no other uses. This is a 100% rule.

- *We need a President who's fluent in at least one language* ✔
  (Buck Henry)
  (who is)
- *Who's eaten the last muffin?* ✔
  (who has)
- *The enemy is anybody who's going to get you killed, no matter which side he's on.* ✔ (Joseph Heller)
  (who is)

Fact. If you cannot replace the *who's* in your sentence with *who is* or *who has*, then it is wrong.

Whose. *Whose* is used to show possession or to ask who owns something. *Whose* usually sits before a noun – see Section 47.

- *Whose bike was expensive?* ✔
- *Conscience is a mother-in-law whose visit never ends.* ✔
  (H.L. Mancken)

Saved from the Grammar. The full grammatical explanation of *whose* could cure anyone's insomnia. I wouldn't dream of boring you with that. But, that's okay, because the explanation of *who's*, as you've just read, is simple. If you cannot substitute the *who's* in your sentence with either *who is* or *who has*, then use *whose*. Just before you stick it in, perform a quick check to ensure it's got something to do with possession. It will have. Job done.

172 YOU'RE AND YOUR

The Quick Answer: *You're* is short for *you are*. *Your* shows that something belongs to "you" or is related to "you" (e.g. your car, your father).

Some writers confuse *you're* and *your*. I see this mistake most often in emails and written notes. I reckon most of them are a result of rushing. That's understandable. However, the same mistake in a formal document constitutes a grammatical howler.

You're. *You're* is a contraction of *you are*. It has no other uses. This is a 100% rule. If you cannot expand it to *you are* in your sentence, then it is wrong. Examples:

- *The trouble with the rat race is that even if you win, you're still a rat.* ✔ (Lily Tomlin)
  (Expands to *you are* – correct)
- *Doing nothing is very hard to do. You never know when you're finished.* ✔ (Leslie Nielsen)
  (Expands to *you are* – correct)
- *You said you couldn't believe you're ears.* ✘
  (Does not expand to *you are* – should be *your*)

 BEWARE Confusing you're and your in a formal document is a disaster.

Your. The word *your* shows that something belongs to "you" (e.g. your car, your arm), is of you (e.g. your picture, your photograph) or is related to you (e.g. your uncle). *Your* is a possessive adjective. (Other possessive adjectives are: *my*, *your*, *his*, *her*, *its*, *our* and *their*.) Examples:

- *Our expert will answer your questions about pensions and savings.* ✔
  (questions belonging to "*you*")
- *Sarah doesn't look like your sister.* ✔
  (related to "*you*")

Yours. The word *yours* is known as an absolute possessive (others are *ours*, *his* and *hers*). There are no apostrophes in any absolute possessives. This is a 100% rule.

- *They say female canaries can't sing. Well, her's can.* ✘

Well, that's it. The end. I reckon that's all the grammar stuff people really care about. If you want more, please visit www.grammar-monster.com. It's got all sorts of lessons, glossaries and tests. Just before I sign off though, I would like to leave you with these thoughts:

Know your team and know yourself. There's a fair chance you won't be able to write a perfect report in one sitting. Let's imagine a perfect report scores 10/10 and a blank sheet of paper scores 0/10. Well, in your team, there will be people who can take your paper from 0 to 6. These are the ones with either the experience or the research skills to get you out the starting blocks. These people are your builders. Arguably, they have the hardest job. Often though, your builders will use too many words (e.g. express ideas twice), say stuff that's too detailed for the audience or fail to structure the document logically.

This is when your plasterers step in. Potentially, these are the people in your team with a bit of a bent for grammar, the bigger picture and slightly more logical minds. (In fact, a plasterer might be one of your builders, but one who isn't tired due to building.) Are you following my analogy? A plasterer will take your report from 6 to 8. If there's any fighting to be done, it'll be between the builders and the plasterers.

Once all the blood has been cleaned up, the polishers can move in. It's their job to polish the words, perfect the grammar and ensure the document is succinct and fit for purpose. In my experience, polishers are bad builders and vice versa. So, you must know who's who in your team, and allocate the work accordingly. Here's my main point though. There must be good communications between builders, plasterers and polishers – both up and down the chain. When something is amended in a document that affects its score, the person whose work is being changed must have the change explained to them – even if it's just a style change. This might seem like a time-consuming practice, but it's a great investment. It quickly ends up with your builders handing in reports that are pretty much ready for the envelope.

If you don't have a team and you're on your own, you have to work out where your skills lie. Are you good at getting started? Do you always get picked up for poor structure or poor grammar? Whatever the answer, allocate more time to your weak areas. If you're poor at structure, start by just writing the paragraph headings to create a logical framework. The best advice for a lone writer though is to take a break between each stage. Be a builder. Rest. Be a plasterer. Sleep. Be a polisher.

Be consistent but, above all else, help your reader. Grammar nuts can get pretty excited about a comma before *and*, an apostrophe to show the plural of an unwieldy abbreviation, the punctuation around *e.g.* and stuff like that. However, something you notice very quickly when you delve into the detail of grammar is that many of the leading grammar references contradict each other and a number of the so-called US and UK conventions aren't well observed in those countries at all. So, my advice is don't expend too many calories worrying about details like those – just be consistent. The only thing that trumps consistency is clarity. If you have to break your consistency or even a writing convention to remove ambiguity or to make your writing clear, then make it so. When questioned about it, fight like a cornered rat.

Don't overuse semicolons. As soon as I explain to folks how to use semicolons, they often start littering their writing with semicolons. Now that you know how to use semicolons, don't. Well, okay, you can if you like. But, don't go crazy. Imagine you have a two-page report to write. Now, think of that report as a posh dinner. Semicolons aren't the salt that you sprinkle over your meal. A semicolon is the glass of wine that you have with it. Often, you won't have a glass at all. However, you might have one. You might even have two. With this level of moderation, the effect is good. Five glasses? No chance. Same deal with semicolons. I have nothing against semicolons. I just think they need trimming back at bit. Used correctly and with some restraint, semicolons are wonderful.

Cheers

– INDEX –